BAND OF SISTERS

American Women at War in Iraq

KIRSTEN HOLMSTEDT

Foreword by Maj. L. Tammy Duckworth

STACKPOLE BOOKS

0 11557 03566 7

Published in paperback in 2008 by
STACKPOLE BOOKS
5067 Ritter Road
Mechanicsburg, PA 17055
www.stackpolebooks.com

Cover design by Tracy Patterson

Cover photo by Karen Anderson, U.S. Marine Corps Reserve captain and owner of Dancing Barefoot Photography.

Printed in the United States of America

10 9 8 7 6 5 4 3 2

ISBN-13: 978-0-8117-3566-7 (paperback)
ISBN-10: 0-8117-3566-4 (paperback)

The Library of Congress has cataloged the hardcover edition as follows:

Holmstedt, Kirsten A.
  Band of sisters : American women at war in Iraq / Kirsten A. Holmstedt. —
1st ed.
    p. cm.
  Includes index.
  ISBN-13: 978-0-8117-0267-6
  ISBN-10: 0-8117-0267-7
  1. Iraq War, 2003—Women—United States—Biography. 2. Women sailors—United States—Biography. I. Title.

  DS79.76.H652 2007
  956.7044'34092273—dc22

                                        2007002680

*To all American service members
past, present, and future.*

Table of Contents

Foreword vii

Introduction xi

Schoolhouse Rocks 1

Shoot Down 27

Not Ready to Be an Angel 53

Call Sign: "Krusty" 81

The Little Bird that Could 115

Little Dee with a Big Gun 139

Who Wants to Be Average? 155

Taking Command of the Herk 185

Live from Iraq 217

The Healers of the Guardians of Peace 253

Roll with It 283

Epilogue 309

Afterword 315

Acknowledgments 321

Index 323

Foreword

On November 12, 2004, Army Captain Tammy Duckworth lost both of her legs when the UH-60 Black Hawk helicopter she was co-piloting was hit by a rocket-propelled grenade fired by Iraqi insurgents. The explosion almost completely destroyed her right arm as well, breaking it in three places and tearing tissue from the back side of it. Duckworth received a Purple Heart on December 3 and was promoted to major on December 21 at the Walter Reed Army Medical Center, where she was presented with an Air Medal and Army Commendation Medal. On November 21, 2006, Duckworth was appointed the director of the Illinois Department of Veterans' Affairs by the state governor.

I WILL ALWAYS PLACE THE MISSION FIRST. I WILL NEVER QUIT. I WILL never accept defeat. I will never leave a fallen comrade. These statements are portions of the Soldier's Creed. They are referred to as the Warrior Ethos. These words were a lifeline that helped me survive my injuries and the tedium of day after day of endless pain in the hospital. They are gender-neutral statements that get at the heart of what it means to be an American Soldier today. I am not a big fan of being identified as a woman anything. I worked so hard not to be different from the other Soldiers for most of my career. Being effective in combat requires only that you place the mission first, that you will never quit, never accept defeat, and that when a buddy falls, you do not leave them behind.

Like some of the women profiled in this book, I have usually been the only woman in an all-male unit. When I first started my career, a generation of women had already pushed through, breaking down the barriers in Army aviation. Like any group of people, some were outstanding Soldiers, while others simply used their gender to gain an unfair advantage. This latter group's actions made life very difficult for the women in my generation. Their over-reliance on their gender to pave the way left a negative impression of female Soldiers in their male counterparts. By the time I came along, these men were in leadership positions and were even less welcoming of female troops than previous generations. We had to break through one at a time by proving we were just as good all over again—this time, by being as tough and gender-neutral as possible. Most of the women in this book are younger than I am, so they may not have gone through some of the stuff that has made me reluctant to have myself identified as a "female" Soldier. I am just a Soldier. Progress is made with each generation.

Regardless of my personal feelings, I know that this book has an important contribution to make even if I don't always agree with all of the statements made by some of the women profiled. When I was recovering at Walter Reed Army Medical Center in Washington, D.C., I was asked to address a group of female legislators (Congresswomen and Senators) on what I felt about a ban on women in combat. I told them it was stupid and unrealistic under the conditions of modern warfare. To have to answer an irrelevant question like that has taught me that perhaps the country needs to know that women are fighting and dying and that we need to move on, just like we don't discuss African Americans' or Japanese Americans' service based on their race as we did in World War II.

The women profiled here are a remarkable cross-section of the women serving in uniform today. I applaud their professionalism and their friendship with one another. My unit had just one other female pilot, and it was always nice to have someone to bunk with. When I was injured, she traveled with me to the hospital in Germany even though I was unconscious, just so I would have a friendly face around if I were to wake up. This act of kindness touches me to this day.

Sometimes, it does just take another woman to understand. In my first week at Walter Reed, I was in so much pain that I found myself counting to sixty over and over again. I didn't have the strength to survive the day, but I was pretty sure I could survive sixty seconds. So I counted the minutes away, one at a time. My husband was my rock of strength in the hospital, my hope for the future. During this time, Sergeant First Class Juanita Wilson came to me in the Intensive Care Unit. She looked down at me in my bed and said, "I know you are hurting. It will get better. Can I stand here for you?" She then took off her artificial arm and stood next to my bed for hours, day after day, as I counted. She radiated a peace and serenity for me that kept me going. She was the only one who could do that for me, a fellow amputee, one Wounded Warrior reaching out to help another. Later, she came to my room, decorated it, and washed my hair. The men all had their heads shaved, but my hair had not been washed in weeks. Sometimes it does take another member of the sisterhood to understand what another woman needs to feel better. She even used conditioner!

The ultimate message of this book is that the stories are not about being women. They are about being tough and professional. This nation is a remarkable place where little girls can indeed grow up to be whatever they want to be. The women in this book have all done their part to protect the freedoms of all the little girls who want to grow up and be nurses, fire fighters, or, yes, even helicopter pilots. As illustrated by Captain Armour's story, it's not about being the first female anything. It's about not wanting to be average. God Bless America.

Maj. L. Tammy Duckworth
Director, Illinois Department of
Veterans' Affairs

Introduction

AFTER THE SHOCKING EVENTS OF SEPTEMBER 11, 2001, I BOUGHT A
TV and ordered cable and Internet service for my home so I
could immerse myself in the military actions unfolding first in
Afghanistan and then in Iraq. Up to that point in my life, I had
avoided following wars closely in the newspaper or on television,
in a book or on DVD. I was born in 1963—too young to grasp
what was happening in Vietnam before the war there ended in
1975. I did take notice of a few brushfires that followed, but it
wasn't until the first Gulf War that I began to pay more somber
attention to Americans fighting overseas.

Along with purchasing cable, I began renting war movies. Not
service comedies like *Stripes* or *Private Benjamin* that treated war as
entertainment, but movies that put me in the middle of screen
carnage—*Band of Brothers* and *Black Hawk Down*—and challenged
me to make sense of the horror. Before Iraq (and Afghanistan),
the ultimate war novel for me was *A Farewell to Arms*, a romance
with a war lingering in the background. Now I read books of fic-
tion and history that directly illuminate the many faces of war: *All
Quiet on the Western Front*, *The Things They Carried*, *Catch-22*, *Flyboys*,
Jarhead, *Piece of My Heart*, and *On Killing*. I consumed war on
screen and in print, sometimes with a glass of wine to numb the

pain I'd feel while watching or reading depictions of humans using deadly force against one another.

Why was I tracking this war so closely and, indeed, examining war itself in more detail than I'd ever cared to before? What had changed inside me? In this war more American women were serving in more combat roles than ever before. Many U.S. military specialties once exclusively open to males had in the preceding decade or two opened up to women. Never in an American war had so many women been assigned to so many roles directly associated with combat. In Afghanistan and Iraq, women for the first time flew attack helicopters and fighter-bombers in close air support of comrades on the ground. During and after the invasion of Iraq, ground transportation and daily military missions performed by women serving as soldiers and Marines were regularly disrupted by fierce insurgent attacks. Following the invasion, women as well as men engaged in nation-building operations of various kinds under fire.

Too old to enlist in the military, but young enough to remember how I felt when I was nineteen or twenty, I could not imagine myself as I was at that age driving a Humvee across the desert in Iraq while snipers hid in trees or on rooftops, preparing to kill me. How would I perform if duty required me to fight for my life and the lives of my friends? How would it feel to stare into the eyes of an enemy prisoner of war? To hold the hand of a dying Marine, embracing the poignant responsibility of being the last living person he or she would see or hear? And how would it feel to *be* that teenaged Marine?

I couldn't help wondering: When had most of the women enlisted—before or after September 11? How scared were they when facing an elusive and vicious enemy? How did they deal with that fear? How equipped were they physically and emotionally for combat—not only for the fight itself, but for combat's less-than-visible traumas?

Throughout the millennia legions of men have gone to war. The men who stayed behind have asked themselves the same kinds of questions I was now asking myself. I would perhaps have had no cause to ask such questions except that now a larger band of sisters than ever was coming under enemy fire day in and day out.

Living in a military community raised my curiosity. For more than a decade, I had called Jacksonville, North Carolina, my home. It's also home to Marine Corps Base Camp Lejeune, the largest such facility on the East Coast. Many of the women in combat lived in or near the very city where I did; in fact, a few were my neighbors. Women that I might otherwise encounter in the grocery store, coffee shop, or workplace were now fighting for their lives. I personally didn't know how *I* would be able to handle the challenges thrust upon them if I were in their place. How were *they* able to do it? I held the women serving in combat in great esteem. I feared for their safety. I wanted them to come home whole to their families.

I started to collect their stories, clipping them from the newspaper and downloading them from Internet sites. I hoped that the articles, the testimonials, and the accounts—not to mention the television news segments, the Internet web pages, and, of course, the movies and the books—would enable me to somehow put myself in their boots.

It didn't work. The more I read, the more compelled I felt to explore in-depth the experience of U.S. women engaged in twenty-first-century combat. The information I acquired through clips and sound bites only scratched the surface of their still inconceivable world. I needed to delve into their heads and hearts, find out what they were thinking and feeling. To do this, I would have to track them down and earn their trust. I would seek permission to hear their stories of war, accounts that at one time had only been shared by men. While I couldn't go through what these women were experiencing, I could open myself up to what they were feeling, seeing, and doing. I could choose to make myself vulnerable.

I began contacting women as they returned from Iraq and asking them to share their combat experiences. Some were interested; others took convincing. I started this book with the naïve assumption that women who had served in combat in Iraq would be thrilled to be featured in a book, but some, especially the pilots and aviators, needed persuading. Some were eager to tell their stories; others chose to remain silent. Captain Amy McGrath, an F-18 back seater, was torn. She had worked hard to establish her niche among aviators in a male-dominated fighter squadron. She didn't want to stand out. On the other hand, she wanted to mentor girls and young women considering careers in military aviation.

Two female helicopter pilots agreed to be in the book and then backed out. One was part of a company of Black Hawks that lost an aircraft in Iraq. Six soldiers in a company of thirty-eight were killed, including her commander, one of her instructor pilots, and four others. The grief was too intense and fresh for her to talk about it. The other had returned from Iraq. We talked while she prepared for a year-long trip to Africa to fight terrorism. Later, her CH-53E helicopter and another one, with crews totaling twelve, crashed off the coast of Africa. Ten were killed, and two survived, including the female pilot I had interviewed.

A young military police officer in the Arizona Army National Guard turned down a spot in the book. She got shot at, returned fire, and was wounded in her arm. She said she was *real* conservative. The topic of women in combat remains controversial, and anything that is contentious could potentially make her commander in chief look bad. She didn't want that to happen. This individual was considering a political career in Texas.

In researching each story, I talked not only to the women in the book but to many other women and men in combat past and present. I spoke with their mothers, fathers, sons, daughters, spouses, childhood friends, co-workers, psychiatrists, doctors, and physical therapists. We communicated by phone and by e-mail. I sat at a kitchen table with a wounded soldier from Fort Campbell, Kentucky, and watched modern-day warfare extend from the battlefield into the private home of a female soldier and her family. We flipped through photo albums, went out for coffee and meals, and walked together. I traveled to Beaufort Marine Corps Air Station in South Carolina and to Pope Air Force Base and Fort Bragg in Fayetteville, North Carolina, to get a close look at an F-18 fighter jet, C-130 transport plane, and Kiowa helicopter. Then I flew in a turbo-prop plane from Norfolk, Virginia, to the USS *Harry S. Truman* off the coast of Florida to get a feel for the challenges and dangers of working on an aircraft carrier. I experienced an arrested cable landing (a.k.a. a controlled crash) and a catapult launch where the plane is shot into the air from 0 to 130 miles per hour in less than three seconds. I modeled float jackets and flak jackets, vests, and helmets. We laughed about the absurd things. But mostly we cried over lost and wounded comrades and over the effects of combat on families.

One of the biggest challenges I faced in writing this book had to do with juggling the women's stories. When the number of stories grew to more than five, and women returned from war only to turn around and go back to Iraq for a second or third time, I did everything I could just to maintain contact. As one came home, I would interview her while her combat experiences were fresh. Then another would return, and I would have to put the former aside, at least for the moment. This went on for three years. On a typical week, I would be interviewing one of the subjects for my book, while also talking to the mother of another woman, and the co-pilot of yet another. It was crazy, but it was important to keep up communication with all of the women in the book, no matter how erratic it seemed at the time.

I remember e-mailing one of the women in the book while she was in Iraq for the second time. I was hoping that she could give me some fresh insight while in-country, while emotions were raw, instead of waiting until she returned home. In the e-mail, I asked, "What kind of danger are you in?" She thought I had asked her *if* she was in danger, not *what kind* of danger.

She wrote, "What do you mean am I in any danger? I spent Easter morning with mortars flying all over, our bus stop was blown up. . . . We can't even get mail because our convoys are being attacked. We've had to clear our building three times within the last two weeks because of IEDs in our parking lot." The line that really got to me was not the one about mortars but the one that started, "We can't even get mail . . ." She has two children.

Later, the same person sent me another e-mail from Iraq. In my journal dated April 21, 2004, I wrote, "Today I received an e-mail from Yolanda (Mayo). It wasn't particularly emotional but as I wrote back to her I started to cry. Up until then, I hadn't noticed how much she, the book, the war were getting to me."

As I set out to write this book, I had no way of knowing where these women's stories would take me. How could I? In fact, in the back of my mind I think that was part of the reason why I started the book in the first place—to find out where they would lead me, you. But I have to be honest: This journey started out as an intellectual and practical exploration of women in combat and turned into much more. It became emotional, personal. While they peeled back the layers of their lives and recounted their stories, I, along with the families, friends, and co-workers of the women in this book, were also forced to look inward. We all had to because to look at women in combat is to take a closer look at who we are as individuals, the mores that shape our lives, society.

☆ ☆ ☆

Early on March 20, 2003, when the desert sky was still shrouded in darkness, stadium lights shone down on Al Jabar Air Base in Kuwait and lit the path to the flight line for a twenty-eight-year-old Marine captain whose jumpsuit I.D. tag bore the name McGrath. The aviator strode briskly across the flight line with other aviators from the Green Knights all-weather fighter/attack squadron. Like millions of U.S. Marines and soldiers before, McGrath was heading into combat. Like any one of the other 130,000 American troops in Iraq, McGrath might not come back alive. Like the hundreds of combat aviators flying from Al Jabar and other air bases in the region that day, McGrath had trained with a squadron to be here, cost the U.S. government $1 million for a year's worth of preparation, and was responsible for a $50 million aircraft. And like nearly 20 percent of the personnel in combat support and service units about to enter Iraq, McGrath was a woman. How she and other women in the U.S. military performed in jets and helicopters, on aircraft carriers, in convoys and in surgical wards, and when they came face-to-face with enemy prisoners of war, would validate or refute one of the most radical, controversial, and public experiments in the annals of U.S. military history. The eyes of the enemy were on her as she took off. So were the eyes of her countrymen. Would she be successful?

Band of Sisters is the first attempt to take a close look at how the experiment of women in combat is playing out. Not in American polls, not in the media, and not on Capitol Hill, but in Iraq, where, as McGrath says, "There are no front lines out there. Let me repeat. There are no front lines out there."

There have always been women in combat, but not in the United States. Female warriors from the Amazons of Greek mythology are said to have found an independent kingdom under the government of a queen and to have trained in agricultural pursuits, hunting, and the art of war. Armed women served as loyal bodyguards in India. In Scandinavia, women who did not yet have the responsibility for raising a family could take up arms and live like warriors. In the history of Bohemia, a large band of women carried on war against the duke of Bohemia and enslaved or put to death all men who fell into their hands. Joan of Arc drove the English out of France. The Dahomey Amazons were a 6,000-strong military unit in West Africa who were active from the sixteenth to the late nineteenth century, and in the kingdom of Siam in the late nineteenth century, the king had a personal battalion of 400 spear-wielding women. In the twentieth century, the state of the Soviet Union and Israel took the initiative to train and use women for light infantry and other combatant roles.

For more than two hundred years, women have served the United States in times of war. They started out as nurses, soldiers, and even spies. Thirty thousand women served in World War I—before they could vote. In their roles as medical support, though, they were hardly embraced as part of the armed services. One of the most profound turning points for women in the military came after the bombing of Pearl Harbor, when Army and Navy nurses worked side by side tending to more than 2,000 wounded servicemen. For aspiring military nurses, this was a wonderful moment and accomplishment. But what about the women who sought to serve their country in other capacities? What about those who dreamed of becoming fighter pilots, MPs, mechanics, combat engineers, and logistical officers?

In many ways, the Gulf War of 1991 was a watershed conflict for women in the U.S. military. More than 40,000 servicewomen went to war and one out of every five women in uniform was deployed in direct support of the Gulf War. The number was a steep climb from the 10,000 servicewomen—mostly nurses—who served during the Vietnam War. One woman was killed by enemy fire in Vietnam, and none during conflicts in Korea or Afghanistan. In the first Gulf War, eleven women were killed in action, and two were taken prisoners of war.

But it wasn't until after the first Gulf War that many combat positions opened up to women in the military. President Bill Clinton signed the military bill ending combat exclusion for women on combatant ships. In 1994 the USS *Eisenhower*, a Navy aircraft carrier, received its first sixty women.

In 1993 Defense Secretary Les Aspin ordered all armed services to open combat aviation to women (in spite of the recommendation by the Presidential Commission on the Assignment of Women in the Armed Forces that Congress reinstate the ban). A year later, the Department of Defense risk rule was repealed. Many units supporting ground combat operations were now open to women. And the services were given the discretion to open even more jobs to women in combat as needed. As a result of the Department's actions since April 1993, women are now eligible to be assigned to some 260,000 additional military positions, many of which involve combat. Altogether, about 80 percent of the jobs and more than 90 percent of the career fields in the armed forces can now be filled by the best qualified and available person, man or woman.

Since the war began in March 2003, more than seventy women have been killed and more than 400 have been wounded in Iraq. With women exposed to battlefield risk for up to a year at a time, and with no end to the war in sight, the debate over whether women should serve in combat support and service units, or be barred from direct ground combat, has been reignited.

The women in *Band of Sisters* come from bases and air stations throughout the United States. They served at different times in the war, and in various cities and towns in Iraq. They are of different ages, races, and ranks. They are single and married mothers, recent high school and college graduates, and reservists. Most of them had precise reasons for joining the military. They sought a career. They needed money for college. They wanted to do something more fulfilling. They were looking for a challenge, an adventure. They were following in their father's footsteps. Some felt strongly about serving God and their country. Others simply needed a steady job.

To find their way into combat, women did what they had done for many years in the home, on the playing field, and in the workplace. They nudged their way in and did their jobs well, and the public began to take notice. Some observers liked what they saw in the first Gulf War; others found it disturbing. Granted, you still won't find women in the infantry or driving a tank, but changes in technology and in the very nature of war have blurred the front lines and the definition of being "in combat."

Plenty of women in support roles have found themselves in vicious fire fights, under attack by mortar and rockets, and taking hostile fire in the air. As one female Marine noted, a missile doesn't target a specific gender. In today's war, women are often as vulnerable as men. They can't drive tanks but they can drive Humvees and trucks. And it's the Humvees and trucks, inching their way through the open desert in long and exposed convoys, that the Iraqis targeted—first with ambushes of mortar and small-arms fire, later with so-called "improvised explosive devices" (IEDs) that can tear a person literally limb from limb.

The capture and rescue of Private First Class Jessica Lynch early in the war pushed women into the spotlight once again. Not because she was a good or bad soldier, but because her capture showed how vulnerable women could be in this war. Just a few days after the war started, Lynch caught the attention of this country and the world when her convoy became lost and was ambushed in An Nasiriyah. The already controversial Iraqi war had produced America's first "hero," an eighteen-year-old woman from West Virginia, and the Army wasn't about to let go. It appeared one hero, and a female at that, was sufficient to the Army's needs. Yet Lynch's story turned into a passive account of mishaps and confusion, a tale of what can go wrong when a driver makes an erroneous turn in the middle of a war. The intent of this book is not to disparage Lynch's experience but to show that one female hero in a war of thousands just isn't enough.

The story of Captain Amy McGrath—indeed of any of the women written about in *Band of Sisters*—will show the outcome of that highly contentious experiment with its life-or-death consequences. How would the women and the individual branches of the military respond in the harrowing days, months, and years to come? Was the Army prepared to send thousands of women into combat? Were the Marine Corps, Air Force, and Navy? And were the women ready for what lay ahead? How willing were they to adapt?

All Marines, soldiers, sailors, and airmen bring their personal histories, idiosyncrasies, and skills into battle. But for the rising number of women in the United States military, there were unusual challenges, unexpected answers, and outcomes that would be full of surprises. There would be plusses and minuses, as the fundamental notion of what a soldier is and the movie version come face to face with reality.

As the experiment continues to play out in the desert, these women warriors insist they are no different from their male counterparts and they don't want to be treated as such. They shrug off the idea that the torture they might endure as a POW would be greater than what a male would suffer. The reason they appear so nonchalant is that they truly believe their bodies and lives are no more valuable than those of the male soldiers. None of the mothers wants to hear that her life is more valuable than the life of a father. Saying a certain number of women have died and some of them are "mothers" cheapens the sacrifices of all the fathers who have lost their lives. All of them are sad, all of them, not just the mothers. These women consider themselves equal, and not greater, in value. Like most soldiers, they don't think of themselves as heroes. All blush at the mere mention of the word.

And yet just their having to insist that they don't want to stand out, or that they are the same as men, may indicate how different they are. They have to be doubly heroic because they are facing many of the same challenges as the men in combat, but they can't draw attention to themselves.

Women can't help but be different from men because of their menstrual cycles, hormones, personal hygiene, fears, attitudes, emotions, strengths, weaknesses, and interests. But do those differences make women unqualified to serve in combat? As long as there are women in combat, people will argue they don't belong in foxholes. Some will say they shouldn't be in combat because they have the ability to reproduce, because a mother shouldn't leave her children for months at a time. Others suggest we have a draft and only allow men in the armed services. Some ask what has this country come to when we let our women fight our battles for us. Are there distinct advantages a woman warrior brings to combat? How is the experience different for her, even if she is equally as effective as a man?

As McGrath configured bombs to be dropped over Iraq, as a female nurse consoled eighteen-year-old wounded and dying GIs, and as a female pilot came face to face with her own mortality while her helicopter fell violently to the ground, none of these women felt as though they were in the wrong place at the wrong time. They may have signed up with the military during peacetime, with little thought of ever having to go to war, looking forward to serving their country on American and not foreign soil. However, they trained for war, knew it was a possibility, and were willing to fulfill their obligation, no matter the cost. "This is our job," Captain Amy McGrath said. "We're there, and we're there to stay."

Lance Corporals Carrie Blais and Priscilla Kispetik,
United States Marine Corps.

Schoolhouse Rocks

Suddenly, a loud crash jolted them from their tranquil positions. A rocket-propelled grenade (RPG) had just smashed the window and wall where the male Marines were sleeping. **Marine Lance Corporals Carrie Blais and Priscilla Kispetik** *dropped to the floor. "You okay?" they yelled to each other. Before they could grab their flaks, Kevlars, and rifles, they heard the whistle of another incoming RPG and crash.*

At ten o'clock on the morning of May 26, 2005, two female combat service support Marines and fifty male infantry Marines sought shelter in an abandoned four-story school in the city of Haditha after spending several hours patrolling streets and searching the homes of suspected Iraqi insurgents. With the thermometer rising to well over one hundred degrees, now was a good time to take a break. They would start up again later, when the sun wasn't so intense.

Before settling down, the Marines had to search each room in the school to make sure it was clear of the enemy. Lance Corporals Carrie Blais and Priscilla Kispetik were ordered to go with two male Marines. The two female Marines would clear one side of the second floor of the building; the two male Marines, the other side. Blais and Kispetik had been with the grunts for only about twenty-four hours but already they were feeling good about how things were going. They figured the grunts had to trust them if they were letting them clear one side of the hall. Little did the grunts know that the women had trained to clear houses and buildings but had never done so during war.

The fact that Kispetik and Blais were even with the grunts was unusual but not unheard of in this war. Operation New Market was a mission that required Marines to surround Haditha and methodically search the city for enemy fighters, weapons, and support structures. The women were "attached" to the grunts to search Iraqi women and children. While patrolling the streets and searching homes, every Iraqi had to be checked, including women and children. There were no exceptions. Women had been known to hide weapons and explosives on their bodies and under their clothing. Since the Iraqi culture doesn't allow men to search the Iraqi women, Kispetik and Blais got the honors. Marine supervisors weren't thrilled about sending their women into combat but they didn't have a choice in the matter. In this war, there was no front line, or every line was the front line. No place was safe in Iraq.

This was a critical mission. Haditha is located on the Euphrates River 140 miles northwest of Baghdad and about a two-hour drive from Al Asad. It was one in a string of towns populated almost entirely by farmers and merchants of Iraq's Sunni Muslim minority. The vast majority of Iraqi insurgents were Sunnis. They had been joined by radical Sunnis from other countries who entered Iraq from Syria to attack the United States and Iraqi security forces and members of Iraq's newly dominant Shiite majority.

Blais was twenty-eight, five feet two inches tall, with brown hair and blue eyes. When she got nervous, she liked to talk a lot.

When she talked a lot, her already funny sense of humor kicked into high gear. Energy drinks and pills kept this Connecticut native wired during most of her stay in Iraq. Kispetik, on the other hand, appeared much more laid back. The twenty-three-year-old from Houston, Texas, armed herself with a dry wit that she fired off less frequently than Blais but it was just as effective. Kispetik was five inches taller than Blais, with short brown hair and brown eyes. When Kispetik got nervous, she stifled her wittiness with Marlboro Milds and Coca-Colas, freeing up the airwaves for Blais's monologues. There would be plenty of tense moments in Haditha to fuel their habits and their humor.

Blais and Kispetik had been working at Al Asad Air Base for several months when they volunteered to go to Haditha. They were tired of being cooped up at the base. Blais, who spent her days outside in the blistering desert heat repairing heavy equipment, had already gotten a taste of what it was like to travel with the grunts when she accompanied 3/25 Lima Company 1st Platoon to the town of Haqlaniya. She was hooked. One night the Marines took fire from an island densely covered with trees. The next day they decided to secure the island but to do so they had to run across a dilapidated bridge that had more holes than a leopard has spots. One grunt ran across, then another. *Oh Lord have mercy*, Blais thought. With her "short stumpy legs," she had to take twice as many steps as the other Marines, doubling her chances of stumbling into a hole. Blais never ran so fast in her life. Although the experience was scary, it was also thrilling because for the first time Blais felt like she was an active participant in the war.

On the same mission, Blais and some other Marines were ordered to patrol an area for improvised explosive devices (IEDs). They were searching for anything in the desert that didn't look like it belonged. Making the search more difficult was the unusual amount of trash that littered the streets and camouflaged the bombs. Marines had to make a conscious effort to not be good Samaritans and pick up garbage. They had to stay alert. After days in the desert heat, it didn't take much to forget about the risks involved in the assignment. That is, until they have a near-death experience that rattles them to the bones and puts them back on the road of caution.

After searching the desert for a while, Blais found a burlap bag. Dig it up, someone said. She started digging and pulling until she couldn't pull anymore. It was stuck. Then she noticed a wire coming out of it.

"Put it down! Put it down!" the grunts yelled as they took off running in the opposite direction.

Blais did as she was told and scampered away.

Later, an explosive ordnance device (EOD) technician blew it up. It caused quite an explosion. If Blais had pulled any harder, she would have been toast.

While Blais had already traveled outside the wire to Haqlaniya, Kispetik had yet to leave Al Asad. As soon as Blais heard about the mission to Haditha, she jumped at the opportunity to get off base again. This time, she was determined to bring along her buddy Kispetik who spent her days in a small air-conditioned room processing paperwork that Blais generated.

In the abandoned school, on her way up to the second floor, Blais thought that maybe the grunts should have put her with a male Marine and Kispetik with a male Marine—with guys who had cleared rooms before. All the doors to the classrooms were closed. With their rifles in the ready position, Kispetik and Blais took turns pushing the doors open and running into the rooms. One ran straight ahead and the other to the side, moving their rifles and their eyes in all directions. If Blais ran inside the room and to the left, Kispetik ran straight. If Blais started shooting, Kispetik wouldn't have to worry about anyone shooting from behind her. She could concentrate on where Blais was targeting.

At one door, Blais thought she saw a big lock. Knowing that she wouldn't be able to penetrate the lock, she kicked the door hard and knocked it down. This got her blood flowing. She was pumped. The force that she used to kick down the door drew the admiration of the male Marines in the hallway but not from Kispetik, who would later tease Blais, saying the door was made of something resembling particle board and not oak. Anyone could have knocked it down. After clearing the rooms on all four floors, most of the Marines settled into a large classroom on the second level.

In the classroom where they chose to bed down, there were two windows—one in the front of the room and one in the back. A curtain covered the back window. Most of the male Marines found a spot at the front of the classroom and stretched out on the floor, or on the desks and chairs. Blais and Kispetik made themselves at home in the back of the room where it was darker and cooler.

It wasn't until they arrived in Haditha the previous day and climbed out of their amphibious assault vehicles (AAVs) that most of the grunts even realized they had female Marines with them. The looks on the grunts' faces revealed their disappointment. Having already gone on a mission with the grunts, Blais was okay with their less than enthusiastic reaction; Kispetik may have been wondering who her real enemy was, the grunts or the Iraqis. At first she felt uncomfortable. She sensed the grunts staring at her and Blais, as if they could will the women away with their intent gaze. Blais tried to reassure her buddy, letting her know that she was scared the first time she traveled with the grunts but not to worry. The grunts never bothered her. They were focused, and not on her. Blais witnessed their intense camaraderie, and the strict rank structure that made the grunts so unique and effective. They were in tune with how each other worked. When they searched houses, the lead grunt didn't have to turn around to see if someone had his back. The trust level was high.

Blais and Kispetik befriended another female Marine on the road from Al Asad to Haditha. Corporal Karen Cunningham of the 4th Landing Support Battalion in Vienna, Ohio, also volunteered to go to Haditha. The twenty-six-year-old reservist was a heavy equipment operator. As she began to connect with the other two women, the comfort level rose. Blais would joke that Cunningham broke the equipment, Blais repaired it, and Kispetik processed the paperwork. At Al Asad, the women didn't work far from one another, but Cunningham didn't get to know Blais and Kispetik until they hit the road.

Cunningham had heard that Blais was cool but didn't go out of her way to get to know her. The reservist had become so attached to her platoon that she didn't see the need to make new friends. Besides, female Marines were known to be tough on one another. Before meeting, they would check one another out: What kind of Marine are you? Are you a slacker? Do you play the female card? Are you good to go?

It seemed all three of these women were good to go. They bonded fairly quickly as there were only a handful of female Marines serving with the grunts in Haditha. Cunningham fit in well with Blais and Kispetik. She was animated and enjoyed imitating people. Blais, especially, liked to poke fun at Cunningham's height. Cunningham is five feet ten inches tall, eight inches taller than Blais. Eventually, Blais would joke that she never went out of her way to talk to Cunningham because she feared her. "I was afraid you were going to stomp on me." Cunningham's other defining feature is her green eyes. Between her eyes and her height, the Iraqi women, like Blais, wouldn't know what to make of her.

Cunningham shared the desire that Blais and Kispetik had to get off base, travel with the grunts, and do what they had been trained to do in boot camp. Cunningham had already spent a week and a half in a remote desert region near the Syrian border for Operation Matador. She was sent there to search Iraqi women but the area was too dangerous so she was sent to Al Qaim. While there, she assisted with mortuary affairs and was told to be on standby to help out with female Iraqi patients. Al Qaim was a short distance from the battle, so the Angels (fallen Marines) were flown there instead of the full distance to Al Asad. Nine Marines were killed and forty were wounded in what was the largest American campaign since militants were driven from Fallujah six months earlier.

In the mortuary, Cunningham searched the Angels for ID cards or dog tags and recorded who they were and the extent of their wounds. In most cases she was able to document only what was left of the bodies. After filling out death certificates, she helped place the Marines in body bags and called for a flight to take them to Al Asad as quickly as possible.

In Operation Matador, the Marines cleaned out the insurgent haven and killed more than 125 militants and wounded many others. One of the people they wounded was a pregnant Iraqi mother. She arrived at Al Qaim after she and her family had been in a taxi that was shot up. Cunningham and another female Marine cut off the mother's clothes to check her wound. The woman who had been shot didn't want to be exposed in front of the men so the female Marines covered her with a blanket while they removed her clothing. All the while they had to remain alert to the possibility she could have a bomb strapped to her body. All Cunningham wanted to do was help, but she had to keep reminding herself that the Iraqis—men, women, and children—had no problem blowing themselves up to kill a few Americans. In addition to seeing the gunshot wound, Cunningham noticed bruises covering the Iraqi woman's body. A male Marine told her that Iraqi husbands liked to beat their wives.

While going through boot camp, Cunningham often wondered why she had to do the exact same training as the male Marines when she was prohibited from serving in combat. As she prepared to head to Haditha with Blais and Kispetik, into a direct combat zone, she heard on television that the House Republicans retreated from a sweeping ban on women in combat support and service units, and instead approved legislation backing the Pentagon's policy barring women from direct ground combat. Knowing they were doing something that not many women got to do, or wanted to do, drew Kispetik, Blais, and Cunningham closer together.

On their first morning in Haditha, the Marines separated into platoons and squads. Cunningham went with 3/25 Lima Company, and Blais and Kispetik went with 3/2 Kilo Company. They all spent a couple of hours patrolling the streets and searching homes. The streets were small and curvy, making it difficult to see who or what was around the corner. And each property had rock walls bordering the streets. While Cunningham was with her platoon, she walked in fear, knowing that at any moment a militant could be on the other side of the wall waiting to ambush her and her platoon.

Small, tan-colored houses stood side by side and blended in with their desert surroundings. On the edge of town were palm groves and a field area that reminded Blais of photos she had seen of rice paddies in Vietnam. As they patrolled the streets, the Marines swatted gnats from their faces. They put on goggles to cut down on the annoyance only to have their eye protection fog up.

Since this was Kispetik's first time on patrol, she didn't know quite what to expect and the grunts weren't forthcoming with information. She opted to stand watch outside while the grunts searched the houses. If they needed her they would let her know. Blais, who was already comfortable with her role and knew some of the Marines, entered the homes.

A house search usually went something like this. A Marine knocked on the door. An interpreter identified the Marines to the occupants. The Iraqis glared at them, especially at two in the morning when the Marines woke them from a sound sleep. The female Marines rounded up the Iraqi women and children into one room while the grunts dealt with the men of the household and searched the homes.

For the most part, the homes were full of clutter. The Iraqis were pack rats. They had piles of things one might find at a yard sale—old suitcases, clothes, pictures, lanterns, paperweights, newspapers, magazines, and furniture. All this "stuff" made the task of finding weapons and ammunition more difficult.

Signs citing adages and prayers to help the Iraqis get through the day, along with posters and stickers that Americans collected in the 1980s, covered their walls. One house had a huge sticker of Wonder Woman. Most of the furniture looked worn and even when it appeared nice, looks could be deceiving. Once Blais and Kispetik spotted what seemed like a nice couch so they sat down only to find out that it didn't have any cushions.

Blais, Kispetik, and Cunningham gradually got used to barging into homes, rummaging through the belongings of strangers, and guarding women and children. They also got accustomed to the different reactions from the Iraqi people. Iraqi women and children, fearful of the male Marines, screamed and cried until they saw female Marines. Then the mood in the house changed; the tension eased. They were happy to see the women. Blais didn't think they could tell she was a woman with all her gear on. The flak jacket hid her chest, and she tucked her hair under her Kevlar helmet. But they knew. Blais was happy that her presence calmed her enemy, but she was also there to do a job and didn't want the Iraqis to think that she was any less of a Marine. She realized the importance of the mission. She knew that anyone could hide a weapon, including the most innocent looking grandmother or child. Sometimes Blais and Kispetik tried to talk to the women in the little Arabic they had picked up and by using an Arabic phrase book Blais carried with her.

If there were no women and children, the female Marines participated in the house search. They would go up on the rooftops to make sure they were clear of Iraqis and weapons. A lot of sniper shots came from the rooftops in this and other Iraqi cities. On one rooftop, Marines found bedsprings, a car battery, and jumper cables. It looked to Blais as if some form of torture had occurred on this rooftop. They also found shells from an AK-47. In another house, Blais didn't believe an Iraqi when he said he didn't have any weapons. She lay down on the kitchen floor and found AK-47s under a refrigerator.

Cunningham went on house searches with another platoon, separate from Blais and Kispetik, so more ground could be covered with the female Marines. She found that in some houses her presence had a calming affect while in others it didn't make a difference or was considered an insult. At five feet ten inches she towered over the Iraqi women.

One household had four women who were amazed and excited to see Cunningham. As she patted them down, they swarmed around her, offering food and water. They'd look at her, clap once, and look at her again. Everyone was welcomed in that house. When she finished patting down the women, Cunningham sat down and the Iraqi women sat around her. The male Marines just laughed and left the room.

During her first few house searches, Cunningham wore her Kevlar. But after a while it occurred to her that no one could really tell she was a woman with all her gear on. So she did her own little sociological experiment in some of the households and took off her Kevlar so the Iraqi women would know she was a female.

After a morning of patrolling the city, Blais, Kispetik, and the grunts drove to a spot on the edge of town where they could bed down during the heat of the day. When Blais went to Haqlaniya, the grunts used Iraqi homes as their forward operating bases (FOBs). The Marine Corps paid the Iraqi people to let the Marines stay in their homes. The Iraqis moved out and the Marines moved in. They slept on mats on the floor. Over the months and years of fighting in Iraq, the grunts had gotten so picky about where they stayed that they wouldn't choose a house unless it had a satellite dish for watching television.

Blais thought housing on this trip would be equally desirable and had wooed Kispetik into going on this mission by telling her that the grunts stayed in nice homes. When they arrived at their destination and got out of their truck, Blais saw a huge house that looked like a mansion. *Sweet.* Then a grunt pointed her in the opposite direction—a palm grove.

Fifty Marines and ten men with the Iraqi Security Forces (ISF) found trees to rest under, to protect themselves from the direct sunlight and the soaring temperatures. Blais and Kispetik found a little nook in the palm groves a short distance from the grunts. Everyone sprawled out on the grass, packs and all. They knew they wouldn't be going back on patrol any time soon. It was too hot. They would stay in the shade and pound water until the sun set. Kispetik was less than thrilled with the accommodations. She had given up her fairly comfortable bed back at Al Asad for the bug-infested woods. Blais, who at best tolerated Kispetik's smoking habit, made an exception in the woods. Since cigarette smoke was a bug deterrent, Blais encouraged her buddy to light up.

While they passed the day waiting for dusk, a staff sergeant approached the female Marines. They exchanged names. He asked the women if they had ever gone on house searches before this mission in Haditha. Blais said that she had. Then the real reason for his visit came to light. He let them know that they were not going to receive special treatment because they were women. They were Marines and every Marine (male or female) was a rifleman, and he expected things to run that way. Blais and Kispetik were grateful for this attitude. For the most part, they didn't want to be treated differently. There was one exception.

Mother Nature was calling. They had to go to the bathroom but the grunts had set up a 360 perimeter around Kilo for protection. There were Marines everywhere and they could see everywhere. Blais and Kispetik didn't know what to do. Finally, after a short debate—short because they really had to go—they walked over to one of the Marines on the perimeter and asked, "Where *can't* you see?"

He said he was "on post" and could see everywhere.

They asked him if he could *not* look in one area for about two minutes. He laughed. That broke the ice, a little.

On another occasion, Kispetik was going to the bathroom while Blais held up her blouse like a curtain for privacy. Kispetik had her back to a tree. Blais teased her, saying things like, "Don't lean against the tree. You're going to get bark up your butt." As she said this, Blais, who was facing the Euphrates River, did a double take. She thought she saw something move on a small island in the middle of the river. "There's a cow in the river," Blais shouted. Kispetik jumped up, nearly exposing herself.

After asking the Marine on the perimeter not to look their way for a couple of minutes, and getting a laugh out of him, Blais wasn't exactly feeling a bond with the grunts but she wasn't feeling ostracized either. Kispetik wasn't feeling as good as Blais about the situation. She imagined the grunts were thinking, *Great, we've got females with us. We're going to have to take care of them.* Kispetik hoped for the best, hoped that she could prove herself to them. That would come in time. But until their patrol that evening, no other grunts came near them.

As far back as they can remember, Kispetik and Blais have wanted to be Marines. Kispetik's grandfather, father, grandmother, and a couple of cousins were all Marines. Blais had chosen to follow in her father's footsteps. He spent twenty years in the Marine Corps as a grunt and served in Vietnam. He died while she was in boot camp. Blais's younger brother, twenty-four-year-old Donald Blais, Jr., joined the Marine Corps before his sister and served during the battle for Fallujah. She hadn't seen him for a year, until she landed on the tarmac at Al Asad in a C-130. He was leaving on the same aircraft. She saw his platoon, and then him, in the distance, and thought, *You son of a gun.* Neither one of their commands would let them visit with each other. Blais would have to wait another seven months before she saw her brother. Seeing her brother was particularly emotional because while he was in Iraq, the Marine Corps had mixed up Donald's Social Security number with another Marine's and had notified Donald's mom that he had been wounded by an IED in Iraq, was in critical condition, and had been flown to a hospital in Germany. They had the wrong person.

As Blais and Kispetik waited out the heat in the shade of the palm groves, they listened to the sound of prayers pouring from the mosques. They watched a car drive up, park, and then speed off as Marines approached. Once the sun set, they started putting on their gear to begin their patrol when they heard a loud blast. A mortar had landed nearby. They didn't see it but they heard it, and they felt its concussion. It happened so fast that all they could do was hit the ground. They were already wearing their flaks and Kevlars. There wasn't much else they could do. No one got hurt. Marines searched the area. Perhaps the worst part of that mortar attack was that it set them back five more hours. Marines had to sweep the area and make sure it was safe. They didn't start their patrol until 11:30 P.M. As they prepared to leave for the second time, the EOD technician asked the women to help him carry a load of C4 plastic explosives. They were already carrying seventy to one hundred pounds everywhere they went because they planned to stay in a different location each night. But they didn't want to appear weak so they agreed to lug the extra weight.

That night on patrol, the Marines looked for Internet cafés that insurgents might have been using to communicate with one another. The grunts ordered Blais to watch the perimeter. She lay down on a pile of dirt beside the road and propped up her rifle. Every time she got comfortable the weight of her pack caused her to slide down the mound of dirt. As she struggled to get into position, a dog caught wind of her scent and headed in Blais's direction. The dogs could be fierce in Iraq. Some Marines feared the canines more than the Iraqis. The dog growled as it approached her. *Do I shoot it*, wondered Blais, who loves dogs. While this was happening, Kispetik sat behind Blais, holding her rifle in one hand and her CamelBack—water container—in another. Fortunately, something distracted the dog and Blais didn't have to shoot it. It went away on its own.

When the Marines began to walk further down the road, they put Blais and Kispetik in the middle of the platoon since patrolling the streets wasn't their specialty. The women didn't mind this too much. They had started to hear rumors that the Iraqis were targeting American female Marines and soldiers. Blais was beginning to feel like a guinea pig in some large experiment, as if she and Kispetik had been recruited for patrol as bait to draw out the insurgents.

After patrolling all night, the Marines found a large abandoned house to sleep in. That morning, Blais and Kispetik got the best sleep of their lives. Blais, who typically does recon before she beds down to make sure the area is rodent-free, didn't give the furry critters a second thought. She was too tired. Both women dropped their packs in the corner of a room and fell asleep. They had been with the grunts for twenty-four hours and were exhausted. They had a hard time imagining their weary bodies spending weeks and months with infantry.

Later that same morning they went on another patrol. The Marines knew which houses they were supposed to search, but in an effort to win the hearts and minds of the Iraqi people they didn't target a specific house because it might make the family look bad. So they searched the houses around their target, too.

In one house, Blais came upon a thirteen-year-old girl crying hysterically and talking in Arabic. Since Blais wasn't fluent in Arabic, she sat down beside the girl and tried to console her in English. All of a sudden, the girl started speaking perfect English with an Arabic accent.

"Why do you love Bush?" she demanded.

Oh Lord, a little help please. Where's the interpreter?

"No, why?" the girl insisted.

Blais explained that she didn't love Bush but that he was her commander in chief—her boss—and she had to do what he said. Blais's loyalty was to her country.

It was after this search and patrol that Blais and Kispetik arrived at the school, opened and kicked down some doors, and made themselves comfortable, relatively speaking. When a Marine asked for volunteers to post security, Blais stepped up. They considered going up on the roof but decided it was too dangerous because of sporadic sniper fire in the area. They opted for the fourth floor instead. While on security with another lance corporal, Blais saw a couple of Iraqi kids throw an unidentified object into the street. A car sped around and picked them up. The Marines sent someone to check it out.

Back on the second floor, Kispetik was sitting next to a big infantry Marine who had acquired quite a tan while patrolling the streets in the hot Iraqi sun. She also noticed that he had a larger weapon than her M-16. It may have been an M-240. The Marine asked her if she had a cigarette. She had about four packs of Marlboro Milds. "Yeah," she said, handing him an entire pack. Cigarettes were fairly easy to come by in Iraq, but Marines still tended to hand them out sparingly. Kispetik's gesture was unusually generous and helped break some of the tension between the genders. The grunt started talking about his girlfriend. Kispetik listened. He had been out there longer than she had and probably needed someone other than another grunt to talk to, maybe even someone of the opposite sex. It made Kispetik feel good to know that he would confide in her. He said his girlfriend was pressing him for an engagement ring but he thought she was mean. All she wanted was his money. Kispetik said he should trust his instincts. She told him that his girlfriend sounded like a gold digger and that he shouldn't have anything more to do with her. Be careful, she warned.

In Iraq, a lot of the male Marines talked to Kispetik and Blais about their personal problems. Blais had a theory about this. They didn't talk to the women because they were better listeners but because they were supposed to be better listeners. And they were somebody different. The grunts needed a new sounding board, a fresh pair of ears. After a while, the Marine that Kispetik had been talking to got called away to provide security. She never saw him again. He was hit by shrapnel and medevaced out.

While engaging in conversation with the male Marines, Blais and Kispetik were careful not to flirt or to give the appearance they were being flirtatious. Blais knew better. In Haqlaniya, she was talking to a grunt when a platoon sergeant spotted them and immediately gave them a dressing-down. The grunts hadn't seen many female American women, and the platoon sergeant didn't want his Marines to get the wrong idea. Blais's lieutenant smoothed things out, but the embarrassing moment lingered. Blais had been forewarned. In Haditha, Blais and Kispetik made a conscious effort to keep their distance from the grunts when they weren't on post or patrol. They spoke when spoken to.

When Blais finished her security watch, she rejoined Kispetik. Some of the Marines who had recently returned from patrolling the streets had a bad feeling that day, like something was going to happen. Even though Blais hadn't patrolled since earlier that morning, she also sensed something ominous. It was about 4:15

in the afternoon. All the guys in the squad had thrown off their packs, unbuttoned their blouses, and untied their boots. They wore only their T-shirts and pants. Their flaks and Kevlar lay nearby. They were either asleep or relaxing.

Blais and Kispetik couldn't sleep even though they were both tired. So Blais wrote in her journal while Kispetik listened to eighties music on her CD player. Kispetik, who had been lying down, sat up to grab another CD. Blais was making a list in her journal of the things she wanted to accomplish while she was in Iraq: pick up corporal, earn a combat action ribbon . . .

Suddenly, a loud crash jolted them from their tranquil positions. A rocket-propelled grenade (RPG) had just smashed the window and wall where the male Marines were sleeping. Blais and Kispetik dropped to the floor. "You okay?" they yelled to each other. Before they could grab their flaks, Kevlars, and rifles, they heard the whistle of another incoming RPG and crash. The second RPG hit the building where the two had been sitting just moments earlier. The window and wall caved in. Both women ducked and covered their faces as the debris fell. Luckily, the wall was made of a light substance like plaster and not brick.

Kispetik ran out of the classroom. Blais was right behind her until she snagged her pants on a desk.

"Come on, Blais," Kispetik yelled.

Blais wiggled herself free and crawled out of the room.

The grunts had moved to the hallway. Someone took roll while the Marines quickly buttoned their blouses and tied their boots. Kispetik stood on one side of the hallway and Blais on the other, facing into the classroom and the corner where the first rocket hit. Two Marines lay there on their stomachs in a pool of blood.

When the RPGs hit the school, one of the heads of the Iraqi Security Forces (ISF), who had been traveling with Kilo Company, ran outside the building and started firing away. A couple of Marines dragged him back inside.

Blais and Kispetik heard AK-47 rounds interspersed with conversations in Arabic. Blais thought the Iraqis were coming in the building, and that she and the other Marines would have to fight their way out. *I don't know if I can do this.* But those thoughts came and left in a flash, and were replaced with action.

The staff sergeant needed two people to go with him into the classroom that had just been hit by RPGs. Blais volunteered. They looked out what were previously windows to determine where the rockets had come from but couldn't see anyone. As they were leaving the room, Blais tripped over something. She looked down and saw a Marine.

"What's wrong with him?" she asked Kispetik.

Blais and Kispetik knelt down and checked for a pulse. Blais thought she felt something. They held his hands and talked to him. The corpsman came over and said the Marine was dead. The Marine was a major who had gone to check on two younger Marines on post after the first RPG hit. The two grunts on post were wearing their protective gear. When the second RPG hit, shattering glass hit the major. He wasn't wearing his flak. The glass pierced his chest and punctured his lungs.

Next, the staff sergeant, Blais, and a couple of other Marines took off for the third floor. Kispetik stayed behind on the second floor. To get to the next level, Blais had to run down the hallway in the direction of the AK-47s. As the Marines ran up the stairs, they stayed low to dodge a barrage of bullets flying over their heads. Training is so lifelike that sometimes the Marines forget when it's real. Not this time. Blais knew this was the real deal. She and the staff sergeant reached a classroom on the third deck and took their positions in a window. From their new location, they had a view of the schoolyard and the stone wall that surrounded

it, a road, a lone house, and then a cluster of houses. Captain
Sean O'Neill came into the classroom and told the Marines there
were no friendlies in the area. Anyone on the street was a possible
threat. The staff sergeant ordered Blais to fire on anyone with a
weapon. Less than two minutes later, Blais spotted a male Iraqi
about 400 meters away. He was wearing a white robe and carrying
an AK-47 as he ran from the one lone house to the other houses.

"There's someone there," Blais yelled to the staff sergeant.

It was Blais's first time firing at someone. She was scared. She
didn't want to take out a random person.

"Shoot," the staff sergeant yelled back.

Without hesitation, Blais fired two shots, hitting her target in
the right leg. His leg jerked and he fell. The AK-47 landed a short
distance away. The Iraqi started crawling toward his weapon.

"Finish it," the staff sergeant yelled.

Blais fired two more shots. The Iraqi stopped moving as his
white robe turned red. The accuracy of her shots surprised Blais.
She could hit an Iraqi on the run but on the firing range, she
couldn't hit a stationary target. She wanted to get out of there—
alive.

The staff sergeant slapped her on the back.

"Nice fucking job," he yelled.

Blais nodded her head. She didn't know what to say. She had
just taken a man's life.

The staff sergeant must have known it was the lance corporal's first kill because he grabbed her Kevlar, turned her head so
she was facing him, looked her in the eyes, and said, "Think of all
the lives you just saved."

It was the first time in her Marine Corps career that Blais felt
like she had made a difference.

"Rah," Blais said back, a short version of the common Marine
Corps expression, "oohrah."

Just then, an Iraqi on a motorcycle came into view. Blais and the staff sergeant "lit him up." When the staff sergeant fired, Blais hit the deck. His weapon was so loud that it startled her. He could have been using an M-16 or an M-240. She wasn't paying attention. But the classroom they were in was empty and amplified the sound of the weapon. Plus she had just experienced two RPG explosions. At that point, even a pin-drop would have unnerved her.

"You okay?" the staff sergeant asked.

"Yeah," Blais said, as she got back up and re-entered the firefight.

A few more targets appeared. Blais heard a lot of firing from the grunts on the fourth deck and from the roof. While Blais countered the Iraqi attack from the third deck, Kispetik was dodging sniper fire on the same side of the building but from the second floor. Tactically speaking, Kispetik was at a disadvantage because she was in a lower position. Every time she got ready to shoot, an Iraqi hidden in a tree or on a rooftop fired the first shot. She fired a couple of rounds but it was hard. She just wanted to keep low because the Iraqis were aiming for her head. The sporadic firefight continued for a while. Kispetik and Blais both felt like they had tunnel vision during the firefight. They saw only what they needed to see.

While Blais and Kispetik were taking fire, Cunningham stood on the rooftop of a building several miles away. She could hear the action but couldn't see it because a hill separated her from her buddies. She was doing surveillance in her immediate area and setting up staging points for snipers. Just as a couple of the Marines were pointing out to Cunningham where Blais and Kispetik's were positioned, Cunningham heard the booms from the RPGs and the *rat-tat-tat* of gunfire.

Cunningham got a sick feeling in her stomach. She hoped her friends would survive the firefight but she couldn't help but think the worst. She had flashbacks of the Marines who had been killed and wounded in Al Qaim. Working in the mortuary, she had seen what happened when buildings crushed people and when AK-47s mangled bodies. Now, on the front line, she heard the RPGs and AK-47s—the deadly instruments that killed and wounded Marines. She hoped the Marines would somehow appear on the top of the hill that separated them but they never did.

After several subsequent booms, Army Black Hawk helicopters flew in. Cunningham and the Marines she was with watched the aircraft for a while, then they moved out to find a better base for their unit—just in case the Iraqis targeted them next. They would need to defend themselves. They left a couple of snipers on the rooftop.

When the firefight settled down, Kispetik and a staff sergeant ran up a flight of stairs where they met other Marines. Now Kispetik was on the same floor as Blais, but at the opposite end of the building. Kispetik felt like she was watching a movie from a window, but at the same time she was in the movie. Tanks and amphibious assault vehicles drove around below her, and helicopters flew overhead.

The Marines determined that the majority of the firing was coming from one house so they contacted air support. Within minutes, a jet dropped a 500-pound bomb on the house. Blais heard the whistling of the bomb as it fell and thought it was headed for her. She didn't hear an explosion when the bomb destroyed the house, but she saw the cloud of dust and debris. Kispetik was at the end of the school closest to the house and only about 500 meters away when it blew up. Both of the women could see the shock wave move toward them. Before it reached her, Kispetik moved away from the window. Blais, on the other hand, did just the opposite. She moved toward it.

Doooooosh—the air pushed Blais backwards.

Holy crap! Wow!

Rumor had it that Abu Musab Al Zarqawi, a leader in the Islamic jihad against the United States, was hiding out in that house and the bomb had killed him. Later reports said he had been wounded in the bombing but escaped.

As darkness set in, the number of rounds fired by both sides dwindled. Blais and Kispetik found one another. Blais got some aspirin to quell an intense headache. Kispetik took an energy pill and was bouncing off the walls. During the firefight, she had a lot going on in her head. After the adrenaline rush and the excitement, when she finally realized things were settling down and no one was shooting at her anymore, Kispetik's mind and body were exhausted and wanted to shut down. She suddenly became so tired that she started to fall asleep but she knew it wasn't the best time to take a nap so she took the energy pill. Militants could still be lurking nearby. There was no telling what might happen next.

Since it was dark and they couldn't turn on the lights in the school, the Marines put on their night-vision goggles (NVGs) and searched the classroom where they had left their gear. They sat in the windows and listened for Iraqis outside. They heard sounds off in the distance but nothing nearby. After a while, the squad Blais was attached to went on patrol but she wasn't invited. It was one of those few times when she didn't mind being treated differently by the grunts.

Once the Marines returned from their patrol, all the Marines in the school walked three blocks down the street to a small theater. They didn't want to press their luck and stay at the school. Before they moved into the school it looked like it had already been in a firefight and shelled by RPGs. The Marines didn't hide the fact they were changing locations. Anyone looking out the window could see them walking down the street, but it wasn't as if they were going to the theater to "hide out." They were looking for a new and temporary staging area.

Most of the Marines found a spot to rest on the floor in the theater. The men in the Iraqi Security Forces set up camp on the stage, which was hollow, and every time they dropped their gear and weapons the Marines thought a bomb had gone off. Some Marines went back on patrol after that. A chaplain stopped by. Although Blais doesn't consider herself a religious person, she jumped in line for communion. *It's true there are no atheists in war. I survived this day—there is a God.*

Later in the evening, Kispetik and Blais were standing on the roof when some of the Marines nearby decided to test their M-240s without warning the others. With nerves still fragile from the firefight several hours earlier, Kispetik dropped down fast. Blais, who had just returned from patrol and taken off her flak and Kevlar, reached for her protection.

The morning after the firefight the Marines visited the house that had been bombed. All that remained was rubble. The bombing was so precise that the house next door had only one window blown out, and Blais wasn't even sure that was from the bomb. The Marines also searched the house the Iraqi was running to before Blais killed him. They didn't find his body and none of the Iraqis would admit to knowing anything about him or the firefight.

Once the realization of her official kill sunk in, Blais began to have mixed emotions about her feat. On the one hand, she felt more than ever that she had made a real contribution to the war effort. Of course her primary job of repairing heavy equipment was important. It was all important. But being in a firefight was different. And even though her father was deceased, Blais felt a new connection to the Vietnam vet whom she had grown up admiring.

Blais also began thinking of her one kill as guilty pleasure. She knew the number of women who actually "fought" in combat was limited. It was an honor to have a kill because in the Marine Corps, your status increases proportionally with your number of kills. But Blais also felt guilty when she thought about the man she killed. She pictured him with a family. Granted, he was carrying an AK-47, but they all had AKs. There is still a part of her that thinks she shouldn't have shot him, she shouldn't have taken his life. She just hopes and prays that she did the right thing.

Captain Robin Brown, United States Army.

Shoot Down

"You always wonder whether you will be able to handle it if something bad happens. Well, I got a chance to find out."

—Army Captain Robin Brown

"MAYDAY, MAYDAY, MAYDAY, WHITEWOLF ZERO SIX, WE'RE GOING down," said a female voice into the mouthpiece attached to her helmet.

Just moments before, Army Captain Robin Brown and Chief Warrant Officer Two Jeff Sumner, pilots of a Kiowa Warrior helicopter, heard a large explosion and then felt their aircraft lurch forward, shake violently, and begin to fall. Warning sounds erupted in the cockpit, lights flashed on the control panel, and instruments trembled. Shattered and uneven rotor blades slowed. They were free falling. The pilots would have to perform an "auto-rotation" maneuver.

In flight school, pilots practice landing when their engine fails. They fly up to 1,000 feet, cut off the engine, and land. At the right speed, 70 knots, they can keep the rotors turning and the air flowing through them. This is called "auto-rotation." It's the scariest thing in the world the first time a pilot tries it, and a good training instructor makes a new pilot do it over and over again until it becomes second nature. When Brown felt the explosion, she and Sumner were at 100 feet, a difference of 900 feet between training and reality. One hundred feet isn't much distance when you could be falling to your death. No time to think—just react and hope the training pays off.

Brown grabbed her shoulder harness and locked herself in. She reached for the microphone, located on the cyclic, which controls the forward, backward, left, and right movement of the helicopter. The cyclic was shaking uncontrollably. It took a second for Brown to grasp it. Sumner had his hand on the collective, a joystick used to raise and lower the aircraft.

"MAYDAY, MAYDAY, MAYDAY, Whitewolf Zero Six, we're going down!" she repeated.

Brown's thoughts shifted into overdrive—had they been hit by a rocket-propelled grenade or were they feeling the vibration of a concussion from a ground explosion? She thought they had been hit. By what, she didn't know.

✯ ✯ ✯

It was December 9, 2003, four months into her deployment in Iraq. Twenty-eight-year-old Brown, thirty-one-year-old Sumner, and another helicopter with two pilots had just provided security for a convoy delivering new currency to Baghdad. They had made an hour and a half flight from Al Taqaddum Air Base to Baghdad. The mission was a success. While the helicopters refueled, the pilots went to the bathroom and ate lunch. They spent about forty-five minutes on the ground.

As they prepared to leave Baghdad, the pilots were unaware that a squad of Iraqi insurgents—two, three, maybe more—hiding in desert brush outside of Fallujah, awaited their return.

Brown stepped into the left side of the aircraft and took her seat. At five feet three inches tall, she couldn't reach the pedals. The pedals were adjustable, so she slid them all the way forward. And although she was lean, weighing just 110 pounds, she had little room to move to the right or left in the compact aircraft. Her small frame had grown bulkier with the addition of armor and a survival vest. A helmet absorbed her head, covering her short brown hair, and barely showing her small narrow face and brown eyes.

Seated to her right was Sumner. He was five feet eight inches tall and weighed 170 pounds. He had blond hair, blue eyes, and a great big smile. Before deploying to Iraq, Sumner had nearly six years of flying experience. Brown had less flight time because she had chosen the path of a commissioned officer, which emphasized leadership skills over flying hours. In Iraq, they would fly together for eight months and complete more than seventy-five missions.

To the unacquainted, Brown and her aircraft looked fragile, delicate, as if they could easily crumble with little force. Unarmed, the Kiowa helicopter weighs only 4,500 pounds, about the weight of a Ford Explorer. That's light compared to Apaches and Black Hawks, which weigh in at more than 11,500 pounds. Yet both Brown and her aircraft were tougher than they appeared. Jet pilots say a helicopter doesn't fly; the earth rejects it. Brown likes to think that her Kiowa flies because it beats the earth into submission.

Brown and the Kiowa were agile, sturdy, and resilient. Rarely, if ever, did Brown look at her size, or the dimensions of her aircraft, as a weakness. Given the choice, she wouldn't trade her Kiowa for another aircraft. Brown may not have given much thought to her small physique but her father did. Biff Messinger was a former elite infantry Ranger who finished his career as chief of operations for the commandant of cadets at the United States Military Academy at West Point. Privately, he worried about his daughter. He knew the demands of the Army. When he recalled his own training, in airborne and ranger schools, it was hard for him to imagine Robin, as small as she was, going through the same. But he never told her that.

Kiowas are scout helicopters. They fly armed reconnaissance missions. Cameras located in a black disco ball on top of the aircraft photograph the landscape below and project the photos on two small television screens for each pilot to see. The aircraft weren't designed to fly into battle, get shot up, and return home unscathed. Nor were they intended to transport large numbers of troops, equipment, or supplies. Five or six Kiowas can fit, with their rotors folded up, into a cargo plane.

As commander of Bravo Company, 1st Battalion, 82nd Aviation Regiment, from Fort Bragg, North Carolina, Brown led a company of twenty-six pilots. In Iraq, their primary mission was to respond to an attack on a moment's notice, a.k.a. quick response force (QRF). The missions were extremely stressful for the pilots, who received information at the last minute, on their way out the door. They didn't have time to mull over the situation, weigh the options, consider the alternatives. Seldom did they know exactly what they were flying into when they arrived at the scene of a conflict. A battle could be ongoing or it could have just ended, with insurgents still fighting or fleeing. Either way, the pilots had to be on their guard, alert at all times.

Once they were airborne, Brown's job was to keep her eyes on all the activity in the sky and on the ground, and to navigate and maintain communication with various entities. This was important because as soon as it took off, the aircraft became a target for shoulder-fired missiles. Kiowas fly low and fast, thirty to fifty feet above the ground (about the height of a two-story house) and at speeds of 85 to 90 knots, although they can travel 125 knots. The trick is to fly slow enough to see what is going on below, on the ground, yet fast enough so nothing can hit them. If they were flying near a city, where there were a lot of wires, they bumped up to 100 feet.

On their flight back to Al Taqaddum, Brown, Sumner, and the pilots in the other aircraft conversed back and forth. They had been flying together for four months and had known each other even longer. Making conversation was effortless. They didn't stay on the radio too long because they couldn't tie up the frequency and they had to pay attention to their surroundings. But when they did talk on the radio, they sometimes sounded like truck drivers on a CB. The pilots usually stuck to two topics—their daily bowel movements and food. Not totally unrelated. Life could get monotonous in the desert but the same couldn't be said for trips to the bathroom. They talked about food because they all missed good chow. They liked to ask the question, "If you could eat any-thing right now, what would you eat?" Answers ranged from Twinkies to filet mignon.

Sex was another hot subject. Having a female and former jun-ior prom queen on board provided Sumner and the two male pilots in the other aircraft with a different point of view. They always asked Brown's opinion when they wanted a female per-spective. She was comfortable jumping into the conversations because she grew up among a family of soldiers, where the men teased and bantered with extraordinary ease. Brown is the grand-daughter of retired Chief Warrant Officer Four Peter A. Merli, a cavalry infantryman from World War II, and of General Edwin J. Messinger, Sr., who served as commandant of cadets of West Point from 1954 to 1956. Plus, her dad and uncle were in the Army. She attended Fordham University in New York on an Army ROTC scholarship, and then joined the Army.

At about two in the afternoon, Brown's aircraft was just south of Fallujah, a five-minute flight from the airfield. The pilots flew over the city nearly every day. They knew the landscape and its potential hazards. Although the city had been identified as a hot spot, the pilots didn't feel threatened because they took a south-ern route. At the time, the most dangerous part of Fallujah was north of the city. The altitude at which the pilots flew, and their knowledge of surface-to-air missiles, gave them an added sense of security. They were flying under the assumption that the Iraqis were afraid of the helicopters and reluctant to shoot at them. The few times the Iraqis did fire at the aircraft, they used small arms or rocket-propelled grenades, which are like bottle rockets. The weapons have no guidance system.

Brown and Sumner, flying at 100 feet and 75 knots, trailed the lead aircraft, flown by Chief Warrant Officer Three Mark Teeden, a veteran pilot at thirty-eight, and Chief Warrant Officer Two Chris Wallace, twenty-six and fresh out of flight school.

The two aircraft flew over open fields and came to a dam they regularly used as a checkpoint to let headquarters at the airfield know they were inbound.

Brown, speaking into her mouthpiece, reported to ground forces that the aircraft were leaving their area of operations and entering the airfield's.

"Blue Devil Seven Four, this is Whitewolf Zero Six. Two KWs passing through your air space. We're now exiting to the west and frequency change to the airfield."

"Roger. See you later."

Then Brown radioed the airfield.

"Pegasus Ops—Whitewolf Zero Six is a flight of two KWs inbound, currently at the dam."

As the lead aircraft started to cross the Euphrates River, Brown and Sumner, less than 500 feet behind, moved from the right to the left, varying their flight pattern so as not be a target.

Just as their aircraft was lined up behind the lead, Brown heard, and then felt, an explosion.

The pilots in the lead aircraft couldn't see Brown's Kiowa when it was hit because the trail was almost directly behind them. Kiowas don't have rearview. They depend on radio communication and line of sight. But as soon as the lead heard an explosion, it broke hard to the left and then back around to the right to vary its flight pattern. If it wasn't a ground explosion and someone had shot Brown's aircraft, the lead could be the next target.

Brown and Sumner knew the engine on their aircraft had been affected because of the way it was losing RPMs. They would have to maintain control of the helicopter to land safely. They looked for a clearing. The pilots were used to practicing their auto-rotation landings on runways so they wouldn't bang up the $8 million aircraft. They learn how to land in a safe environment to minimize casualties during training and hope that the training will transfer to a real-life situation. The purpose of auto-rotation is not to save the aircraft but to save the pilots inside. There was no runway for this real-life emergency landing but there was a freshly plowed field.

The helicopter had lost its engine and hydraulic power. The only way to get the Kiowa safely on the ground was to use centrifugal force. Sumner put the aircraft into auto-rotation, relying on air going up and forcing the rotor blades to turn, like a windmill. The rotors were already turning, and the air kept them rotating. At the same time, Sumner carefully lowered the collective to slow the blades. If he reduced the speed of the blades too quickly, the aircraft wouldn't have enough lift and would smash to the ground like a dropped egg. The key was to achieve a state of optimum air speed and auto-rotation. He was also pushing the cyclic forward to gain air speed and get the wind to go through the rotor system for some extra lift.

They're falling

falling

falling.

The auto-rotation was working fine even though the aircraft was still vibrating violently. Sumner strained to keep the helicopter as steady as possible. Otherwise, the aircraft could gain forward motion and flip over when it hit the ground.

For a split second, as the helicopter dropped, Brown thought, *This could be it. This could be bad.* However, she didn't really think she would die and she wouldn't let herself be captured. She knew in the back of her mind that to *not be captured* she had to do certain things. She would rely on her instincts and her Army training when she hit the ground, if she got out of the aircraft alive.

As the aircraft dropped to the ground, Brown focused on the positive. This might work out. She considered all the steps as they were happening. It felt like the action was occurring in slow motion and very deliberately. While she thought through each step, she felt calm and detached. She didn't have time to think about anything else. Only, *What's my next step?*

Right before they hit the ground, with the aircraft still shaking out of control, Sumner pulled up on the collective at the last second, flattening the blades. This skillful maneuvering, as well as the plowed field, helped to cushion what would have typically been a jarring landing. Instead of wheels, the Kiowa has landing skids, or legs, that look like two skis. The aircraft fell slowly to the plowed field and landed slightly on the back of its skids. The skids sank into the field like skis pressing into thick, deep snow. Then the momentum of the fuselage pushed the aircraft slightly forward. If they had been any higher when they were hit, the helicopter wouldn't have stayed together.

By the time the pilots in the lead aircraft came back around, Brown was on the ground. Teeden identified the position of the downed Kiowa and radioed the airfield to report a "lame duck"— an aircraft down. Wallace switched to an emergency frequency and waited for Brown to radio him.

It felt to Brown as if fifteen seconds had passed from the time they were struck to when they hit the ground. It was more like half that time. In combat, senses come alive and perception of time slows down. Like a car accident, everything seemed to happen in slow motion.

They survived the crash but Brown and Sumner weren't out of danger from their aircraft and from whoever had shot them down. When the aircraft rocked forward, its rotor blades were still spinning furiously, all wobbly and bent and out of whack now. The blades hacked at the ground and beat themselves up, sending up a furious din. At any moment, they might fly apart and whip into the cockpit, and Brown knew it. Those out-of-control blades could slice them to pieces. Both pilots put their hands over their heads to protect themselves—an instinctive and useless reaction.

The blades are made of composite material and are very light. When a helicopter goes down, the blades beat themselves into the ground and shred. The pieces fly into the cockpit. Many people who die in helicopter accidents are killed by the blades shooting into the cockpit.

All Brown heard during this period was the sound of the blades slicing into the dirt and the noises emitting from the control panel. When the blades at last stopped spinning and the pilots uncovered their eyes, the cockpit was full of sand. Brown and Sumner sat back for a minute. Brown's first thought was, *We made it*. Neither had been injured. They both smiled big—they couldn't believe it.

They seemed fine, but the same couldn't be said for the helicopter. It was already on fire. Black smoke billowed from the engine. The pods that held the rockets were also aflame and might blow any second now. Time to go. As they crawled out of the cockpit, they had to step up because the aircraft had sunk so low.

They were wearing their helmets and dressed in desert flight suits, which are light and made of a fire-resistant material called Nomex, the same fabric worn by firefighters and race car drivers. But they're not light once they add their armor, made of Kevlar and a ceramic material, and weighing about thirty pounds, and a survival vest, which adds another forty-five pounds. Everything Brown needed to survive over a twenty-four hour period was tucked somewhere in one of her vest's many pockets—flares, smoke canisters, water purification tablets, razor blades, a mirror for signaling, flash light, matches, knives, candy, wet wipes, toilet paper, and a radio. The pilots could add anything they wanted to their vests. Brown normally stored extra food in hers. Long-term survival kits, including pup tents, were kept in the aircraft.

Brown was carrying about three-quarters of her weight when she got out of the helicopter and ran for cover to a large irrigation ditch near the field. She and Sumner also had firm grips on their 9mm pistols. Still in shock, they crouched in shrubbery not far from the aircraft. They knew they had to get farther away from the Kiowa. They didn't know who had shot them down or how close they were. They had to get out of there as quickly as possible—but where would they go?

In the sky, Wallace and Teeden circled around a second time. Teeden didn't know if his trail had been to his right or left rear when it was hit because they operate on what's called a free cruise. The trail is given the latitude to cross behind the lead, as long as it stays within forty-five degrees on either side. The freedom to move from one side to the other makes the trail less of a target. When Teeden didn't see the other Kiowa in the air, he scanned the ground for smoke. Initially, he assumed the worse. Then, as he continued on his flight path and looked down 150 yards from his turn, he saw the aircraft sitting upright, smoking.

Teeden's survival instincts kicked in. Standard operating procedure dictated that if an aircraft went down, the sister ship in the sky was not to fly over the same location for fear of being shot down, too. But at the same time, Teeden and Wallace didn't want to leave their trail aircraft behind. Teeden thought that if Sumner and Brown made it to the ground, he would land next to the aircraft. If it was on fire, and the pilots were still in the aircraft, he and Wallace would pull them from the burning Kiowa. He started to tell Wallace to look for a place for them to land when they spotted Brown and Sumner running. Seeing them was a relief for the pilots overhead.

Wallace knew the downed pilots had hand-held radios in their survival vests and immediately tried to reach Brown on two frequencies, UHF and VHF, which the pilots share. "No luck," he said, frustrated, when no one answered on the other end. "No luck. No luck."

Adding to the strain of the situation was the close relationship of these four pilots. They were like family. The four had flown as a team for the past 120 days and hoped they would fly together for the remaining 120 days of the deployment. In combat, pilots were closer than when they were back in the States. When they were in the States and they got off work, they went their separate ways. In combat, they walked together to chow, to the showers, to the phone. They ate, worked, and slept together. They lived together. Naturally, they became closer. They knew what was happening in one another's lives on and off the airfield, in and out of the sky. When someone received mail or a package, they all shared in the excitement. The camaraderie was exceptional. It had to be that way.

They knew Brown's husband, Jason, who was also a Kiowa pilot stationed at Fort Bragg. They knew that the young couple was restoring a 1921 home. That they had already painted the interior aqua walls white and turned three small rooms into one big room. That they had revamped the bathrooms, master bathroom, and laundry room. They had probably heard Brown quote Home and Garden TV and could easily imagine her curled up on a couch with magazines such as *Home*, *Metropolitan Home*, and *Dwell*.

On the ground, Brown continued to make Mayday calls over the guard frequency. Anyone who had a UHF radio would hear her. For some reason her radio wasn't communicating with the sister ship, Teeden and Wallace. However, an Air Force A-10 was flying nearby and picked up the call. An A-10 can be used against all ground targets, including tanks and other armored vehicles. It was specially designed for close air support of ground forces.

Having the A-10 around was reassuring for the pilots because once they hit the ground they were out of their element. Being on the ground was fine if you were in the infantry. Pilots felt safest in the familiar surroundings of their aircraft, in the air.

They took turns covering one another with their 9mm pistols as they moved, one at a time, away from the helicopter. As they distanced themselves from the Kiowa, they were unaware of the attackers, who had had a similar notion.

From the air, Wallace spotted a couple of Iraqis fleeing the crash site. They hid in a ditch, about 200 meters up the river from Brown and Sumner. Wallace couldn't see whether they had any weapons. Teeden turned the aircraft in the direction of the Iraqis. He could have fired on them but decided against it. The suspects were fleeing the area. Rules of engagement stated that if you were in direct fire you could return fire. Even though the pilots were sure the Iraqis they had in view were the perpetrators, they weren't in direct fire. They also considered that there might be other Iraqis nearby, serving as spotters like those shown in the movie *Black Hawk Down*, who used cell phones to signal that aircraft were approaching. Or they could have had missile systems hidden in the tall grass.

Other Iraqis, wanting a closer look at the downed aircraft, began walking and driving along the main road that led out of Fallujah toward the crash site. Brown and Sumner weren't aware of the growing number of spectators as they were tucked away in shrubbery. They thought they had found a good spot until the A-10 notified them that a mob had arrived at the aircraft, which was now engulfed in flames. Vehicles had also started to arrive. They needed to be on their guard.

The pilots were trained that when they were shot down, they should move around as much as possible so as not to get trapped in one location. They sprinted from one spot to another to get into a better position, not knowing exactly what was happening around them and how long they would have to be out there.

Then they started to hear gunfire, lots of it.

Brown looked at Sumner. They both started to laugh and couldn't stop. It was a nervous reaction.

"Jeff, tell me that's our fifty-cal cooking off from the heat of the aircraft on fire."

He looked at her but didn't say anything.

"Is it or isn't it?" she asked, giggling. "Are they shooting in the air?"

They were accustomed to seeing Iraqis fire their munitions into the air as a sort of celebratory fire.

"Tell me it is," she said.

"Yeah it is," he said, but neither one knew for sure because they couldn't see the helicopter from their position. It might be Iraqis shooting at them or their rescuers. Later, they discovered that it was .50-caliber ammunition from their aircraft.

Still laughing, they joked about whether the Army would send them home since they had been through the trauma of being shot down.

Just as Brown was thinking they had found a safe spot, Sumner poked her and pointed up. A boy, no more than fifteen, was standing next to his bike and staring down at them. They didn't know whether to shoot him or let him go. They let him go, knowing that he was probably going to ride back and tell someone he had found the two American pilots. In the meantime, trucks had converged on the site of the downed helicopter and they were honking their horns. Brown assumed they were part of a posse dispatched to find them. These feelings were heightened by a big white Suburban that pulled up next to the aircraft and just sat there.

The kid on the bike rode back toward them. Brown was sure that the boy was going to reveal their location. They were in a tough spot. They could either stay where they were or cross the road in the hopes of concealing themselves better on the other side. Either way they were taking a risk. They had no idea what they would find on the other side of the road. Yet they felt exposed in their current position, hiding in the brush.

Finally, they decided to go for it, together. They raced up the hill. The Iraqis who had gathered to see the helicopter were walking away from the pilots, toward the aircraft, and they didn't see them. They ran across the street and down into an embankment of twelve-foot grass along the Euphrates River. For the first time, they felt good about their position. In the grass, they were totally hidden, perhaps a little too concealed. Their sister ship—Wallace and Teeden—lost track of them.

Both the sister ship and the A-10 continued to fly big circles around the pilots on the ground. They didn't want to fly overhead for fear they would give away their location.

Within fifteen to twenty minutes of the helicopter going down, American troops began moving toward the site. A quick response force of Kiowas had been launched. Three aircraft from Brown's company would participate in her rescue.

The sister ship lost sight of Brown and Sumner for about ten minutes, when they made their way from the ditch through an area of shacks and palm trees to the river. The A-10 let Brown know that the sister ship couldn't find them. Sumner pulled out a two-by-two-foot fluorescent orange panel that he had purchased and tucked in his survival vest for this very situation. He laid it out and when Wallace and Teeden flew overhead, they spotted it.

"I GOT HIM! I GOT HIM!" Wallace shouted to his co-pilot. He pointed to Sumner so the pilots on the ground would know they had been spotted.

When the ground elements arrived, they secured the aircraft and got rid of the crowds. Wallace and Teeden found a safe location for two Black Hawks to land and pick up the pilots. With an A-10 providing security, as well as three Kiowas now on the scene and one incoming, the Black Hawks landed with a security force from Brown's company. Their job was to secure the site, get Brown and Sumner, and take them directly back to base. Teeden's aircraft was running out of gas but he refused to leave until he saw his friends board a Black Hawk.

When the Black Hawks landed, a dozen soldiers poured out of each helicopter and formed a circle around the aircraft. They had already been told the approximate whereabouts of Brown and Sumner. The pilots had trained for this. They had practiced a lot of downed pilot scenarios, and escape and evasion situations, where they put an aircraft on the ground, got out, and ran away. They'd be handed a map and told to rendezvous at a certain point. When they reached their destination, they knew they were supposed to get down on their knees and wait for the soldiers to come to them. They weren't expected to run out of the tall grass because even though the soldiers had been given coordinates, they couldn't be certain there weren't bad guys in the area ready to rush out at them.

After what felt like a long time, Brown and Sumner began to worry that their rescuers couldn't find them. They were hidden in a ditch. A berm up above separated them from the Black Hawks. They couldn't see the Black Hawks or the soldiers from their position. Meanwhile, the soldiers from the Black Hawks couldn't find the downed pilots. Brown and Sumner decided to go to the Black Hawks. They ran up to the ridgeline. Team members in Kiowas were talking to them on the radio, urging them to hold their position when they got to the top of the ridge.

The soldiers fanned out, facing away from the Black Hawks and carrying M4s, automatic weapons, and grenade launchers. One soldier was responsible for looking for the downed pilots, going to Brown and Sumner, touching them, pulling them into the circle, and closing back in on the aircraft. Less than four minutes passed from the time the Black Hawks landed, picked up the pilots, and took off.

On the Black Hawk, Brown and Sumner sat side by side. They were bursting with adrenaline and relief. Brown was so happy they had made it through the ordeal together that she kept slapping Sumner on the leg. She was proud they had remained calm and rational.

As much as a pilots train for such circumstances, they never really know how they're going to react until they are faced with the situation. Sumner was proud they were both so rational and focused. After surviving the attack and the crash with Brown, Sumner felt a new and intense bond with his co-pilot that one would typically associate with a sibling. Brown was also proud of the other Kiowa pilots who participated in the rescue. Knowing that her entire company was up in the air securing the area made her feel a lot better.

Brown's helicopter was hit around 2:10, and they arrived back at the airfield at 3:30. When she learned how long they had been on the ground, Brown couldn't believe it. She felt like she had been on the ground for four or five hours. It seemed like forever.

As soon as they returned to the airfield, the pilots were taken to the first aid station where they had physicals and were debriefed. They weren't allowed to talk to anyone en route. It wasn't until Brown sat down in the station that she realized she was bruised from hitting the dash.

Several hours after she was shot down, Brown called her parents in Texas. Her father said that if Robin hadn't told him she had been shot down, it would have been like any other conversation. Nothing about her voice, tone, or attitude was different from any other conversation they'd had. It started out like any other call.

"Dad, what's up?

"Hey Robin, it's good to hear from you. What are you doing?"

"I'm just calling to check on you, see what you're doing."

"I'm getting ready to go to work." It was 6:45 A.M. Texas time.

"Oh, working banker's hours?"

Robin had made fun of him ever since he'd joined the civilian world. She thought 6:45 A.M. was late.

"Cut that out. Why are you calling at this hour in the morning?"

"I have to tell you before you hear it someplace else. First of all, I'm okay and so is Jeff."

"What?"

"Well, we got shot down today over Fallujah. We think it was an RPG."

"How long ago was this?"

"Three hours."

She wanted him to know she was okay before he saw a news report on TV about a chopper in the 82nd Airborne being shot down. She didn't want him to have to worry about whether it was her, and whether she had been wounded or killed. It was her and she was fine.

Brown's dad was speechless. He looked over at his wife, Kathleen, who was still in bed.

"Robin's okay," he told her.

"What do you mean Robin's okay?"

He handed the phone to Kathleen so she could talk to her daughter.

Her dad walked into the living room, turned on CNN, and sure enough there on the television screen was a picture of Robin's helicopter burning, looking much like a piece of crumpled foil. The announcer reported that the condition of the crew was unknown. Had Robin's parents seen the helicopter on the television and not known their daughter was safe, they would have thought the worst. Instead, she had called them upbeat and positive. Perhaps because of the lingering adrenaline, Robin's voice, attitude, and delivery at the time of the call could have led anyone to believe she had just won a marathon.

In the days immediately after the Kiowa was shot down, Brown and Sumner were sore and achy, mostly in their backs and necks. They also had bruises from where the seatbelts had restrained them. The medical staff gave them muscle relaxants to dull the pain.

Brown, Sumner, Teeden, and Wallace were ordered to take time out from flying for a few days. Since they flew as a team, they also took breaks as a team. Consistency among who flew with whom was essential for maintaining team integrity. Switching pilots meant having to learn someone else's personality and habits. This could be taxing if done often. The Kiowa pilots already felt overworked. The last thing they needed to worry about was each other's personality and what the other was doing.

During their break, the pilots spent time digesting what had happened. The airfield was situated on a plateau. They suspected that the Iraqis had informants reporting when aircraft took off and returned because the airfield got mortared fairly often—never when the aircraft were out. The Iraqis knew the airfield had a device that could automatically home in on the origin of the mortars once they were fired. If the aircraft were shut down, it would be twenty minutes before the pilots were up in the air and the attackers would be long gone. If there was an aircraft out, the pilots could receive the coordinates and respond quickly to that area. If the people firing the mortars happened to stick around, they could be found. The Iraqis got pretty smart. In the last four months that Brown was at the airfield, there were no aircraft out when they were mortared.

Prior to the incident, the pilots had received an increasing number of intelligence reports that there was going to be an Iraqi stationed on the northwest of Fallujah for forty-eight hours waiting to shoot down an aircraft. But nothing ever happened. The pilots started to realize that, especially at night when it was more difficult to see, the Iraqis were probably shooting RPGs at them. RPGs weren't a serious threat because they weren't very accurate. But they were beginning to sense that an increasing number of RPGs were probably being fired at them and they weren't aware of it.

The Iraqis were always shooting off something, especially celebratory fire and flares. When the pilots were flying, there was stuff going off all the time. They just assumed that most of it was from innocent people messing around. And then every once in a while something came a little closer and they wondered if it was meant for them. They didn't know—there was no way to know.

Before Brown was shot down, she didn't fly with fear. Any fear she had she learned to control. She had a duty and was going to fulfill it. After she was shot down, she felt vulnerable. She wasn't the only one. Teeden compared the fear level of flying over Fallujah to being thrown into a tank with a great white shark and only a raft to float on. "It's just a matter of time before he comes and eats you. We knew they were there. We knew they were trying to engage us on a day-to-day basis and we just dealt with it."

During their three-day break, the pilots also reflected on their reporting point, the dam. When they were coming into the airfield from the east, they always checked in at the dam. In hindsight, they realize that wasn't very smart because the Iraqis knew where to expect them. The pilots did away with reporting points and varied their approach into the airfield.

After their crash, the sooner Brown, Sumner and their sister ship got back in the air, the better. They started flying again three days after they were shot down, but it wasn't easy. Brown was scared to death but knew she had to overcome her fear.

This was one of many times Brown appreciated having Sumner beside her in the cockpit. He helped to calm her nerves even though he was scared as well. "I can't say I wasn't," he said. "We had to be strong for each other."

Brown was shot down by an SA16, which is a shoulder-fired, heat-seeking missile. The goal of an SA16 is to lock on to a heat signature, such as the engine of an aircraft. Kiowas have what looks like a disco ball on top of the aircraft to confuse a missile by projecting heat behind the helicopter and away from its engine. If the ball works, the missile will miss its target. The SA16 got very close to the body of the aircraft but never hit it. Instead, it veered off and hit a rotor blade, exploded above the aircraft into the blades, and down into the engine.

Brown and Sumner were fortunate because had the SA16 hit the aircraft, they wouldn't have survived. Since the ball was able to distract the missile, they were able to get the helicopter on the ground before the damage totally destroyed the aircraft. The enemy was not only getting smarter by shooting at the trail aircraft, but they were also getting luckier.

Prior to this deployment, Brown spent three months in Iraq at the start of the war. As part of the 82nd Airborne Division, she followed the Army's 3rd Infantry Division during its march toward Baghdad. The infantry stormed through towns in a matter of days and took down Baghdad. Brown's unit worked on the ground, securing the towns behind the infantry so supply trains with gas, ammunition, and food could get through to Baghdad without being attacked.

In her unit, Brown had five trucks, twenty people, some fuelers, and ammunition. As they advanced, the aircraft, which were stationed at an airfield to their south, would fly up, refuel, and conduct operations in support of the ground units. At the end of the day or of a flight, the aircraft flew all the way back to the airfield, which was about an hour away. Once an airfield was out of range from Brown and the fuel for the aircraft, the Kiowas jumped to a new, secure airfield.

Brown did that for about forty-five days, until the Army decided that everything was secure and they weren't needed anymore. This was welcome news for a battalion that thought it was going to be in Iraq for a year and was being sent home after three months. They returned home thinking they would not deploy again.

About a month after returning from her first deployment, Brown was talking to some other pilots during a social at the Officer's Club at Fort Bragg when Captain Kimberly Hampton, a twenty-seven-year-old female Kiowa pilot from another battalion, approached her. Brown didn't know Hampton very well but had seen her around. Hampton was attractive, with long blonde hair, blue eyes, and fair skin.

Brown had yet to receive official word that she would be returning to Iraq.

Hampton said she had heard Brown was being sent back.

"You did?" Brown asked.

"Yeah."

"I don't want to go back," Brown said. "You can have it."

"Are you kidding?" said Hampton, who had served in Korea and Afghanistan, but not Iraq. "I'd do anything to go."

Brown understood Hampton's enthusiasm for going to Iraq because she'd felt the same way the first time around. As a military pilot, Brown was accustomed to training every day. In most jobs, employees do what they are trained to do. Combat pilots don't put their training into action unless the United States is at war. Brown looked forward to testing her training.

But she wasn't excited about returning to Iraq. She detested the living conditions in the desert. She felt dirty, miserable, and hungry all the time. She would have liked to have gone to Afghanistan because she hadn't been there. Having just come from Iraq, she knew exactly what to expect.

However, there was one big plus about possibly returning to Iraq. The first time Brown deployed she held a staff position and planned what everyone else was doing. If she traveled there a second time, she would be in command and spend a lot of time flying.

Hampton couldn't wait to go and got her wish. Before Brown made her second trip to Iraq, two companies joined her battalion. One was Hampton's.

On her second deployment, three weeks after she was shot down, Brown was eating lunch in the chow hall when her first sergeant rushed up to her.

"Did you hear about Captain Hampton?"

"What?" Brown asked.

"She was shot down."

"What?" exclaimed Brown and the men in her company.

"Yeah, there's one KIA [fatality]."

Brown dropped her food and raced to the operations center, where she listened to the radio. Calls flooded the frequencies about what was happening on the ground. At first reports from the crash site indicated there was one KIA but they didn't say who it was. Then they reported that both pilots were okay. There were a lot of conflicting reports. Finally, someone said there was one female KIA. The same type of missile that had hit Brown's aircraft had struck Hampton's Kiowa, only this time exploding the engine and the tail boom. The pilots had no control of the aircraft as it was flung into the ground. Hampton was the first KIA in their unit during the war with Iraq. The other pilot survived the crash with minor injuries. The shoot down was unimaginable to Brown, who all that time kept thinking that it couldn't possibly be happening again.

Coping with Hampton's death was the hardest part of Brown's eight-month deployment. It was even more difficult than her own near-death experience. Not necessarily because the two women were such good friends. They hadn't had a lot of time to get to know one another because they flew on different shifts and had hectic flying schedules. They did have a chance to talk when they first arrived in Iraq, when there was only one woman's shower open at certain times of the day. Brown and Hampton walked together to and from the shower. And their tents were side by side when they arrived. They also saw each other during their daily meetings and briefs.

But it was the parallels between the two incidents that Brown found so disturbing. They were both female commanders flying trail. Hampton was only two kilometers from where Brown had been shot down, flying the same type of mission, at the same time of day.

After Hampton was killed, Brown recalled a short conversation she'd had with Hampton following her own accident. When Brown got off the Black Hawk, Hampton walked up to her and gave her a big hug.

"I want to tell you your guys were so in control," Hampton said.

"What do you mean?" Brown asked.

Hampton told her that when they got the call that Brown's helicopter had been shot down, Hampton tried not to burst into tears. She asked the guys if they needed help. They told her they were taking care of it. They were going to get Brown.

Brown was shocked that Hampton would admit to being on the verge of tears because she appeared so tough. The admission made her seem weak and vulnerable. Brown didn't know of any pilots who would own up to thinking about crying, never mind actually cry. Saying you almost cried was a funny thing to admit, Brown thought at the time. Not only that, but it was a funny thing to feel. Brown thought that way because she, like so many other pilots, trained herself to turn off her emotions. And that works, until someone says there was an aircraft shot down.

It wasn't until Brown learned that Hampton's Kiowa had been shot down and there may have been a KIA, that she appreciated Hampton's admission. "Then, of course, I totally understood it when her call came in and I became very emotional," she said. "I went through a very hard time when Kimberly was killed." Any thoughts Brown had about Hampton being weak had been washed away by her own tears for the fallen female comrade. Brown knew several male pilots who had been killed in Iraq, but she never mourned for them the way she did for Hampton. Perhaps she was seeing herself, her own mortality, in Hampton.

Brown spoke at Hampton's memorial service at the airfield in Iraq. She described her fallen comrade as someone who was always focused and raised the bar. "Kimberly wasn't out to prove anything to anybody. She just wanted to serve her country. She loved to fly and she loved being Cav. The Army lost a great warrior on January 2, but her spirit remains in those of us who were privileged enough to serve with her." Later, Brown mourned in private.

Hampton was shot down three weeks after Brown. She and Sumner were just getting their confidence back. Once again, they had to put a crash behind them. They reminded themselves that there were ground troops, many in their teens and early twenties, who were scared to death and being shot at every day. They were relying on the Kiowa Warriors.

When Brown returned home from Iraq after her second deployment, she and her husband, Jason, talked about the shoot down a couple of times. Then they made a point of putting it behind them and moving on. In Jason's opinion, the fact that his wife was shot down was strange, but it happened and everything turned out fine. "I don't think we'll ever revisit it," he said. "It was very normal, like a car wreck."

Other pilots who had been shot down called the Brown residence to express their concern for the couple. One former pilot, who had been shot down twenty years earlier, said he still has nightmares. Jason said Robin doesn't have nightmares and she won't.

The couple takes what happened seriously, but they won't dwell on it. They don't bring it up in public and hope others won't, either. They don't like it when something happens to someone and it becomes the framework for the rest of their lives. "Neither of us wants that," Jason said.

On the other hand, Brown *is* very proud of how she and Sumner responded to being shot down. "You always wonder whether you will be able to handle it if something bad happens. Well, I got a chance to find out. I feel very lucky that I know that about myself. That's the only way it defines me."

Specialist Rachelle Spors, United States Army.

Not Ready
to Be an Angel

Army Specialist Rachelle Spors *had one thought:*
I'm going to die.

TWENTY-THREE-YEAR-OLD ARMY SPECIALIST RACHELLE SPORS' DAY
often started with a phone call in the basement (a.k.a. dungeon)
of the hospital at Al Asad Air Base. The basement was where Spors
and the other medics passed the time of day while waiting for an
emergency call. The room looked as if it had been furnished by a
flea market and a high school carpentry class. They stored their
gear in wooden crates and open-faced wooden lockers that stood
against two walls; several beds leaned against another wall. Non-
matching vinyl and metal folding chairs were scattered near a
round wooden table in the middle of the room. While waiting for
a call, some of the medics watched TV, played Xbox four-player,
or read magazines; others slept. Spors, who has blonde hair, blue
eyes, and lightly freckled skin, and was dressed in her desert
camouflage uniform, liked to stretch out on one of the beds, sit at
the table and watch a movie on her laptop, or write a letter to her
boyfriend.

Inevitably, a call would cut short the games and movies and
jolt the medics back to reality, like now. The hospital command

center upstairs called to report an incoming medevac with at least one wounded Marine. Usually when the medics got the call, the helicopter was at least fifteen minutes to an hour away. Still, they all dropped what they were doing, grabbed their flak jackets and Kevlar helmets, and maybe their earplugs.

They ran to the top of the stairs and out the door, staying close to the building until the Black Hawk landed, and the aircrew gave the medics the okay. Then they ran with a litter—a stretcher—to the medevac.

On this evening, Spors couldn't hear anything over the noise of the helicopter's engines and rotors, and it was dark outside. At first, all she could see was a male Marine lying on a litter. Once the medics pulled the litter out of the helicopter, Spors saw that the patient was about twenty-five-years-old and had an above-average build. He appeared strong and muscular—invincible. He looked to Spors like the type of guy who couldn't, or wouldn't, get hurt. But he did get hurt by the shrapnel of an improvised explosive device (IED) or a land mine. The Marine was pale from the loss of blood and grimaced from the pain. His uniform remained intact except for the material around his damaged leg, which had been cut away and replaced by several tourniquets.

Spors and her three partners quickly grabbed corners of the litter—two in the front and two in the back—and walked as fast as they could without causing more harm and discomfort to the patient.

Spors took the back left-hand side of the litter. From there, she had a good view of the patient. She could see how, from the knee down, his leg was turned and wrapped in several tourniquets to stop the bleeding. But the temporary bandages weren't doing the job. The wound left a trail of blood as the medics made their way to the emergency room.

"It HURTS. It HURTS," the patient cried out.

The medics kept quiet while they ran. They didn't know what to say. There wasn't anything to say.

"OW!" the patient shouted when they jostled him. "OW!"

The sound of a grown man crying out in pain troubled Spors, a young medic from Minden, Nebraska. Only five years had passed since her junior year in high school, when the Army recruited her for the 313 Medical Company, a National Guard unit from Lincoln, Nebraska. She enlisted in the National Guard in February 2000, graduated from high school in May, and left for basic training in Fort Jackson, South Carolina. Once Spors finished her military training, she enrolled in the University of Nebraska at Kearney full-time to study education and become a teacher. She had just started her student teaching in Houston, Texas, when she received a call from her unit saying they were going to Iraq. Her part-time job would soon become full time. Her career as a teacher would have to wait. She arrived in Iraq in November 2004.

Now Spors was transporting a man who was going to have his leg amputated, and she had no words of comfort. What do you say to a man who is going to lose half his leg? What do you say to make him feel better? This was when Spors realized just how hard her job could be. There was nothing she or her comrades could say to this patient to ease his physical or emotional pain. Nothing! Not even the military could improve on this situation. The Marine might get monetary compensation from the government for having his leg blown off, but he'll never get his leg back. The money will never be enough.

Spors had seen worse wounds before, but this was definitely the bloodiest one she had ever seen. It was also the first time Spors could remember smelling the strong metallic scent of blood. When they arrived in the ER, the medics put the patient down on a short makeshift wooden table that looked and felt more like a workbench than a bed. Blood was everywhere. It pooled beneath the patient on the floor, soaked his pants and the litter, and formed a clot on his leg.

Spors stayed with the patient for a while and tried to calm him but it was hard because the ER was small and there were a lot of people around. It felt crowded, hectic. She didn't want to leave the Marine for fear that he might pass out from the pain or from losing too much blood. Before long, the medical staff carried the patient to the operating room (OR) to remove the lower half of his leg. He didn't know what was going to happen but he suspected. Spors could see the fear in his eyes and hear it in his trembling voice. She helped the OR staff roll the patient onto his side and cut off his clothes. Then she left.

While she was in Iraq, Spors was a litter bearer for some 300 wounded Marines, soldiers, and Iraqis.

Spors had two primary functions as a medic in Iraq—to transport patients from the helicopter to the hospital and to travel in an ambulance in Army convoys in case someone got wounded and needed immediate medical attention. During the convoys, soldiers complained of bruises and constipation, types of problems that Spors could treat with a pill. She wanted to give the whiners a small dose of advice with their meds: *Suck it up. Have a drink of water. You're alive.* But she would never say that because for the most part, the soldiers were tough. They didn't have many problems so when they tracked her down she gave them the benefit of the doubt.

On May 29, 2005, her twenty-fourth birthday, Spors drove in a convoy from Al Asad Air Base to Camp Korean Village (Camp KV). Camp KV is located in a remote stretch of Iraq's western desert, close to the Syrian border, and near the highway that connects Jordan with Baghdad. It got its name because it once housed Korean laborers who paved the Amman-Baghdad highway during Saddam Hussein's regime. Camp KV, surrounded on all sides by miles of sand, now served as a base camp for Marines helping Iraqis run checkpoints along the Syrian and Jordanian borders, and patrolling western Iraq.

Spors was traveling with Army Specialist Christopher Linneman, who was a paramedic back in Omaha. Because of his medical background, Spors would look to Linneman now and then to make sure she was following proper procedure.

They were driving on a road known for having land mines hidden in the rough along the shoulders. Two vehicles rode ahead of Spors, both driven by third country nationals (TCNs). As they were driving, the first truck hit a double stack of land mines, setting off a huge explosion. The convoy came to an immediate halt.

"Someone's hit," Spors shouted into her radio to the convoy commander. "Do you want us to check it out?"

"No, wait a minute," the commander radioed back.

A few minutes passed.

The commander called back. He ordered Linneman and another soldier from the vehicle directly behind Spors' ambulance to find the driver of the truck that had exploded. They only had to find one person because the TCNs usually rode alone. They didn't need any help driving old semi trucks from the 1970s.

Spors stayed in the ambulance by the radio. She waited for her partner and the other soldier for a few minutes but quickly grew impatient and joined Linneman with a litter and ambu bag—a bag-valve-mask resuscitator used to help provide artificial ventilation to patients who are having difficulty breathing. The explosion blasted the driver through the window on the passenger's side and into a ditch about ten to fifteen feet from the vehicle. When the medics found the driver, his breathing was shallow. They couldn't see a lot of blood but brain matter oozed from a cut on his head. To help the TCN breathe, the medics inserted a combitube in his throat. That would secure the patient's airway and help to ventilate his lungs. Then they put him on a litter and carried him to the ambulance.

Spors radioed the convoy commander to request immediate air support. Neither she nor Linneman thought they could save the patient but they kept trying. This was their first serious patient in the field. They didn't know how long they were supposed to try to keep him alive. As time passed, the TCN didn't appear to be breathing. Spors thought she felt a weak pulse, then nothing. She tried to start an IV. She did chest compressions. She tried to give him oxygen.

Forty-five minutes later, when the medevac arrived, an air medic told Spors and Linneman that they shouldn't have spent so much time and effort trying to revive the patient. It was obvious to the air medic that the TCN had died right away. Combat medics often have to make quick decisions for medical situations they've never encountered before. Spors thought, *Okay, we'll know that for the next time. Everything is a learning experience.* The medics moved the dead TCN from the litter to a body bag. He was flown away.

Once or twice a week, Spors and another medic convoyed with the 57 Transportation Unit from Fort Drum, New York. They drove from Al Asad to Camp KV, a distance of about 300 miles that could take as little as six hours or as long as two days, depending on the number of IEDs they encountered along the way.

Camp KV was made up of a small collection of concrete buildings intermingled with Marine Corps tents. The population fluctuated but had several hundred troops including support staff for amenities such as the post office, post exchange, and disbursing office. There was also a small detachment of sailors comprised of a general surgeon, anesthesiologist, trauma doctor, nurse, and several corpsmen at the camp to provide medical care to anyone who needed it. They would stabilize patients from the local area for transfer to higher-level medical facilities at Al Asad or Baghdad. The facility served as the first point of treatment for soldiers wounded in the region. From Camp KV, Spors escorted the TCNs to the border to retrieve new trucks and supplies, and then back to Camp KV.

On July 14, 2005, Spors and thirty-two-year-old Staff Sergeant Tricia Jameson drove to the border and hung out with other medics and truck drivers from 57 Transport in a large concrete parking lot while the TCNs got their new trucks and supplies, and had their vehicles searched for contraband. When all this was accomplished, sometime in the afternoon, they would return to Camp KV.

Spors was eager to get back to the camp because she and some of her friends had made plans to watch a movie that evening. She was especially excited to see Aswald Hooker. He was a handsome twenty-four-year-old Navy corpsman, five feet eleven inches tall, nearly shaved head, bulging brown eyes, Colombian brown skin, and an athletic body.

They met a month and a half earlier, while Spors was working at Al Asad. Hooker, who was stationed at Camp KV, had a week-long layover at Al Asad before departing to Qatar for some R&R. It just so happened that Spors had been granted R&R for the same week. They met in Al Asad two days before their departure and hit it off right away. They were on the same flight to and from Qatar. Hooker sat across from Spors on a C-130 plane, but they couldn't talk. The noise from the engines made it impossible to hear one another. Plus, they were wearing headphones to protect their ears and dampen the sound around them. They exchanged looks instead.

Camp Qatar catered to members of the armed services who were on leave from the war—a respite before returning to the fight, to the bloodshed. The camp had a pool, a gym, computers and video games, a Chili's restaurant, pizzeria, and a nightclub that served alcohol. The American service members weren't allowed to drink alcohol in Iraq. At Camp Qatar, they could have up to three alcoholic drinks a day.

When he woke in the morning, Hooker and Spors' ambulance partner, Linneman, walked over to the women's barracks and got Spors. Then they'd spend the entire day together, from eight o'clock in the morning to ten o'clock in the evening. One day they spent on the beach; another day Hooker and Linneman went sand boarding. Spors watched.

After a blissful week in Qatar, Hooker stayed at Al Asad for a few days before returning to Camp KV. Prior to leaving, he told Spors that he liked her and wanted to stay in touch. That wouldn't be easy but it wasn't impossible, either. They could see each other a couple of times a week when Spors convoyed to Camp KV. When they were apart, they couldn't e-mail or phone one another. But they could write letters on their computers and save them on thumb drives, portable memory storage units that fit into any USB port on a computer. The drives are small, about the size of a human thumb, hence their name. When Spors and Hooker saw one another, they exchanged thumb drives. Hooker wrote a page or two every day about what was happening at Camp

KV. He described the patients he saw, their conditions, and whether they lived or died. He reminded Spors to put on *all* her protective gear before she went out on a convoy. He also teased her about being in the Army and hailing from Nebraska. Written and oral bantering worked well on the battlefield. It took the edge off the stress of their jobs.

Spors, who wasn't as comfortable expressing herself in writing, started out typing about five lines a day but increased her correspondence as she began to treat it more as a journal of their relationship. The writings taught them a lot about each other and enabled them to stay in touch even when they were apart.

A month and a half had passed since their week in Qatar. Spors had convoyed to Camp KV six or eight times since then, but they were short visits, a day or two each. She and Hooker looked forward to this trip because Spors was scheduled to spend a week at Camp KV.

While Spors waited for the trucks to be inspected, a driver who was standing with a few other soldiers about fifty feet away yelled, "Hey Spors, we need you guys. Quick! We've got to go outside the wire."

"Okay," she shouted back. Then she repeated the order to her partner, Jameson. "We have to go outside and help someone."

"Get in your vehicle and follow me," the truck driver yelled. "A few Marines are hurt. We're going to help them."

Spors jumped in the driver's seat of her ambulance. Jameson climbed into the passenger seat. As she drove to the camp's gate, Spors put on her protective gear—Kevlar helmet and flak vest. She followed the truck and was the second vehicle out of the camp. Normally, the ambulance wouldn't be the second vehicle in a convoy. Driving that close to the front increased a medic's chance of being hit by an undetected IED. The convoys preferred to keep the medics and their ambulance in the rear where it was safer. But in this situation she didn't have much choice. Only one truck seemed to be responding and it had already left, and the trucks were much faster than the ambulances. She would have to catch up. She pushed her boot down on the gas pedal. She had no idea where she was going. The driver had said, "Follow me" and took off.

Inside the ambulance, Jameson turned to Spors and said, "Hey, we're actually going to do this."

"Yeah, we're actually going to help some patients," Spors said.

Jameson had yet to help any wounded Marines or soldiers. She had arrived in Al Asad just three weeks earlier. She drove with Spors because Linneman was going home that day on leave. They were all from the same National Guard unit in Nebraska.

In the ambulance, Jameson pulled on her medical gloves. She wanted to be ready to jump out of the vehicle as soon as they met up with the hurt Marines.

Earlier that same day, one or more soldiers thought they had seen at least one IED on the side of the road when they were driving into the border camp. But instead of following up on their instincts right away, they decided to give it a closer look on their way out.

A mile outside the gate, Spors heard a tremendous BLAST.

Three 155 rounds and two 137 incendiary anti-tank rounds (land mines) had just exploded beneath the rear passenger side of the ambulance. Anti-tank rounds are most effective when they explode directly beneath a vehicle because they can penetrate the armor in Humvees. It takes only one land mine to blow up a Humvee and one 155 round to blow an average sized person off his feet.

The explosions threw the ambulance five feet into the air, sent it into a violent spin, and blew the wheels off. The ambulance spun three times in the middle of the two-lane road, and then shot off onto the shoulder, where it spun a couple more times before coming to a stop and facing the road. Flames engulfed the back half of the vehicle.

Inside the ambulance, Spors felt everything slow down. The explosion caused her ears to ring and her eyes to see everything in red. All she saw out the front of the vehicle was concrete. While still in the air, Spors didn't have time to think about taking her hands off the steering wheel. Instead, she kept turning the wheel as if she were trying to escape this hellish nightmare. She had one thought. *I'm going to die.*

When the vehicle crashed to the ground, Spors did a quick check of her body. She touched her arms. They were still there. She tried to lift her legs but couldn't move anything from the waist down. Then she slapped her legs. She still couldn't feel anything. She was terrified. She thought she had been blown in half.

Oh God, how am I going to get out of here? Spors looked to her left and saw flames shoot past her window. She could feel the heat intensify as the blaze closed in on her.

Then she looked to her right, at Jameson. Her head was slumped. She didn't look conscious. Spors had a bad feeling that her buddy hadn't made it through the explosion. She also had a sinking feeling that she herself wasn't going to survive. *I've got to get out of here.*

She couldn't move.

"Somebody help me, somebody help me," Spors yelled over and over again.

Watching the explosion from just thirty feet away was Specialist Matt Martin, a truck driver with 57 Transport. He was close enough to feel the blast. As the ambulance spun in the air, Martin moved his truck to within ten feet. As soon as the ambulance landed, he and his gun crew ran to it. Martin could hear Spors calling for help. He followed the screams into the fire and opened the driver's door. He immediately recognized Spors because he had driven on convoys with her before and she had patched him up a few times after he had received small injuries.

It took Spors a little longer to recognize her rescuer. She didn't take a good look at Martin when he flung her door open. She was just thankful someone was there and threw her arms at him.

Spors didn't appear hurt to Martin, but she told him that she couldn't feel her legs. With the flames inching closer to the front of the ambulance, Martin paused for only a moment to determine the best way to lift her. He didn't want to move her in such a way that he would cause more harm than good. Whatever he did, he had to do it fast.

As soon as Martin started talking, Spors recognized her rescuer as the guy she had fixed up just the day before after he scraped his hand playing football. She stopped screaming and said, "Martin, get me out of here." He told her everything was going to be okay. Then she stopped talking. She may have blacked out. He grabbed her flak right above the chest and pulled Spors out. Then he spun her away from the fire, placing himself between the burning vehicle and its victim. (Martin received third degree burns on his right arm when he pulled Spors from the ambulance. Later, he would earn a Purple Heart for his combat-sustained injuries.) He dragged Spors to the front of his truck, which was a safe distance from the ambulance, and laid her down on the ground.

"Are you okay?" Martin asked. "Is there anything I can do?"

"I can't breathe," said Spors, who had regained consciousness. "I can't breathe."

He loosened her flak and saw blood. She wasn't bleeding that badly but it was enough for Martin to determine that Spors had been seriously wounded in the blast. He felt under Spors' shoulder. His pinky finger touched a hole where shrapnel had entered, but he couldn't find an exit wound. Shards of shrapnel were stuck in her flak and Kevlar, and a piece of shrapnel had wedged itself into the neck guard attached to her vest. If she hadn't been wearing the neck guard the shrapnel could have cut a jugular vein and killed her.

While Martin tended to Spors, two Army sergeants tried to get to Jameson. The blast had caused part of the roof of the ambulance to collapse so they had to lift the burning roof and then pry the door open. After pulling Jameson out, they moved her behind Martin's truck. Spors was in front of the truck. The soldiers didn't want to add to her already fragile physical and mental state by allowing her to see her dead partner.

"I'm going to die," she told Martin.

"No you're not," he said. "No you're not."

A few minutes after the women were pulled from the ambulance, rounds of ammunition in their vehicle started popping off, so Martin and the gun crew dragged the victims farther away. Army Sergeant Cory Lennon showed up, and then Army Sergeant Sharita Robinson, both combat life savers (CLS). They started an IV bag on Spors.

After lying on the ground for about fifteen minutes, Spors regained the feeling in the lower half of her body. She could move her legs again. Apparently, she had suffered spinal shock. In the force of the blast, she had broken two spinous processes off her vertebrae that caused everything from her waist down to go numb.

Spors thought she had broken her shoulder and ribs. She knew from the blood that a piece of shrapnel had cut her on the edge of her shoulder blade. She was in excruciating pain lying on her back so she asked Martin to roll her onto her side. As he rolled her, Martin reassured Spors that she would be okay. With Lennon and Robinson there to take care of the patient's medical needs, Martin set up security, called for medevac, and then found a place away from Spors to vent. He was furious. He yelled. He wanted to kill someone, an Iraqi. He was angry that Spors had been wounded but he was even more upset about Jameson. He couldn't understand how someone could be killed on her first convoy when he and his battle buddies had rolled on the same roads for a year. It wasn't fair.

After starting the IV, Lennon and Robinson bandaged Spors' side to slow the bleeding. Spors concentrated on trying to keep herself comfortable until a helicopter arrived. She talked to the sergeant in charge, pumping him for information about Jameson.

"How is Jameson?" she asked. "How is she doing?"

"She's fine," he said.

Spors knew he was lying, but she had neither the energy nor the desire to press the subject.

"Are they coming," she asked, growing impatient for the medevac. "Are they coming?"

"Yeah, they're coming," the sergeant said.

Eventually, Spors stopped talking. She was tired, couldn't breathe well, and hurt all over.

She kept telling herself that the medevac would be there soon and that she was going to survive. They would put a tube in her chest to help her breathe. Then they'd send her back to the barracks where she could sleep it off.

Someone told her she would be okay.

"I love you guys," she said.

The soldiers rolled Spors onto a litter and waited. When the medevac arrived, the patient was barely conscious. The air medic took her pulse and instructed her to sit back. She didn't want to.

She wanted to sit up because she thought it would alleviate some of the pain. She lay down and coughed up blood.

The flight from the border to Camp KV took about twenty-five minutes. While she was in the air, Spors began thinking about the medical staff at Camp KV and who she might see.

When the IEDs and landmines blew up Spors' ambulance, Aswald Hooker was hanging out with his buddies in a house he shared with about seventeen other corpsmen at Camp KV. In this dwelling for the male enlisted medical staff, someone was always charged with manning the phone. If casualties were being flown in from the battlefield, the helicopter would radio the command medical center at Camp KV, which in turn would call the corpsmen. During these phone calls, the corpsmen seldom learned the exact number of patients or the extent of their wounds. They'd have to wait until the helicopter landed and they actually saw the patients. One time an air medic told Hooker that he was incoming with two patients and the helicopter arrived with eleven.

Hooker had been thinking about Spors because before she left for the border, they had made plans to watch a movie when she returned. It was about time for her to get on the road and head back to Camp KV. As soon as he heard that there was a helicopter incoming with one wounded, Hooker got a bad feeling but he tried to push the thought out of his mind. Dressed in shorts and a T-shirt when the call came in, Hooker quickly pulled on his pants, blouse, and boots, grabbed his gear—flak, pistol, Kevlar—and ran to the ambulance. It was customary for the corpsmen to joke around during these anxious moments to release tension, but this time was different for Hooker.

"Where's Spors?" asked one of the corpsmen after observing that Hooker wasn't his usual self. He was quiet, and he wasn't participating in the customary banter.

"She's on the road," Hooker said quietly.

The corpsmen drove two ambulances to the airfield, which was less than a mile away, parked, and waited. Hooker's job was to care for the patient in the back of the ambulance while he or she was transported to the Shock and Trauma Platoon (STP). Once they arrived, he would scrub and participate in the surgery. He sat in the back and got his supplies in order. He had to be prepared for anything. He opened his medical bag and set up an IV. *I'm ready.*

Over the radio in the ambulance, the corpsmen listened in on conversations between the medevacs and the medical command center. They learned that there were two helicopters. One had a wounded patient and the other had four Angels—that is, KIAs. Three of the Angels were probably the Marines that Spors was going to help when her ambulance hit the IEDs. The fourth Angel—her partner, Jameson.

Hooker kept his feelings from the other corpsmen. He didn't want them to know he was panicking. He sent the other ambulance to pick up the Angels because he knew that if Spors was dead, he couldn't do anything for her. However, if she was still alive, he wanted to be with her. Also, he had seen his share of Angels, their mangled and marred bodies. He didn't want to see another one, not right now, and especially not if it was Spors.

Angels arrived by helicopter or plane in body bags. They were transported to the STP, where the medical staff opened the bags, checked the bodies for wounds to determine the cause of death, cleaned them up, put them back in the body bag, placed a folded flag on them, and put them in the freezer in the galley until they were flown home.

As the helicopter landed, Hooker got a sinking feeling. When he signed up to be a Navy corpsman, he never imagined that he would go to war, never mind fall in love with an Army medic who could be seriously wounded or killed in combat. If that's what happened, if his girlfriend was inside one of those medevacs, it would be too much for him to bear.

Hooker and three other corpsmen waited for the door of the helicopter to open. Hooker was so nervous that his heart felt like it was beating out of control. A liberal amount of sweat dripped from his body. The door opened, and a medic inside motioned for the corpsmen to take the patient.

Spors lay on her side and faced away from Hooker. A bandage covered her chest wound.

Hooker saw the pants of an Army uniform. *Please let it be somebody else.*

Spors figured that Hooker would be one of several corpsmen coming to get her. When she heard him giving instructions to the other corpsmen, her hunch was confirmed. She felt him touch her feet, then her back as if he was trying to roll her over to see if it was really her.

Hooker saw her Gerber. *It looks like her knife. Don't be silly. A lot of soldiers carry that same knife. It's not her.*

Then he saw Spors' blonde hair, free of her Kevlar helmet.

It was clearly Spors, but he told himself that it wasn't. He looked away. He didn't want to see any other clues confirming that the wounded soldier was his girlfriend. Hooker held the front of the litter as he and the other corpsmen carried Spors to the ambulance. He didn't look back.

Once inside the ambulance, Hooker took off his helmet and goggles. He looked at Spors for the first time. An oxygen mask covered her nose and mouth, and there were splotches of blood on her face. He was speechless.

"Hi, honey," she said.

"Holy shit!" he said. "Fuck."

"Is that Spors?" the driver shouted back.

"Yeah."

"Fuck," the driver said. "Fuck."

They drove through the narrow streets of Camp KV, dodging pedestrians and other military and civilian vehicles. Dinnertime was close, and the streets were busy. The driver, eager to get the patient to the clinic, sped up and yelled out his window, "Get out of the way! Hurry up!" The ambulances didn't have lights and sirens to alert people that they were coming and even if they did they wouldn't be able to use them because they would attract unwelcome attention.

Spors, still lying on her side because any other position hurt too much, tried to turn back toward Hooker without hurting herself. She wanted to comfort him and to let him know she was all right. She reached back for his hand and found it.

Hooker was at a loss for what to do. Intellectually, he knew exactly what to do. But his hands and fingers wouldn't move. All he could do was kneel down beside Spors and hold her hand.

He just looked at her and said over and over again, "Honey, what do I do? I don't know what to do."

He rummaged through his medical bag.

"How do I fix you?"

"You don't have to do anything," she said. "I'm fine."

Already hooked up to an IV bag and oxygen, Spors believed that there wasn't anything else Hooker could do for her until they got to the STP. That may have been true, but she wasn't fine. She had a collapsed lung and was having trouble breathing. She needed help, and she needed it fast.

Hooker was an experienced, and at the moment, an overwhelmed corpsman. If it had been any other person, his hands and mind would have kicked into autopilot. He'd know exactly what to do and he'd do it. In the time it took to drive from the airfield to the ER, he would start an IV, look at a wound, assess it, and wrap it. When he arrived at the STP, he would easily and effortlessly list the patient's vital statistics and medical condition. But this time when the ambulance pulled up to the STP, Hooker was crying and didn't know his patient's status.

The door swung open.

"What do we have?" someone shouted.

Hooker looked away. He couldn't talk.

The medical staff converged on the ambulance. They didn't know Spors well but the staff was a small, tight-knit group and they quickly recognized her as Hooker's friend. And when they did, Hooker heard them say in unison, "Holy shit."

The senior chief climbed into the ambulance.

"Get her out of here," he shouted.

Then he turned to Hooker.

"You're not going in there," the chief said, referring to the ER. Hooker had to get a hold of himself, of his emotions.

Spors seconded the chief's command. She yelled back, "Don't let him come in." Of course, she wanted Hooker to be with her, but she knew he was hurting. Spors never had to guess what he was feeling, including now.

Inside the ER, Spors doubled over. She couldn't breathe. Always the medic, she told the medical staff what she thought was wrong with her, and they let her know that they had it covered. Corpsman Michael Shane Plummer was standing nearby. He was friends with Spors and Hooker. They all joked around a lot. He was part of the group of corpsmen who had planned to watch a movie that evening. Plummer, in an effort to lighten the mood, said, "I guess this means we're not going to watch a movie tonight?"

Overcome with emotion, Plummer left the ER crying. He walked outside and hugged his buddy, Hooker. "She's fine," he said. "She's fine."

Every so often, someone from the medical staff would leave the ER to update Hooker on Spors' progress. "She's awake." "She's responding." "They're not giving her anything for pain." "They're intubating her."

At Camp KV, the aim of the medical staff was to stabilize their patient's breathing, make sure she wasn't losing too much blood, and get her to a higher level of care to treat her life-threatening wounds. Still on the operating table, Spors blacked out and stopped breathing. Her lung had collapsed. The medical staff put a chest tube in Spors by poking a hole in her lung. This procedure re-opened her lung, and drained any blood or fluid that had seeped in. Spors doesn't remember much after that. She was given a paralytic and a hypnotic anesthetic.

Spors had a lot of other wounds. Most of her pain came from the shrapnel that had lodged in her lung, her fractured scapula (shoulder blade), broken and cracked ribs and vertebra, and the small burn on her right arm from the fire that was closing in on her as she was pulled from the burning ambulance.

After about an hour in the ER, an unconscious Spors was carried on a litter to another helicopter and flown to the hospital in Al Asad. She never saw Hooker walking beside the litter to the aircraft.

At Al Asad, Corpsman James Ping had stopped by the hospital command center on his way to chow when he heard over the radio that there was at least one casualty and one Angel incoming. Then the command center received a call from Camp KV saying that the incoming wounded and Angel were two of their own—female Army medics based out of the hospital. For security reasons, no names were mentioned on the radio, but it wasn't dif-

Marine Lance Corporals Carrie Blais and Priscilla Kispetik hang out with the gang at Al Asad Airfield.

Lieutenant General Ronald S. Coleman shakes hands with Blais.

A dynamic foursome that includes Lance Corporals Priscilla Kispetik and Blais.

Blais on her first patrol.

An interpreter sits beside Blais.

A dusty Corporal Karen Cunningham of the 4th Landing Support Battalion of Vienna, Ohio.

A street in Haditha.

Break time in Haditha.

Army Chief Warrant Officer Two Christopher Wallace, Captain Robin Brown, Chief Warrant Officer Two Jeff Sumner, and Chief Warrant Officer Three Mark Teeden at Al Taqaddum Airbase.

A row of Kiowa helicopters at sunrise at Al Taqaddum Airbase.

Army Captain Kimberly Hampton, a pilot and friend of Robin Brown in the 82nd Airborne, was killed when her OH-58 Kiowa Warrior helicopter was attacked near Fallujah, Iraq, in January 2004. PHOTO COURTESY OF U.S. ARMY

Army Captain Robin Brown washes her clothes in a drum of water and soap.

Army Specialists Jessica Sefzik and Rachelle Spors at Camp Korean Village.

Spors with Navy Corpsman Aswald Hooker on R&R in Qatar.

A medevac helicopter.

Wounded Army Specialist Rachelle Spors is transported on a litter from a helicopter to an ambulance at Camp Korean Village.

The ambulance that Spors was driving when she drove over a stack of IEDs.

Spors models a medical vest over her pajamas at Fort Riley in Kansas.

Marine Captain Amy McGrath.

Petty Officer Third Class Marcia Lillie, aviation boatswains'mate, sits on a tractor on the flight deck of the USS *Dwight D. Eisenhower.* PHOTO COURTESY OF MASS COMMUNICATION SPECIALIST 2ND CLASS MATTHEW LEISTIKOW

Lillie participates in a foreign object damage (FOD) walk down on the flight deck of aircraft carrier USS *Dwight D. Eisenhower.* PHOTO COURTESY OF MASS COMMUNICATION SPECIALIST 2ND CLASS MATTHEW LEISTIKOW

Four Marines
in their combat
gear.

Army Black Hawk pilot
Captain Jen Ahl and
Chief Warrant Officer
Three Marc Latimer,
both of B Company 2-3
Aviation Regiment, at
Jalabah Airfield, Iraq, in
March of 2003, several
days after the initial
ground invasion by the
3rd Infantry Division.

Captain Ahl in February
2003 before a routine
training flight at Camp
Udairi, Kuwait.

Marines with the Lioness Program refill their rifle magazines at Camp Korean Village, Iraq, July 31, 2006. Eight female Marines from different units within 3rd Marine Aircraft Wing volunteered for the program to conduct searches of women crossing into Iraq. PHOTO BY SERGEANT JENNIFER JONES / COURTESY OF U.S. MARINE CORPS

Female Marines who participated in Regimental Combat Team 2's Lioness Program at Camp Ripper, Al Asad, Iraq, February 2007. The training is designed to prepare female Marines for future operations. PHOTO BY CORPORAL ADAM JOHNSTON / COURTESY OF U.S. MARINE CORPS

Marine Captain Amy "Gargle" Roznowski of HMLA-267 in front of her Super Cobra attack helicopter.

At a hospital in Balad less than 24 hours after Marine Gunny Sergeant Rosie Noel was wounded by an explosion caused by a rocket-propelled grenade. In one hand she is holding the shrapnel that pierced her cheek and in the other, her guardian angel. Coincidentally, they are both $1\frac{1}{2}$ inches long.

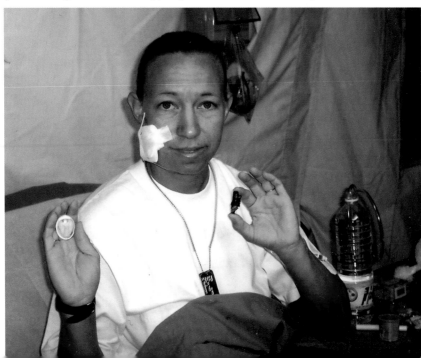

Air Force Captain Jennifer Wilson, a B-2 Spirit pilot, is the first female B-2 pilot to fly a combat mission, which she performed as part of Operation Iraqi Freedom.

Army Master Sergeant Margaret Furman worked as an agent for the Coalition Provisional Authority and was part of an acquisition team that supported the 3rd Infantry Division.

Army Sergeant Leigh Ann Hester, a team leader in the 617th Military Police Company, stands over a captured weapons cache after her squad repelled an insurgent attack on a supply convoy on March 20, 2005, about eighteen miles southeast of Baghdad. For her actions in this engagement, Hester won the Silver Star, becoming the first woman since World War II to win that award.

Captain Karen Anderson (right) speaks with an Iraqi woman during the Iraqi Women's Engagement Program. The program pairs female Marines with local women to give the women a chance to voice opinions and concerns.

A Marine searches an Iraqi woman, a job only female troops are allowed to perform because of Islamic restrictions on male-female contact.

ficult to figure out. Only two female medics from Al Asad had traveled to Camp KV. One had to be Spors. The other, Jameson.

Dr. Necia Williams, a forty-four-year-old Navy anesthesiologist, lived in a cement building across the street from the hospital. There were three barracks—one for officers and senior enlisted (both male and female), one for female enlisted and some male enlisted, and one for male enlisted. Williams lived in the officers' barracks. She was hanging laundry on a clothesline when the field phone rang in her barracks. The sound of the phone ringing always raised the staff's heart rate, if not from the annoying crackling sound then the fact that no one ever called the barracks with good news.

The caller asked for the OR team and the flight nurse, and said there was one "immediate"—the word used to describe an emergent patient with a life- or limb-threatening wound—coming in. "Delayed" indicated someone with a wound that needed attention but was not an immediate threat to life or limb. "Routine" might be used for someone with a wound that could wait awhile.

The entire surgical team headed to the OR. Williams ran to her room and put the rest of her laundry on the floor and signed out to the OR. Each staff member kept a small whiteboard on their door that they used to sign out whenever they went anywhere— chow hall, PX, for a run, hospital. There was also a green log book at the desk at the entrance of each of the three barracks. They had to put their names, dates, time out, and destinations for every place they went. If their plans changed, they were responsible for either going back to change the entry or making sure that someone on the way back to the barracks would change it for them. They were on call 24/7 for seven straight months and were accountable for their whereabouts at all times. Al Asad is a huge base and it would be difficult to find someone if no one knew where to look.

When she arrived at the hospital, Williams stopped at the command center. That's where she learned that the incoming patient and the Angel were both female Army medics who worked out of the dungeon. On her way to the OR, Williams ran into the executive officer (XO). The reservists from Spors' unit all worked out of the dungeon of the hospital. They worked, ate, and berthed together. Their purpose, when they weren't performing their individual specialties, was to stand by for incoming litter support. The command center always called them when a helicopter came in.

The XO told Williams that he didn't want the Army medics from downstairs off loading the helicopter when it arrived. Instead, a team of Marines would be the litter bearers for the stretchers coming off the bird. Later, among themselves, the Army medics would question the XO's decision not to have them carry the litters. Williams supported the decision not only because the XO was senior to her, but also because she trusted that he made the decision with the mission and everyone's best interest in mind. The XO was a former Marine who went to nursing school and joined the Navy. Williams knew that having one of their medics wounded and another killed affected the XO deeply but he kept the corpsmen and medics mission focused.

Williams was both anesthesiologist and head of surgical services, which meant she was responsible for the OR. She made sure everyone was ready to do their job—that they had the information and supplies they needed, sterilized instruments were available, and they were "good to go" (a Marine term) at all times. She made sure the OR techs and nurses, the anesthesia team, and the surgeons were available. Jose Hernandez, the certified registered nurse anesthetist (CRNA) who worked with Williams, would turn on the oxygen cylinders and double-check the field anesthesia machines while Williams headed to the Shock Stabilization and

Trauma Room (SST), field name for ER. It was there, in the SST, that Williams learned that it was Spors who had been wounded.

Williams knew Spors as a friend and a colleague, someone who was energetic, friendly, and interested in learning. Spors had observed several surgeries and had even "scrubbed" in on one of the more minor cases, meaning she scrubbed her hands at the field sink, put on a sterile gown and gloves, and had stepped up to the OR table with the surgeon and a surgical tech. She had handed instruments to the surgeon, held retractors, and was allowed to be part of the surgery. Of all the enlisted medics who had served with Williams and her staff, Spors was the only one who had participated in a surgery in the OR. How ironic that only a few weeks later, Spors arrived as a critically wounded patient.

As the OR crew prepared themselves and their equipment for the patient, they were unusually somber and quiet. They had gotten word that the patient was "one of our own." Even though the medical staff in the hospital was Navy and the medics were Army, they all worked together every day and considered each other family.

Spors was taken immediately from the SST to the OR. Her vital signs were relatively stable (i.e., she had a pulse and a blood pressure) given the degree of her wound. She was already intubated and had a chest tube. The medical staff hooked her up to the monitors.

Ping noticed that Spors had dried blood around her neck and arm. Particles of sand clung to her clammy skin. It was still too soon after the accident for the swelling to start. She looked uncomfortable and was moaning from the pain. Her presence as a patient humbled Ping and others on the medical staff. Up to this point, none of their own had been wounded or killed. Seeing Spors in this position was a sobering reminder of their own mortality.

When Spors arrived in the OR, she heard the familiar voices of the medical staff and that had a significant calming effect on her. Since she was a member of the National Guard and not a full-time soldier, Spors had practiced her medical skills only a couple of weekends a month. The high demand for medical care in Iraq often left her frustrated. Instead of feeling empowered by her training she felt limited, inadequate. She had asked the medical staff at Al Asad if she could observe and participate in some of their medical procedures and they acquiesced. Having seen them in action, she knew they would be able to help her. She couldn't speak but if she could she would have told them, "I'm going to be fine. Thank you, guys." She thought about her buddy, Jameson. Although no one had told her, Spors knew in her heart that she was dead, that she had gone fast, and that it wasn't painful.

Williams gave Spors anesthetic drugs to induce sleep, rolled her on her side, and stuffed tightly rolled blankets around her so the doctors could cut a seven-inch incision below Spors' breast to her side to "explore" the chest cavity and to extract a piece of shrapnel about the size of a small Matchbox car. If the shrapnel in her chest had been just an inch away from where it was, Spors could have been an Angel, too.

As the medical staff performed the emergency surgery, Ping was struck by the concern on their faces and the lack of chitchat in the SST. People weren't talking over one another. Everything was cut and dry and to the point.

Patients almost always want to see the pieces of metal that are removed from their bodies so the OR nurse took the shrapnel, cleaned it off, and put in a container to send with Spors. Williams could usually decide fairly early in the surgery whether a patient would be extubated after their surgery or whether they would be left intubated to fly to the next higher echelon of care. Spors was left intubated and given high doses of drugs to keep her unconscious not only through the surgery but following its completion throughout "packaging" for flight.

The flight nurses had written protocols and physician orders that they followed during flight to continue administering drugs to help the patient maintain an unconscious state, and to prevent the patient from moving and self-extubating—a potentially life-threatening event. Weather conditions prevented Spors from being medevaced for quite a few hours after the completion of her surgery so she was moved to the ICU where she could be monitored by the ICU nurse and flight nurse until a medevac helicopter and accompanying gunship helicopter could take her to the next echelon.

Once Spors was flown away, the reality of what the staff had just experienced set in and they started talking about it. It definitely affected those close to Spors. They dealt with the reality of war every day, but treating Spors was especially difficult for the corpsmen. Some were angry, some were quiet, and some prayed, but all were affected.

From Al Asad, Spors was flown to Baghdad to Balad to Germany and finally to Walter Reed Army Medical Center. She slept during most of her flights. She woke up in Germany long enough to talk to her commander and to her good friend, Army Specialist Jessica Sefzik. That's when she learned that Jameson had died.

She also woke up on a bus on the way to Walter Reed. She could hear the people around her engaged in normal conversations. Spors wondered why she wasn't more conscious and why she couldn't move. And why were they talking about mundane things and not taking care of her? She tried to stay calm. Her medical background taught her to remain quiet and let the machines do the breathing for her.

Spors spent the next several weeks at Walter Reed. At first, just sitting up in a wheelchair was difficult. She was in excruciating pain. Adding to her pain were her sore ribs. Even with morphine, she felt like she had been stomped on by an elephant. Two chest tubes helped her breathe. Bandages covered her shrapnel wounds, chest tubes, and the burn on her arm. It wasn't until a week after the explosions that she found out she had had emergency surgery back in Al Asad.

As the medical staff weaned Spors from morphine and as her physical health improved, the patient began to think more and more about her partner. While the morphine was in Spors' system, it concealed her pain—both physical and emotional. When the drug wore off, Spors struggled with guilt. She blamed herself for Jameson's death. She thought she should have seen the IEDs before she hit them and swerved out of their path.

After Walter Reed, Spors went home for a month on convalescent leave and then to Fort Riley in Kansas to be put on medical hold. A month later, she returned home to work at an armory in Kearney, Nebraska, near her hometown, until she was well enough to be released from active duty.

In the dungeon at Al Asad, Spors' day often kicked into action with a phone call. When she returned to the States, she was reminded that not all phone calls transmit bad news. While she was recovering at Walter Reed, Hooker called. It was a welcomed surprise. In the months ahead, Hooker's visits and phone calls helped Spors recover. They gave her something to look forward to.

The band of sisters lost one, almost two, of its medics when Spors' ambulance drove over the explosives. It's a day Spors will never forget. There are the physical reminders. Her chest still gets tight and she still has difficulty taking deep breaths. She does a lot of shallow breathing exercises. She can't run like she used to and is more susceptible to getting pneumonia when she is sick. And there are the emotional reminders. She can't help but reflect now and then on that fateful day of July 14, 2005.

But exhibiting the same courage she showed after losing a fellow medic and being seriously wounded, Spors was able to rebound and pick up where she left off before she deployed to Iraq. She went on to graduate from the University of Nebraska at Kearney with a bachelor's degree in Spanish education and English as a second language. Now she's teaching high school Spanish in Omaha, Nebraska. When she recalls her experience in Iraq, she prefers not to think about her near-death experience. Instead, she chooses to focus on the friends she made and the fun they had.

Captain Amy "Krusty" McGrath, United States Marine Corps.

Call Sign: "Krusty"

"The killing aspect is hard. It's also very difficult for me to talk about. There really isn't a day that goes by that I don't think of the human toll. No matter what side, we're all human."
— ***Marine Captain Amy McGrath***

JUST GETTING OFF THE GROUND THAT MORNING WAS A CHALLENGE.

It was March 20, 2003, and the war between the United States and Iraq had officially begun. At 2:30 A.M., the desert sky was shrouded in blackness, except for Al Jabar Air Base in Kuwait, where stadium lights shone down and lit the path to the flight line for twenty-eight-year-old Marine Captain Amy McGrath and three other aviators.

Dressed in her tan flight suit, helmet, and black boots, and carrying a flight bag, McGrath walked purposefully toward her jet. A flight suit concealed her athletic body. Her helmet, with the name "Krusty" across the front, covered a head of short thick curly brown hair that when exposed, stood out in a squadron of shaved heads. A military identification tag, along with a pendant of St. Michael, the patron saint of Marines, hung from her neck.

Although McGrath had been flying nearly every day for a month to enforce a no-fly zone in southern Iraq, on this morning there was a greater sense of urgency as the military was now on high alert. A heightened sense of danger pervaded as McGrath and her fellow aviators went on the attack. This was the real thing.

McGrath was preparing to fly in the first round of missions for the Green Knights, one of five Marine Corps squadrons with twelve F/A-18 (Hornet) fighter jets each stationed at Al Jabar. Marine and Air Force, along with British squadrons, were represented. Like McGrath, many of the aviators had been awake since the previous day, anxious to receive their orders, to get their jets in the air, and to do what they had been trained to do.

As a weapons' systems operator, also called the "back seater" or WSO (pronounced *wizzo*), one of McGrath's primary responsibilities on this and every other mission would be to punch in the correct coordinates for bombs and missiles before her pilot flipped the switch to release ordnance on a pre-designated target. If she did her job well, they would hit their targets. If she got rattled, they would miss, the human factor complicating the already intricate calculus of destruction.

McGrath and the other aviators neared their jets just as a Scud alert sounded, stinging the air with deafening sirens. A Scud is a surface-to-surface missile that can deliver chemical and biological weapons. The threat of an incoming Scud posed a serious threat at the beginning of the war. At the sound of the sirens, the people who normally cranked the engines and prepared the jets for take-off grabbed their chemical protective gear, gas masks, flak jackets, and helmets and ran into nearby underground bunkers, leaving McGrath and the other aviators to fend for themselves.

The aviators had already walked a half mile, too far to turn back and retrieve their safety gear. They left their protective clothing and equipment behind because it wouldn't fit in the cockpit. So once they started walking to their jets, they were extremely vulnerable. And while the sirens shrilled out the imminent danger of incoming missiles, McGrath and the others couldn't take off running. Their flight gear, which included a harness and survival vest, was heavy and made for sitting in a cockpit. It wasn't designed for standing up and walking, never mind running.

During wartime, the jets always flew as a "section" of two aircraft. Walking beside McGrath was Lieutenant Colonel Jason Richie, the pilot of the lead jet and a veteran of the first Gulf War. He calmly instructed his WSO, Major "Gomer" Pylant, McGrath, and her pilot, Major "Cherry" Innocenti, to keep walking and to press on. His low-key manner and tone helped to soothe McGrath, who shared his outlook, to press on, no questions asked. Aviators would rather take their chances in a jet in the air than on the flight line. And on that first morning of the war, nothing was going to stop McGrath and the other aviators from launching when Marines on the ground up north were counting on them. Once they arrived at their jets, they split up, Innocenti and McGrath walking to their F-18.

Each aircraft was assigned an enlisted plane captain who ensured that the jet was ready for take off. Normally, this Marine followed the pilot around the jet. If the pilot had any questions or saw that something wasn't right, he could tell the plane captain to fix it. It was the enlisted man's job to make sure the windshield was clean, the switches were where they needed to be, and the safety straps in the cockpit were laid out neatly so the aviators could put them on with ease. If there were any questions about the ordnance, the plane captain knew who to call to get the answer.

During the Scud alert, the plane captains were nowhere in sight. They, too, had retreated to the bunkers. However, at least one other enlisted person stayed behind. He ran from jet to jet, arming the weapons and putting up the ladders, the last duty of a plane captain before a jet departed.

McGrath's first mission that morning called for close air support (CAS). While the name implies a specific distance, CAS actually refers to the detailed coordination and integration that occurs between air and ground troops so the correct targets are hit with precision and no friendlies are killed. This kind of coordination is necessary because from the air, the aviators can't distinguish between friendlies and enemies. If the Marines fell into harm's way, there was a good chance McGrath would have to engage her weapons—a military euphemism for taking out bad guys.

She and Innocenti walked around the aircraft at the same time, in different directions, performing their preflight check. They had to ensure the bombs and missiles loaded on the jet were secure. An F-18 can carry up to 8,000 pounds of armament at one time. All bombs (laser-guided JDAM, dumb bombs, or any air-to-ground rockets) hang from the fuselage or the wings of the jet. The number and variety of bombs and missiles the jet carried differed depending on the mission. The jet also has 500 rounds of 20mm bullets and a gun that fit inside the F-18's nose.

As the Scud sirens continued to blare, McGrath quickly verified that each bomb had two correct fusings. One fusing armed the bomb after it was dropped, and the other told it when to go off. Sometimes it was more efficient for a bomb to explode above the ground than below it. If there were hostile troops in the open, the bomb could have the most devastating impact if it were set to go off twenty to thirty feet above the ground, showering troops in the open with shrapnel, its concussive force not dampened by tons of sand. If McGrath's mission called for destroying a bunker or a runway, she would set the fuse to go off after impact, enabling the bomb to travel through the target and blow up beneath it. The timing of the explosion depended on what she was going after that day.

Once she finished her preflight inspection outside the jet, McGrath climbed the ladder and slid down into the narrow, cramped quarters of the cockpit. From the back seat, she had a view of the back of the pilot's head and the highly technical control panel that surrounded them. McGrath, who is five feet seven inches tall, adjusted her position by raising the seat all the way up. F-18s are designed for male pilots, or for individuals consistently taller than the average woman. All aviators, male and female, have to fall within a certain size to fly jets. They can't be too small or too large. Reconfiguring the jet to be more female friendly probably won't happen in the near future, if at all, because the number of women flying fighter jets hasn't increased significantly, even moderately, since military aviation opened up to women in 1993. In 2003 there were 113 female Marine aviators, and only seven were fighter pilots.

Beside her seat, McGrath had just enough room for her flight bag, which held maps of the area, a book of emergency procedures for jet malfunctions, a list of frequencies the aviators could talk on, checklists for systems that she ran and set up in the jet, and satellite photos of pre-planned targets. She also had a night-vision goggle (NVG) case she carried on evening missions. McGrath pulled safety straps tightly across her body to be as close as possible to the ejection seat in case she had to use it. The straps weren't painful but they weren't comfortable, either.

Within twenty minutes of starting the preflight check, the F-18 taxied away from the airfield without the clearance of the tower operators, who had also chosen to wait out the Scud alert in the bunkers. The pilots and WSOs, now on their own, were flying $50 million jets and carrying thousands of dollars worth of ordnance. They had already been briefed about their mission. The technology was the best that money could buy and the latest in pinpoint destruction. It was mounted and maintained by some of the best-trained crews in the world. But once they left the ground, the success of their attack was in their hands and their hands alone—a matter of steady nerves, cool judgment, flawless coordination, and old-fashioned instinct.

As soon as they were airborne, the aviators were relieved to have left the Scud threat behind but they pressed north not knowing exactly what danger lay ahead. The first Marine aviation strike of the war occurred during McGrath's flight, but she was not a part of it. She had been sent on another mission. Some members of the Green Knight squadron led the strike on Safwan Hill, an Iraqi military observation post a couple of kilometers across the border. The destruction of Safwan Hill was a priority since it had sophisticated surveillance equipment near the main highway that ran from Kuwait up to Basra and then Baghdad. The attacking forces couldn't attempt to cross the border until it was destroyed.

As one section of jets destroyed Safwan Hill, McGrath and her team provided close air support for Marines crossing the Kuwaiti border into Iraq. Since it was early morning and still dark outside, McGrath wore her night-vision goggles. They allowed her to see everything clearly, including anti-aircraft artillery, surface-to-air missile launches, ground artillery, and even small arms fire. As she flew north of the border, McGrath watched what appeared to be a huge fireworks display. The goggles, which don't have the best depth perception, gave the illusion that she was the target of incoming missiles and artillery.

The Marines that McGrath protected that morning were only twenty to thirty miles north of the border. McGrath communicated with a Marine officer on the ground to find out what kind of aid, if any, they needed. During these missions, military aviators targeted anything and anyone who posed a threat to the Marines, including enemy tanks, artillery, and personnel who were firing on coalition forces.

McGrath may or may not have destroyed anything on that first mission. This may sound strange, but modern war is fought at the speed of sound from 17,000 feet above the earth, a fast-paced round-robin of missions that all run together. Her recollection of the early days of the war is a blur. Other aviators in her squadron are similarly vague about this period. As the aviators transitioned from policing the no-fly zone to flying combat missions, chaos prevailed. McGrath had planned to keep track of the number of missions she flew and the bombs she dropped, but that became difficult early on. Once the war started, her squadron flew round-the-clock missions for three months straight. McGrath, herself, flew thirty-seven missions in twenty-four days. She flew multiple flights nearly every day, each flight two to three hours long, and she often fired missiles and dropped bombs and obliterated places where the enemy was presumed to be. The pace was so frenetic in the beginning of the war that the doctors handed out dextroamphetamines, known by the brand name Dexedrine, to help aviators stay awake. They were also referred to as "go pills." The doctors wanted the aviators to at least test the pills on the ground in case they had to fly three to four missions back-to-back. McGrath tried one but didn't like the effect it had on her. It made her feel as though she had drunk ten cups of coffee. She preferred coffee to pills, maintaining that the Al Jabar cafeteria had the best cappuccino machines. She enjoyed French vanilla cappuccino before the early morning briefings that preceded each flight mission. McGrath did take the "no go pills" that were used to help the aviators sleep between missions. She said they were so strong she could have slept through a nuclear war. They had to be potent to shut down the aviators' adrenalin.

For the first twenty-four hours of the war, everyone in McGrath's squadron was either flying or getting ready to fly. Having finished her initial flight, McGrath went to the squadron tent, only to find her name on the whiteboard for another mission five hours later. On her next mission, she and her pilot were tasked with destroying a bridge in southern Iraq. If they succeeded, the Iraqis would have more difficulty traveling south, where Marines were securing oil fields during the first forty-eight hours of the war.

To destroy the bridge, McGrath employed a laser-guided bomb. A Marine on the ground radioed the coordinates of the target to McGrath, who in turn recorded the information and displayed the target on what looks like an infrared TV camera. Then she directed a diamond pointer to the target to indicate the destination of the bomb. A sensor on the bomb picked up the laser and tracked it to the target. With McGrath's okay, the pilot pressed the button to drop the 2,500-pound ordnance. As the bomb departed the jet, McGrath felt a quick jolt in the aircraft.

When the bomb struck the bridge, McGrath didn't hear the explosion. One of their last tasks before take-off was to pull the canopy down over the cockpit and latch it. Once an aviator fastened the canopy, it was so quiet in the cockpit that McGrath may as well have been in a soundproof room. She couldn't even hear the deafening noise from the jet's engines. But she could see a flash from the explosion, followed by smoke. The visual results depended on the size of the bomb and the target, and on the time of day. Explosions were most visible against the dark landscape. Early one morning, McGrath took out a suspected ammunition depot. Seven hours later, while flying another mission, she could see the complex—many miles away, still burning.

Danger is inherent in war, whether you are in combat in the sky or on the ground. Some argue that because Saddam Hussein didn't have an air force, American pilots and their crews weren't in danger, especially those in fighter jets flying five miles up in the air. Kiowa helicopter pilot Robin Brown's experience should be proof enough that the sky above Iraq was far from safe. Granted, McGrath, who flew much higher than Brown, never felt as though she was being directly targeted or that a missile had locked onto her aircraft. However, flying over Iraq was no flight over the Rose Bowl. The Iraqis had surface-to-air missiles and anti-aircraft artillery. McGrath knew her jet was the target of barrage fire and that she could be shot down and captured. If that happened, she would probably be raped and killed, and her male pilot would be beheaded or beaten to death.

Women were once prohibited from flying in combat because of the possibility of being sexually assaulted. In 1993 they won the right to fly fighter jets. McGrath thinks it's ridiculous to say a woman shouldn't fly jets because she may endure more pain than her male counterpart if her aircraft is shot down. She contends, "It's going to be as shitty for guys as it is for women. It's war. Horrible things happen." Still, many people have difficulty imagining and accepting the sexual abuse that captured women would probably have to endure. They envision their mothers, wives, and daughters in those situations and it's simply incomprehensible. It's still easier to think of a father, husband, or son in similar situations even though they too can be raped. Some don't believe that war is the proper work environment for women who have, can, or will give birth to their children and grandchildren.

But as far back as the Civil War, there have been female POWs. In the War Between the States, several women were taken prisoner on both sides. In World War II, Lieutenant Reba Whittle, an Army nurse, was on a medical evacuation plane shot down over France. The Germans captured Whittle and held her in a prisoner-of-war camp until Germany surrendered eight months later. At least seventy-nine American women, nearly all Army or Navy nurses, were taken prisoner when the Philippines fell to the Japanese in May 1942. All survived captivity, and were treated less harshly than male prisoners.

Two women were among the twenty-three Americans taken prisoner during the first Gulf War. All of the prisoners, male and female, were tortured or abused. One of the women, Major Rhonda Cornum, said she was sexually abused. Cornum, a flight surgeon, was captured when her Army helicopter crashed. In the war that McGrath was fighting, she and her female counterparts were well aware of the hazards of their profession.

In its 2002 report, Amnesty International cited political prisoners and detainees in Iraq who were subjected to systematic torture. The bodies of many of those executed showed signs of torture. Common methods of physical torture included electric shocks to the genitals, cigarette burns to the soles of their feet, pulling out of fingernails, rape, long periods of suspension by the limbs from either a rotating fan in the ceiling or from a horizontal pole, beating with cables, hoses, or metal rods, and *falaqa* (beating on the soles of the feet). In addition, detainees were threatened with rape and subjected to mock execution. They were placed in cells where they could hear the screams of others being tortured and were deliberately deprived of sleep.

Early in the war, McGrath and thirty-four-year-old Captain Andrew Larsen took time out from their busy flight schedule to grab a bite to eat and address the dangers of war head-on. They had a choice between the Marine Corps and the Air Force chow hall. Where they ate depended on which chow hall they were closest to at meal time. Although the food was similar, the Marine Corps chow hall was in a tent and the Air Force facility was in a building. For this meal, they ate at the Air Force chow hall, which on the inside resembled a big reception hall with rows of long tables and folding chairs. From the front of the hall, the staff dished out the food cafeteria style.

Seated at a table, McGrath tuned out the uniformed service members around her to focus on a casual conversation that had suddenly turned serious. She was talking to Larsen about what they would do if they were shot down over enemy territory. The two had met the previous year when Larsen checked into the Green Knights, an all-weather fighter/attack squadron at Marine Corps Air Station Miramar, in San Diego, California. Since then, they had flown together in Afghanistan, and although they didn't fly together all the time, they would team up in Iraq for more than twenty flights.

Larsen was a typical fighter jock—six feet two inches tall, handsome, muscular, and confident. He had green eyes and his shaved head hinted of brown hair. He was someone McGrath had come to trust. Larsen flew the jet and kept them away from any surface-to-air fires. He ensured the jet was within all the parameters to drop the ordnance—a fancy way of saying that he was a top-notch flyer who kept control of a very complicated high-performance aircraft in harrowing conditions—kept sight of their lead aircraft, and safely took off and landed the jet.

Larsen had also come to rely on McGrath. He had to be able to trust her with his life because the back-seater controlled the ejection seat. If McGrath pulled the handle, it would activate both seats and punch the aviators out of the jet. The pilot had to have confidence that when faced with imminent death, McGrath would know when to pull the handle. He had to believe that if the

Iraqis launched a MiG, McGrath, after receiving the initial coordinates, would be able to find the MiG, track it, and input accurate coordinates to return fire. Then she'd tell the pilot whether to fire or not. Failure to execute these steps could lead to a MiG wiping out civilians or friendly troops.

Finally, the pilot had to rely on the back-seater to keep a good lookout. Larsen knew that if McGrath saw a surface-to-air missile coming off the deck, she would give him a good call. Break right. If she was asleep on the job, they'd get blasted out of the sky. No second chance.

In wartime, it was common for aviators to have a plan of action in case they were shot down. They had several options. Some military aviators chose to save their last bullet for each other. Others decided to save their last round for themselves. This is what McGrath and Larsen were discussing between themselves in the chow hall. They came up with their own solution. They preferred to spend their last rounds on the enemy. If they were shot down and Iraqis were closing in on them, these flyers would not surrender. They would blast away and likely get blasted themselves in a hail of bullets.

Larsen leaned forward. "Hey, I've got fifteen rounds in my nine millimeter and another fifteen right here next to me. If we go down, I'm using all thirty."

"I'm using all thirty, too," McGrath said. "And I've got a knife after that."

When the conversation ended, they didn't shake hands. It wasn't that kind of pact. Nor would the subject come up again. It was clear where they each stood. Their eyes told the story: "We will not be captured alive."

If McGrath sounds tough, it's because she is. If she sounds confident, even arrogant, maybe it's because she is. Her self-reliance has grown over the years as her skills, various roles, and their situations have warranted—from an athlete on the soccer field who would rather trample than be trampled, to her training, first as a Marine officer and then as a fighter pilot. You don't earn your wings as an F-18 aviator through meekness, low self-esteem, and second-guessing yourself—which by the way are characteristics often applied to the female gender. Some argue that women don't possess the attack mentality and ego necessary to be a successful fighter aviator. McGrath contends that they do and that these women can be found not only in F-18s, but also in board rooms, courtrooms, and operating rooms throughout the United States. Having a killer instinct isn't unique to flying jets. She also believes that any woman can be just as triumphant as a man at anything, including being a fighter pilot, if she has the same educational and physical background, desire, and work ethic.

Amy McGrath began preparing for a career in military aviation back in the seventh grade at St. Pius X Middle School, a Catholic school in northern Kentucky. That's when she decided to be a pilot—and not just any pilot. She wanted to fly fighter jets. Her class was studying World War II. McGrath's topic was aviation. She had wanted to focus on jets but quickly discovered that there weren't any jets in World War II, except for a few German Messerschmitts at the tail end of the war, which were hardly more controllable than rockets with pilots. This revelation both disheartened and inspired the twelve-year-old. She didn't do well on her project, but she knew what she wanted to be when she grew up.

Aimee Molique, who met McGrath at St. Pius that same year, recalled a childhood conversation about what they wanted to be when they grew up. Molique thought she might be a teacher. "I'm going to fly F-18s," said McGrath, referring to one of the hottest combat jets ever built. That night at the dinner table, Molique told her family about the new girl in her class who planned to fly fighter jets someday. "I laughed about it," she said. "I thought, 'Yeah, right.'" Years later, Molique replaced that laughter with admiration for a friend who "knew what she wanted to do and stuck with it."

At any age, McGrath's decision to become a fighter pilot would have seemed unusual because of her gender. She does have three uncles who served in the Marine Corps but they didn't influence McGrath's decision toward a military career because she rarely if ever heard them talking about their service. Her father, Donald, is a retired high school teacher, and her mother, Marianne, is a medical doctor and a psychiatrist. Donald retired after teaching high school English in Cincinnati for forty years. Marianne was a pediatrician at Children's Hospital in Cincinnati for many years before starting her own private practice.

Less obvious influences guided McGrath toward fighter jets, such as trips with her family to Wright-Patterson Air Force Base, which is home to the oldest and largest military aviation museum in the world. During her family's several visits to the museum, McGrath fell in love with the jets. She would have liked to have spent a summer or two there.

By the time McGrath reached the seventh grade, fighter jets had been around for more than forty years. Female jet aviators were another story. Just as she had chosen a history assignment about a subject that didn't really exist—jets in World War II— McGrath had selected a profession that wasn't open to women.

Twelve-year-old Amy wrote to the U.S. Naval Academy to find out when women would be allowed to fly in combat. She composed the letter without the knowledge of her parents. In her letter, McGrath had not included her family's unlisted phone number. So when a representative from the Academy called her, all he could find in the phone book was the number for her mom's medical practice. He left a message on the answering machine.

Her mom was surprised when she heard the message from the Naval Academy, not for her oldest or her second-oldest child, but for the youngest. She thought it was some kind of a joke. McGrath returned the call and talked with the official from the Academy for about thirty minutes. During the conversation she asked the caller if he thought women would be able to fly fighter jets someday. He replied, "No." The year was 1987.

McGrath took this response as a personal challenge. They were trying to tell her that she couldn't fly fighters because her name was Amy and not Andy. *Oh really. We'll just see about that.* From that moment on, she was determined to become a very good fighter pilot.

It's clear why McGrath chose a profession in military aviation. What's less obvious is where she found the fortitude to succeed in a career where so few women had gone before her. Growing up, most of McGrath's role models were professional athletes such as Johnny Bench, Terry Bradshaw, and David Robinson. There weren't many female sports heroes. Her aviator heroes included John Glenn, a retired Marine pilot and astronaut, and Alan Shepard, a graduate of the Naval Academy and retired naval pilot and astronaut. Both were also part of NASA's first high-profile program, Project Mercury, to learn if humans could survive in space.

Since female role models were few and far between in military aviation, McGrath looked closer to home. She found one in her mother, whose work ethic and intelligence have always impressed and motivated her. McGrath attributes her positive attitude and perseverance to her mom, Marianne, who contracted polio at the age of ten. When the acute phase of the illness had passed, Marianne was left with a weakening of her left arm, trunk, right leg, and paralysis in her left leg. Over time, as Marianne seemed to be getting better, she moved from crutches, to a cane, to a limp.

Amy was about thirteen when her mom started showing signs of post-polio syndrome. Marianne went back to wearing a leg brace and to using a cane. She couldn't walk more than a block without severe muscle spasms and pain. When walking became more difficult for Marianne in the 1980s, she could no longer continue her practice as a pediatrician. She returned to school and became a psychiatrist, which allowed her to see patients while sitting.

Marianne was an inspiration to her daughter throughout Amy's schooling and military training. While playing and excelling at high school basketball and soccer, McGrath would tell herself, "Amy, don't ever feel sorry for yourself." Her mom had conquered more than McGrath could ever dream of overcoming.

Mom's ability to persist became a driving force for McGrath and her own success. While training for a half-triathlon in Florida, McGrath was asked by a guy in flight school why she put herself through such rigorous training. The only answer she could give him was, "Because I can." She never wanted to take her athletic ability for granted. She didn't want to sit around on a couch. She needed to do everything she could because there were a lot of people who didn't take advantage of their opportunities or who simply couldn't.

In 1993, six years after being told that women would never fly fighter jets, and following a successful academic, basketball, and soccer career at Notre Dame Academy, an all-girls Catholic high school, McGrath entered the U.S. Naval Academy at Annapolis. She was the first woman accepted for the class of 1997. Each of the nation's military academies has a limited number of discretionary appointments that can be offered, which means the applicant doesn't have to go through a congressman or senator to secure a nomination before being accepted. McGrath had learned early in her senior year of high school that she would receive a superintendent's discretionary appointment. That same year, the military lifted the ban on female fighter aviators. McGrath wouldn't have to fight that battle.

At the Naval Academy, McGrath revised her dream of flying fighter jets after learning she didn't have the 20-20 eyesight necessary to become a pilot. She chose the next best thing—a career as a weapons' systems operator. Instead of flying the jet, she would coordinate its weapons, including two of the military's best air-to-air missiles, AMRAAMs and heat-seeking Sidewinders, to be launched. The AMRAAM can locate its targets beyond visual range and be launched at any angle and speed. The guidance section of the Sidewinder enables the missile to home in on the engine exhaust of a target aircraft.

McGrath could have flown for any branch of the armed services but she chose the Marine Corps. Traditionally, the F-18 has been one of the least popular aircraft for female aviators to fly because of its aggressive role in combat—dogfighting, air-to-air combat, and dropping bombs. Also, the road to becoming a Marine fighter pilot requires the most rigorous and physical ground training of all the military branches.

During Leatherneck, the equivalent of Officer Candidate School (OCS) for those who attend the Naval Academy, cadets travel to Quantico where they spend the summer between their junior and senior years showing the Marine Corps what they have to offer. One of the toughest challenges for McGrath during this period was the endurance course. It wasn't a question of whether she could pass it. She wanted to be first. The endurance test is a four to four-and-a-half mile obstacle course through the woods, with participants carrying rifles and full packs. There were obstacles every quarter mile. Toward the end of the race, McGrath's rifle, which was slung over her shoulder, caught on a net. The rifle sling jabbed her in the neck and broke skin. She didn't even notice it until she finished the race and a corpsman pointed it out. He saw blood dripping down her neck and asked her what happened. She was so focused she hadn't felt a thing. She still has the scar.

Another time, the 120 people going through the training were split up into four-man fire teams. There were only ten to fifteen women, so not many teams got a female. McGrath was put with three men who were not happy to have her on their team. One of the best athletes in Leatherneck at the time, Scott McCloud, was on her team. On the last day of fire team exercises, the teams raced against one another. McCloud wanted to win. Wearing full packs, team members had to complete a ten-mile forced march/run through the woods. And the clock didn't stop until the last person in the team finished. Early in the race, McGrath was in the middle to back of the pack. That wasn't good enough for McCloud, who was up front. He ran back to her and shouted, "Come on, McGrath. You want me to take your pack for you?" He knew exactly what to say to push her buttons. She raced forward to the front of the pack and stayed there until she finished.

When she graduated from the Academy, McGrath went through ground and flight training. She was one of those rare female Marines who underwent every single day of training with her male counterparts. In training, Marines are graded on much more than their physical abilities. Some people are bigger, stronger, and faster than others just like some people shoot better, some retain knowledge and take tests better, some function on less sleep better, and others take pain better. These are all attributes that the Marines are "graded" on in training. A male Marine may run three miles in twenty minutes and McGrath may only be able to run it in twenty-four minutes, but she may be able shoot an M-16 at 500 yards more accurately than he can. That doesn't mean that either one of them doesn't belong and doesn't have anything to contribute to the fight.

When McGrath arrived at her F-18 training squadron, the commanding officer held her up for four and a half months until another female officer showed up so they could begin their training together. The commander knew Marine fighter aviation was a tough community and he believed the women would be better off going through training together. That way, they could support one another. He thought he was doing the right thing. He'd never worked with female aviators before. McGrath thought it was the worst thing he could have done because he was sending a couple of bad messages to the male aviators. First, that the women couldn't hack it on their own, even though they had made it to that point on their own. And second, that the women were special, which was the last message McGrath wanted sent to the other aviators in training. If you want a unit to work, everyone has to be equal.

Once McGrath completed her F-18 training, she was ready to enter a gun squadron—a unit of twelve aircraft and thirty aviators whose mission was to shoot down other planes and destroy targets on the ground. One hundred Marines supported this endeavor, along with two Navy corpsmen and a flight doctor. McGrath, who had played on co-ed teams throughout her young life, was ready for them, but were they prepared for her? Since the number of female F-18 pilots is so low, that also means there are few women in a gun squadron such as the Green Knights. It's not unusual for a gun squadron of more than 150 military personnel to have only one female aviator—or none at all. How readily the squadron was willing to accept McGrath and how well she performed would have an enormous impact on her future as a Marine aviator—and the future of other female aviators.

In March 2001, fourteen years after being told women would not fly in combat, McGrath and another female aviator, Jaden Kim, joined the Green Knights. They were the first female aviators to become members of the squadron. When they arrived, their presence gave the squadron the distinction of being the only one on the West Coast, in that month and year, to have female aviators. One of the first tests the women faced had to do with accepting, or learning to tolerate, the call sign assigned to them by the other aviators in the squadron.

In the Marine Corps, call signs are a key component in the humbling process that precedes building up a young aviator. Typically, the aviators who have been around for a while in the squadron will test out several names on a pilot before they choose one. Selecting a name is usually an informal, and oftentimes spontaneous, process. Someone may refer to a new pilot as "Beavis," and the next thing he knows, the name has stuck and his call sign is Beavis. The name that sticks tends to be the one the new aviator likes the least. In the training squadron, McGrath was given the call sign "Chia"—for Chia Pet—because of the way her curly hair stuck out from beneath her cover (the military's name for a hat). That name gave way to "Guns," for her overly aggressive behavior during an air-to-air training flight. During her final training flight,

McGrath inadvertently broadcast some hawkish behavior over the radio. Each day there are certain rules of engagement and on that day, the aviators had to actually see the enemy aircraft, and not just pick it up on radar, before killing it. In the heat of the battle, McGrath forgot the rule. She spotted the enemy on radar and couldn't figure out why her co-pilot, who was responsible for pulling the trigger, wasn't shooting the enemy. Instead of talking on the intercom, where only her co-pilot would have heard her, McGrath went over the radio. During training, everything on the radio is taped, including McGrath saying, "Hey, why aren't you shooting? Shoot him! Shoot him!" The tape was played during the debrief. The name "Guns" was okay for a training squadron, but it was short-lived in the Green Knights, her operational squadron. One pilot said the call sign was "way too cool." "Krusty," another reference to her hair and to Krusty the Clown from *The Simpsons* won hands down. The guys thought that was pretty funny, but McGrath didn't like it too much. She begged them not to give her that name, which of course made it official. Kim, who is Asian, was named "Mulan."

After reluctantly coming to terms with her permanent call sign, McGrath moved on. There would be many more tests to come. The members of the male-dominated squadron weren't accustomed to welcoming women into their domain, fraternity, and team. As is the case with many established alliances—male, female, or mixed gender—the onus fell on the newcomer to fit in.

When McGrath and Kim entered the Green Knights, it was a huge deal, according to Captain Jeffery Chiow, a WSO who graduated with McGrath from the Naval Academy and joined the squadron at the same time. Everybody was apprehensive and thought the end was in sight for the all-male squadron.

Michael Folgate, then the captain in charge of the squadron's safety department, shared Chiow's sentiment, saying the Marines in a gun squadron are like a bunch of guys on a football team. They're great guys, but sometimes it's like being around a guy's locker room. Everyone thought that might end.

But in truth, nothing ended when McGrath joined the squadron. While the male aviators continued to fly, McGrath negotiated her way into the squadron and gained a reputation as a highly qualified competitor and aviator, and a go-getter.

Folgate was quick to recognize McGrath as a high-caliber individual with a strong work ethic. Her peers, on the other hand, reserved judgment until McGrath had proven herself in combat. That time would come soon enough.

Until then, McGrath trained and worked on building a rapport with the male aviators. A big part of joining a squadron has to do with becoming "one of the guys," an expression often used around the squadron to imply trust, camaraderie, faith, and dependence on one another. Any male or female aviator right out of flight school isn't "one of the guys" until he or she has been tested and observed by senior aviators. It's that way with any tight-knit group of individuals or team.

Six months after McGrath joined the Green Knights, terrorists attacked the United States, plunging this country into war, first in Afghanistan and then in Iraq. The Green Knights were ready for combat. McGrath, who never thought she would go to war, was now eager to put her training to the test. She wanted to get back at the people who had attacked the United States.

McGrath didn't focus on the danger ahead. What aviators do in the jets in wartime is exactly what they do every day in peacetime. It wasn't as though they made a huge jump from training to combat. Flying is inherently dangerous. Everybody who McGrath had known who had been killed had been killed in peace time.

The Green Knights deployed to Manas, Kyrgyzstan, just north of Afghanistan. There were four female officers in the squadron—two aviators (McGrath and Kim), and a maintenance and an intelligence officer. None of the junior aviators, male or female, had yet proved themselves in combat.

Since it rained a lot in the beginning, the aviators spent their evenings sitting around in their rain-soaked tents and talking. The topic of women in combat came up and before long the discussion turned into a heated debate. In the end, many of the aviators expressed their opposition to women in combat. To some people, Krusty still hadn't proven herself. Chiow said they all had to prove themselves, but no one else was starting the race from two blocks back like she was.

Four junior captains, including McGrath, flew the first mission in Afghanistan. Despite all her training, McGrath wasn't quite sure what to expect. And while there are all sorts of unknowns in war, her fear didn't hinge on meeting the enemy head-on. She worried more about making a mistake than about getting hurt. She didn't want to embarrass herself, the squadron, or the Marine Corps.

On her first mission in March of 2002 into Afghanistan, McGrath became the first female Marine to fly in an F/A-18 in combat. Kim, the other female in her squadron, became the second when she flew her first mission in April of 2002.

Over the next six months, McGrath flew eight- to nine-hour flights in Afghanistan. About eighty percent of that time was droning around in the air space, waiting to see if the troops on the ground needed help. She flew close air support for convoy escorts, special operations convoys, and helicopter assault support. When the Marines were fired upon, the jets provided support. Sometimes, though, McGrath couldn't drop her bombs or fire her missiles for fear of wiping out small American Special Forces units mixed in among the Afghan and Taliban forces. Special operations forces had infiltrated the country in search of the Taliban and Al Qaeda.

To stay alert on the long flights, McGrath talked with her pilot over the intercom. Often times the male pilots drank Cokes to get an extra boost from the caffeine. McGrath didn't drink anything on her flights. She had to keep her bladder empty so she wouldn't have to urinate. While they flew, the male aviators urinated in a "piddle pack," a plastic zip-seal bag with a sponge in it. Something similar has been adapted for female aviators, but McGrath hadn't looked into it because she didn't like having extra contraptions around. She already had enough stuff strapped onto her. Plus, the female version of the piddle pack wasn't in the Navy/Marine Corps inventory of flight equipment, and it wasn't something McGrath would go out and buy on her own. None of the women she knew had used it.

McGrath either dehydrated herself or held it for a long time. Some of the flights could get real uncomfortable, but she had become pretty good at holding it. As a precaution, she bought adult diapers for the transatlantic flight.

Under the best of circumstances, flying fighter jets was stressful. When a unit went into combat that stress increased and it was trying on everybody. In Afghanistan, Folgate observed McGrath taking the initiative to become more tactically proficient. Each person had a certain amount of responsibility. "It's noted when people not only pull their own weight but help everyone else out as well," Folgate said. "Krusty did that."

One way McGrath proved herself was by learning to brief combat missions. A typical brief is one hour long and filled with lots of tactical details. McGrath took the time necessary to learn what was involved in a brief, how to present the information to a group of aviators, and how to assume the overall responsibility for ensuring that all information for the flight was ready to be presented. McGrath had not briefed many flights up to that point in the squadron. She asked for the responsibility, which normally wouldn't have been given to someone with so little experience, especially since they were combat and not training flights.

By taking the initiative, McGrath gained a fair amount of recognition while in Afghanistan. Toward the end of the deployment, her superiors were deciding who would work toward which qualification. Some qualifications are extremely competitive because of the level of difficulty and the respect they receive from the aviation community. One such qualification requires the aviator to gain an increasing proficiency at dog fighting, then turn around and teach combat flying to the new aviators. McGrath was granted the opportunity to train to become an air combat instructor.

Folgate couldn't think of any other woman who had been selected for that role. Successful completion put McGrath in position to attend the Navy's TOPGUN school or the Marines' Weapons Tactics Instructor school. The training also put McGrath in the top four or five people in the squadron that Folgate would want with him when flying a combat mission.

By the time the squadron left Kyrgzstan, McGrath was considered one of the guys, part of the team. Any experience and confidence she lacked in combat McGrath gained in the six months she flew in Afghanistan. That knowledge would serve her well in Iraq, where the flying missions were more frequent and intense.

Several days after the war started in Iraq, McGrath was flying a routine reconnaissance mission when she and Larsen received orders to fly close air support near An Nasariyah. It was an extremely dangerous time for Marines on the ground. Two bloody battles near the city had raged for hours as U.S.-led forces made a relentless advance to Baghdad.

In one area, a paramilitary group loyal to Saddam Hussein had been attacking Marines on the ground for a day and a half. The Marines were taking constant fire from rocket-propelled grenades and automatic weapons. The troops had reached a point where they needed air support to take off the pressure. They had determined that these attacks were being launched from a compound several kilometers away. The compound had to be destroyed. On the ground, Dennis Santere was responsible for relaying the coordinates of the target to the aviators, a critical job. Two F-18 fighter jets already in the area carried out the mission. McGrath was the WSO for the second jet.

Communication was sporadic between land and air as many agencies were trying to use the same frequency. Santere (call sign "Mouth") had to get off his radio a couple times because he was taking incoming fire from the paramilitary group.

A few minutes after the aircraft received the coordinates for the compound, the first fighter jet began its attack from the south, followed by McGrath and Larsen. The lead jet dropped a 2,000-pound bomb, which failed to explode. Instead, it skipped off the roof of the compound and left a cloud of dust.

Hearing the results of the first bomb, the lead aircraft ordered Larsen and McGrath to press to the target and drop their bomb immediately. Santere made a small correction and gave McGrath new coordinates. Flying at an altitude of 25,000 feet and somewhere between 500 and 600 miles per hour, McGrath dropped her bomb on the compound. A silence filled the radios. It seemed like

forever to McGrath. Then she heard a mike click, followed by Santere's excited voice. "That was a shack." The bomb had hit square
in the middle of the building.

McGrath's lead now trailed her by ten miles for his last pass
when he asked Santere for a correction from McGrath's hit.

"Say correction from Wing's hit for my last bomb."

Santere replied, "The building is gone. Dash-2 leveled it. No
one is firing on us anymore."

Nothing else was said over the radios as the frequency was in
constant use. McGrath's aircraft was running out of fuel and had
to return to Kuwait immediately. At this time in the war, there
were no friendly divert bases nearby to refuel.

Meanwhile, on the ground, Marines stood and cheered. They
couldn't believe that after a few concise radio conversations
between ground and air forces, the enemy had been wiped out.
The enemy—who had them pinned down—just vanished.

For McGrath, that mission represents everything that is good
about being a fighter aviator. She and her pilot were in the area
when they got the call to support Marines who were in danger on
the ground. The aviators were able to respond quickly and accurately, and successfully fulfill their mission—no doubt saving the
lives of Marines in the process.

A month after the mission in An Nasiriyah, Santere returned
to Al Jabar Air Base. He looked back through the records to find
out who had flown on March 24. He searched for the call sign of
the aircraft and the squadron. Then he went to the squadron and
asked who dropped the bomb over An Nasariyah on March 24.
He learned it was Captain *Amy* McGrath. Santere didn't know the
voice on the other end of the radio came from a female. He could
have been unaware of McGrath's gender because of the stress of
the situation or because of the way a voice can be distorted over
the airwaves.

Santere tracked down McGrath to let her know he appreciated her help. The compound was definitely a staging area for a paramilitary group, and the Marines on the ground believe that taking out that target helped to break up the resistance. After March 24, Santere and his fellow Marines didn't experience a whole lot of organized resistance from the enemy.

McGrath was working at a computer in the mission planning tent when Santere walked up behind her and tapped her on the shoulder. She looked up at a young Marine captain dressed in cammies. She was quite sure she hadn't seen him before. His nametag read Dennis Santere.

He introduced himself as "Mouth" and asked her if she remembered him. It had been a few weeks since the bombing over An Nasiriyah and a lot had happened during that time. She was about to tell him she had no idea who he was when it hit her. She stood up from the chair.

"An Nasiriyah, right?" she said.

"Yes," Santere said, as he stuck out his hand. "I just wanted to thank you."

"You're more than welcome," McGrath said, shaking his hand.

Santere said McGrath's bombing of the compound was "one of the biggest explosions I've ever seen on the ground."

Following their introductions, McGrath escorted Santere around the squadron and introduced him to the other crew members in the flight—Virge, Tuck, and Mongo. Later that night, Santere brought two Cokes to the ready room tent. He and McGrath sat outside behind the tent and drank the Cokes while sharing combat stories and experiences at the Naval Academy (he graduated a year before her).

"I always thought that was the coolest thing, sitting outside that tent, chilling out, drinking a Coke with the ground forward

air controller that we directly supported one month prior,"
McGrath said. "It was such a contrast to our first meeting over the
radios when he and his unit were taking fire and my section was
flying overhead."

That was McGrath's most rewarding moment during the war.
When it came time to leave Iraq, all her flights and missions ran
together. But she'll never forget meeting the person she supported, and putting a face to that voice on the ground. It person-
alized the war and gave her some perspective.

McGrath has completed more than 85 combat missions and
350 combat flight hours over Kuwait, Kyrgyzstan, Uzbekistan,
Afghanistan, Bahrain, Egypt, Iraq, Saudi Arabia, Pakistan, and
Tajikistan. Since returning from Afghanistan and Iraq, McGrath
has expressed mixed emotions about her role in the war. For military aviators, a certain amount of satisfaction goes along with
destroying a target. After all, taking out a target is one of their primary goals. It is what they train for and what they get paid to do.
And that is true of McGrath, to a certain extent.

"When you have a target and you shack it, it's awesome
because it means you did it right," she said, "and that's good. It
feels great. My best missions were close air support where someone was firing on our guys, and I was able to take them out. In that
case, I'm not thinking so much of the enemy. I'm just happy that
our guys are okay and that I can be of help to them. Every time
you go on a mission, especially in combat, you want to go up there
and do something. You don't ever want to bring your stuff back."

On the other hand, she didn't get a tremendous amount of
satisfaction from dropping bombs on defenseless individuals.
"The missions where I had to take out underground barracks first

thing in the morning—that was a little different." The F-18s have a forward-looking infrared (FLIR) system, or Nighthawk, on the side of the aircraft's fuselage. The FLIR looks like a small missile but it's really a camera that takes pictures using the infrared portion of the electromagnetic spectrum. It helps aviators see heat, which is hard to camouflage. McGrath punched in coordinates that targeted barracks where Iraqi troops were sleeping. Then she watched as the missiles launched and destroyed the barracks. On the FLIR monitor she could see Iraqis running for their lives. Watching those white figures against a green background made the war personal in another way. It forced McGrath to see those objects as humans. If she had just seen a bunker and no people, it would have been different.

When she returned from Iraq, McGrath brought the war with her. Like so many generations before her, she would have to learn how to cope with the emotional scars of combat. The difference—she is female and most war veterans are male.

The personal side of war has recurred in McGrath's dreams. Her mom, a psychiatrist, encouraged McGrath to talk about what happened. This wasn't easy for McGrath, who is a very private person, with deep convictions and with an intense loyalty to family, friends, God, and country. But she did start to talk about what she remembered most—the things that were the hardest.

As any intelligent person would do, McGrath was trying to process what had happened in Iraq. When you're at war, the emotional and intellectual sides of a fighter have to be in sync. The intellectual side of an aviator can't question the emotional side and vice versa. To do so would lead to indecision and death. That's why Marines and soldiers are taught to follow orders. However, when McGrath returned home, the emotional and intellectual sides started to separate and question one another. She was no longer under the pressure and stress of war. She had time to reflect.

At first, McGrath experienced waves of guilt. She felt as though she had been put in a position to kill people because they believed something different from what she believed. She knew this was an oversimplification, but at the same time she was brought up to respect other people's right to live and right to think even if their opinions were different from her own. Here she had been fighting against people who felt as strongly in what they believed as she did in what she believed.

She has taken that thought process to another level. On September 11, 2001, the United States was attacked without provocation and the conspirators were said to be preparing weapons of mass destruction to do the same thing again. They don't value human life the way Americans do. Yes, they have a right to their beliefs, but they don't believe she has a right to her beliefs.

McGrath knows that she was doing her job, that it was an important job, and that she did it well. And that in the process, she saved many Marine lives. At the same time, she destroyed cars, convoys, buildings, and barracks, and anyone inside those vehicles and structures. "The killing aspect is hard," she said. "It's also very difficult for me to talk about. There really isn't a day that goes by that I don't think of the human toll. No matter what side, we're all human. I can't tell you how many Arab guys are out there trying to make a living in the Iraqi army and I killed them." Knowing she destroyed innocent lives is something McGrath says she will have to learn to live with. People tell her that she did the right thing, and that she was justified, but McGrath isn't so sure.

She's aware that a lot of male aviators may look at her ambivalence toward killing as a female weakness, but she doesn't see it as a gender issue. For the most part, McGrath believes that she and the guys are more alike in combat flying than they are different. She knows both male and female aviators who have felt rage and anger toward the enemy, as well as pity for the innocent who have been killed or wounded during operations.

It may be true that more male aviators join the military because they have an overwhelming desire to fly in combat and destroy the enemy. When questioned about McGrath's attitude toward killing people, one male aviator said he was the wrong person to talk to about the subject because he had joined the military specifically to destroy the enemy. Larsen, on the other hand, didn't necessarily choose military aviation for combat purposes. He just wanted to go fast and was tired of getting speeding tickets on his motorcycle. However, he has little sympathy for the enemy. He accepts the unfortunate part of war—that a percentage of good guys will be killed. "It's not my job to sort them out."

While McGrath may not share Larsen's matter-of-fact attitude toward killing, her empathy for the enemy hasn't affected her performance on the job. In fact, Larsen was surprised to learn about McGrath's ambivalence. "I know her," he said, "and she would bomb the target no matter what it was. Whether she liked it or not, she would do it. And she wouldn't have a choice in the matter. I know she wouldn't even hesitate. She may not like it but she'd do it. I never really got any of that from her. She always does her job."

Two months after returning home from Iraq, McGrath flew from California to Breckenridge, Colorado, for a family wedding. McGrath comes from a large Irish-Catholic family, and this was the first time she had seen a lot of her family since returning from the war. Everyone was happy to see her. They thanked her for her service and commended her for her courage. Some wanted her to recall her experiences on the battlefield. All this attention overwhelmed McGrath and transported her mind from the wedding to the war. *My God, I've just killed hundreds of people and everyone is congratulating me.* It didn't make sense to her. McGrath stood in the doorway between the wedding reception and the patio. Used to being in control of her emotions, this tough Marine aviator was now close to tears.

McGrath wasn't in the doorway long when her uncle, Dave Vogel, a Vietnam vet who served in Da Nang from 1968 to 1969, spotted her. He saw a look in her eyes that he recognized. It was a look of sadness, of flashbacks of bombs exploding, of people dying. He was concerned that McGrath was getting down on herself for her role in the war. He knew how hard it was when you left the battlefield, returned to the States, and were left alone to rationalize the role you had in killing others. With hundreds of people eating and drinking and laughing and celebrating, he alone could empathize with her pain. He knew that she probably did things in Iraq that she wasn't proud of. He knew that she was probably questioning her actions. But he also knew that, more than anything, she needed to trust herself.

He walked over to her and in a soft voice, said, "I know. I know."

Petty Officer Third Class Marcia Lillie, United States Navy.

The Little Bird
that Could

"You always have to have fear in your heart on the flight deck. If you don't, and you get comfortable, something will go wrong."
— *Navy Aviation Boatswain's*
Mate Handler (ABMH) Marcia Lillie

THE FLIGHT DECK OF A CARRIER LAUNCHING AND RETRIEVING AIR-craft is one of the most hazardous working environments in the world. During wartime, when the flight deck is in full operation, jets and helicopters are launching and landing round the clock on a small, pitching, rolling deck on the ocean. Jets are catapulted into the air from 0 to 150 miles per hour in two seconds. And they are traveling at more than 150 miles per hour as they aim for a three-foot window on the flight deck and catch their tailhooks, if they're skillful or lucky enough, on arresting cables that bring them to a screeching halt on a flight deck that could almost fit between the goalposts of a football field. More than fifty aircraft, six tractors, and hundreds of sailors, whose average age is nineteen, contribute to the traffic and busyness on the flight deck.

The flight deck crew, dressed in a rainbow of yellow, blue, red, green, purple and white jerseys, wearing cranials (helmets) to protect their heads, and thick headphones to block out the constant din of jet engines, manage the flight deck and coordinate the movement of ammunition, bombs and rockets, and fuel for the aircraft. The crew works shoulder to shoulder with whirring engines, moving aircraft, highly volatile fuel, and explosive ordnance. The slightest step in the wrong direction can lead to instant, violent death. Legs have been crushed under wheels, hands broken under shifting bomb racks. Objects as heavy as bombs, tanks, and fuel carts, and as weightless as flash lights and wrenches, when not properly stored have flattened or knocked out crew members. When the deck becomes slick from hydraulic fluid, oil, or salt from the sea air, sailors and vehicles slide around, and there's not much room to slide before you reach the edge—a steel cliff pitching and yawing above the sea. Fall overboard, and it's a hundred-foot drop into the ocean. Survive the fall and you'll drown in the ship's wake—too much air for the water to hold you up, too much water to catch a breath.

Marcia Lillie's fear of the flight deck was realized on Thanksgiving Day 2001, when she reported for duty on the USS *Harry S. Truman*. Lillie, an E-4 aviation boatswain's mate handler (ABMH), was just beginning her naval career on the aircraft carrier. When the twenty-three-year-old African American arrived on the ship, she was five feet seven inches tall and weighed a mere ninety pounds. The ship was docked at the Naval Air Station in Norfolk, Virginia, so it wasn't moving at the time. Hundreds of sailors mustered on the flight deck, dressed in their utility attire—light blue blouse, dark blue trousers, a navy blue belt with a silver buckle, black boots or leather shoes, and a blue baseball cap with the name of the sailor's command. It could have been quite easy for Lillie to blend into the crowd. Instead, she tripped and fell into the ship's catwalk, a metal grating that wraps around the perimeter of the flight deck—a sailor's last chance at staying aboard before falling one hundred feet to the water and to their death. That day, all she wounded was her pride. Her body was fine. Others have fallen into the catwalk and severely injured their backs or broken their limbs. Ironically, Lillie was prone to tripping and falling before she ever arrived on the ship, yet she chose to work in an environment in which one misstep on a platform that constantly rocked, pitched, yawed, and rolled could end her life. She would need to find her balance and her sea legs quickly. Soon, the ship would be heading to the Middle East.

When the war started in March 2003, the *Truman* and the USS *Theodore Roosevelt* were stationed in the Mediterranean Sea to support U.S. infantry and special forces in northern Iraq. The *Truman* was the daytime carrier and the *Roosevelt* operated in the evening. As the daytime carrier, the *Truman* had to have its aircraft over the beaches at the break of day.

Over the first thirty days of the war, the aircraft stationed on the *Truman* would fly 1,280 missions and use bombs, missiles, and rockets to strike 588 targets. Each day, about seventy aircraft flew just from the *Truman* and dropped more than 700 tons of ordnance (more than any other battle group supporting the war) in one month on targets in northern Iraq.

During those early days of the war, Lillie woke up at two thirty in the morning to support aircraft launching by four o'clock. The aircraft carrier has eighteen levels. As part of the flight deck crew, Lillie slept in a berthing area directly under the flight deck, on the 03 level, for easy access to and from work. She worked in the flight deck control room as an aircraft elevator operator.

The aircraft on the *Truman* flew twelve- to fifteen-hour missions, and the crew supported them with twenty-two hour workdays. Lillie worked such long hours that by the end of her shift she was so tired even the thundering sound of aircraft launching and landing one level above couldn't keep her awake. But she would never get used to the noise in her berthing area that was generated by the women ages eighteen to forty. Nor would she get accustomed to the lack of privacy. Since the crew worked different shifts, people were awake at all hours. The women always seemed to be talking, arguing, venting, or celebrating. The voices in the nearby passageways, and the sounds of steel doors screeching loudly as they opened and moaning as they were bolted shut, were harder to block out than the aircraft. It was easy to see why the majority of sailors are so young. Few older people would be able to tolerate such living conditions. The ship was a floating city that never slept.

The sleeping accommodations were so snug it's tempting to resort to the cliché "packed in like sardines in a can." Lillie couldn't stretch out or sit up because she slept on the middle bed in a three-tiered rack and had less than two feet of space separating her mattress from the ones below and above her. Until she got used to her cramped quarters, Lillie suffered several lumps on her head. The three showers for a berthing area of forty women was a short walk down the hallway. Other berthing areas had up to one hundred women.

After her shower, Lillie put on her socks, a pair of green or blue flight deck pants, and a blue jersey indicating that she was either a plane handler, aircraft elevator operator, tractor driver, or messenger and phone talker. In the Mediterranean, when the temperatures hovered in the forties and the fifties, Lillie wore long johns, two pairs of socks, an extra jersey, two pairs of gloves, a flight deck jacket, and a ski mask. She buckled her belt and laced her black boots. She had two pairs of black boots that she shined herself. She didn't iron her jerseys. Instead, she gave them to a friend who worked in the laundry room and pressed the jerseys for her, imprinting a crease down the middle. She brushed her teeth and fixed her hair and makeup. She skipped breakfast because the mess hall wasn't open yet. Prior to leaving the berthing area, Lillie took one last glimpse of herself in the mirror. Then she walked up the steps to the "fifty-yard line" on the flight deck for a briefing.

Before stepping onto the flight deck, Lillie put on her cranial and goggles to protect her head from moving objects and debris, and her eyes from the sting of jet fuel and fumes. Headphones enabled her to hear what others were saying about movement on the flight deck while shielding her ears from the noise of the planes. During the briefing, leaders informed the crew of the day's plan, including the sequence of aircraft launching, goals, safety, looking out for the people who they work with, and doing good for the country.

On a ship that supported more than 5,000 sailors and Marines, Lillie was one of ten tasked with operating the carrier's four elevators. The elevators on an aircraft carrier are not your typical hotel elevators that hold a maximum of 3,500 pounds. And Lillie was no bellhop, escorting passengers to and from their rooms via the elevators. These elevators are enormous hydraulic lifts that can shuttle 150,000 pounds of aircraft at one time, or two F-18 jets, a helicopter, and bombs and missiles between the flight deck and the hangar bay. Giant locks that look like sliding deadbolts hold the elevators securely in place on the flight deck.

Lillie operated the elevators from the flight control room, a miniature Grand Central Station and a constant hub of activity. The twenty-one by twelve foot room is situated at the base of the "island"—the control tower for the ship. It stands 150 feet tall— about as tall as a fifteen-story building—and bristles with radar and radio antennas. And standing just to one side of the utterly flat deck, it does indeed appear as an island.

Seven people worked in the flight control room on a regular basis—the handler, elevator operator, air wing maintenance coordinator (big daddy), fuels petty officer, the squadron chief and his assistant, and an aviation ordnance petty officer. From where Lillie stood, there were two video monitors to her left and one to her right that displayed the movement of aircraft on the flight deck. Radios lit up red and green. Phones rang constantly. And a steady flow of pilots, flight deck crew, and squadron reps came and went, shouting orders and asking questions about an aircraft's launch or recovery.

Operating these elevators is a huge responsibility. If a jet on the flight deck needs ammo from the hangar bay and the elevator gets held up, the jet won't depart on time. There's no sense in the jets leaving without their ammo, since their mission is to provide close air support for Marines and soldiers on the ground and that often requires dropping bombs on the enemy.

One time an elevator malfunctioned on Lillie's shift, leading to serious structural damage. It was two o'clock in the morning. Lillie was communicating by radio with the spin operator, who worked above her on the seventh (07) level of the island, in the camera room. With a view of the whole flight deck, the crew in the camera room recorded aircraft launches and landings. Lillie relied on the spin operator to tell her what was moving on the flight deck because she could see only a portion of it from the window of the control room and even less when it was dark outside.

Lillie was also talking with Top One (the person in elevator one on the flight deck), Bottom One (the person in elevator one on the hangar bay), and the elevator operator in the hangar-deck control room. The top and bottom elevator operators were trying to decide which aircraft to move from the flight deck to the hangar bay. First, they thought they would move two aircraft and had them loaded onto the elevator, then one, and then none. All this indecision wasn't good for the yellow shirts on the flight deck who seemed to be spending a lot of time loading and unloading the aircraft for no apparent reason. They were using up precious time that could have been spent setting up for the next flight operations, doing maintenance, and bringing up other aircraft.

With frustration levels already running high, more aggravation lay ahead. As soon as the elevator was powered up, it lost power. Lillie called the pump room to report the loss of power which was restored and then lost again. She looked up at the camera that pointed to the elevator to get a visual of what was happening. That's when she saw the massive elevator tilt and drop down to the hangar deck one story below her, taking chunks out of the flight deck along the way. Moments later, the door to the flight deck control room flew open and in ran a scared elevator operator. Luckily, no one and nothing was on the elevator at the time.

In the past, a plane captain or a brake rider rode in an aircraft when it was lowered to the hangar bay and one of those individuals would move the jet or helicopter into place. If the aircraft and a plane captain had been on the elevator, both would have fallen into the sea. Now no one is allowed to ride in the elevator at night. In the daytime, the plane captain or brake rider can ride in the elevator, but they can't be in the cockpit of the aircraft.

In the flight deck control room, sitting on a swivel chair across from Lillie, was the handler, Commander R. D. Jones, a.k.a Hollywood Handler. He ran the show. He was in charge of the movement of aircraft on the flight and hanger decks, as well as the catapults and arresting gear operations and aircraft fueling. Jones had an engaging personality, one he would need to oversee a staff of 750 sailors.

He and Lillie hit it off early and worked well together throughout the deployment. Both had a quick wit that they unleashed in their fast-paced work environment. Jones became Lillie's mentor, and although she was half his age and lacked his experience, Lillie also became someone who Jones could trust. He relied on her so much that sometimes he would bypass her supervisor and go straight to Lillie. When something wasn't working like it should and he needed things to happen right away, Jones knew he could rely on Lillie to take care of it.

When someone else was running the elevator too slowly, Jones would replace that person with Lillie. Jones and his crew couldn't operate in a wait-and-see mode or in slow motion. They had to act and react, act and react. When a broken Viking jet landed on the flight deck and was scheduled to fly in the next mission, Jones, Lillie, and the flight deck crew had to pool their resources to get the pilot out of the plane, repair the plane or find a replacement, and make sure whichever aircraft they used was prepared for its mission. If the spare aircraft was in the hanger bay, Lillie would power up the elevator, lower the Viking jet, wait for it to be repaired or for another one to take its place, and see that a functioning plane was ready to go on the flight deck for the scheduled departure.

With Lillie across from him, Jones was confident that the elevators would run smoothly. He saw Lillie as someone who could do whatever she wanted to do in life. Where some people say they want to do something but they don't have the ability or desire to see it through, Lillie had it all. She was smart, caught on fast, and like the handler, she had a way with people.

When the *Truman* got underway in 2003, women had been serving on ships for nearly a decade. In fact, Jones served on the first ship—the USS *John C. Stennis*—to be built from the ground up with a female crew in mind. Ships that hadn't been designed for female sailors had to be refitted. Male berthing areas and heads were refurbished to accommodate women. And when that was finished, the number of women on the ship had grown to where they needed even more space for the female sailors.

It wasn't long after women started serving on the ships that the vessels became known as the love boat. One way the Navy addressed sexual activity on the ships was by anticipating the behavior and building in controls. For example, in areas that had been dimly lit they turned up the lights. They put locks on remote areas. And they enforced the two-person rule, which meant that if you were going to be in a room with someone from the opposite sex you kept the door open. Jones believes the controls have deterred some of the unwanted actions but he knows he would be naïve to think that no one is fooling around on the ships.

Lillie may have gotten hit on a lot but it didn't get out of control and she never felt as though she was being harassed. She actually found the men easier to get along with than the women, who were full of drama and spent a lot of time getting into arguments and fights. She didn't have many female friends on the ship but she did have a couple of acquaintances with whom she would hang out.

Jones wasn't worried about Lillie. He knew she was picky about who she dated and she was focused on her work. He'd seen her turn down the advances of many sailors. While he couldn't account for her time when she was off duty, he saw Lillie as an independent thinker and someone who was going to blaze her own path. She was in control.

As the elevator operator, Lillie performed another crucial role. She operated a so-called "Ouija board" from the flight deck control room. The Ouija board is a two-by-six-foot flat board that represents a dynamic, moving map of the flight deck. It's used by the people in the flight control room who need to see what's happening on the entire deck but can't because they are on the same level as the flight deck, which is as long as the Empire State Building is tall. The board is a one-sixteenth model of the flight deck.

Unlike some operators of an Ouija board, Lillie wasn't trying to interact with supernatural forces—but in some ways, she was trying to control the future. Like an Ouija board, this map had objects Lillie had to manipulate and control. She rearranged templates representing the fifty jets and helicopters on the carrier's flight deck, as well as nuts, bolts and screws representing ammo, bombs, rockets, and fuel.

As one jet prepared to launch and another to land, Lillie used the tip of her fingers to slide two-inch templates in the shape of jets onto and off the flight deck. After the plane launched, she moved the tamplate to the side of the board with others that had already taken off. When a jet was out of commission, she flipped the template. These are just three of many scenarios she had to learn for the fifty or so aircraft on the flight deck at any given time.

In addition to knowing where the aircraft were at all times, Lillie also had to be aware of what the jets and helicopters were carrying for ammunition and ordnance and what they needed. Piggybacking some of the templates were nuts and bolts representing the ordnance and ammunition on the aircraft, or the condition of an aircraft. A washer indicated that the aircraft needed to be washed. A purple nut meant the aircraft needed fuel. A large nut specified that the aircraft was up on a jack. About ten different colored push pins represented other needs of the aircraft. A black pin meant an aircraft needed to be moved from the flight deck down to the hanger bay, a pink pin indicated the aircraft had no brakes, and a clear pin meant the aircraft was immobile. The crew members referred to this as nutology.

By putting each template in its correct location, Lillie was doing her part to keep the flight deck safe and available. This was especially challenging during the first month of the war, when the pace was so fast and aircraft were coming and going non-stop. If Lillie misrepresented the location of an aircraft by moving its template to a parking space when it was on the flight deck preparing to launch, an incoming aircraft could be informed that the flight deck was clear when it wasn't, leading to a collision.

No one worked better or harder for Jones than Lillie. They were a team, working at a fast pace and in sync. Jones and Lillie were similar in that they liked their work space to be just so. No one was allowed to touch Lillie's Ouija board and no one was permitted to touch her life, except for Jones. Lillie believed that the more people who touched her board, the more room for error. The same could be said for her life. The more who got involved, the more room for mistakes.

Born in Chicago in 1981, Lillie moved several times in her childhood, to South Carolina, back to Chicago, to Arkansas, and then Iowa. As a child, she liked to climb trees, race the boys barefoot down the street, play in the woods, and jump out of the barn behind her house. She had a tendency to get into fights with boys. When her brother, a non-fighter, mouthed off to others, Lillie would step in. Sometimes those fights in elementary school led to a paddling.

One day she got in a fight, and the principal said he was going to paddle Lillie but he didn't do it right away. So every day for a week she wore three pairs of pants to school for extra padding. After a week, Lillie figured the principal had forgotten about her punishment so she wore shorts to school. It seemed her bus was always the last to arrive at the end of the day. This day was no exception. While she was waiting, the principal came outside and gave her barely covered bottom a paddling.

During the third grade, a teacher's reading of *Charlie and the Chocolate Factory* made a bibliophile out of Lillie. She always had a trunk full of books, and to this day, she takes books with her on deployments and reads during her spare time. She's been singing since she was old enough to talk. She sang in church, at home, in talent shows, and in choir competitions. She also played basketball, wrestled, and ran track.

Her parents split up when she was seven. Although she loves him, Lillie rarely saw her father, who worked in construction, drove a truck, and spent some time in prison for selling drugs. She doesn't remember her mom working but does recall her being on welfare, and this memory has had a profound affect on Lillie.

What Lillie knows about welfare she learned firsthand. Her friends called her "little rich girl" because she was living in a big white house that her grandfather had built in Arkansas. But nothing could have been further from the truth. It wasn't long before Lillie moved into Section Eight housing and had to start using food stamps—fake money—to buy groceries. When the other kids in the neighborhood learned that she was on food stamps, they began teasing her. It was painfully embarrassing.

Lillie had twin brothers. One twin died at a young age from a wound sustained in an incident with a BB gun. The trauma from that event caused Lillie's mom to have a nervous breakdown and enter a treatment center. When Mom returned home, friends offered their assistance, including an elder from Lillie's church. The elder and his wife would take care of her mom and cook for her family. He took them to the Laundromat and taught Lillie new songs to sing. In addition to the elder's kindness, Lillie also remembers his clothing. He was in the Army and always wore his decorated military uniform with medals.

"After that I had this thing about wanting to go into the Army," Lillie said. The way he carried himself and wore that sharp uniform, even in church, made a big impression on the then six-year-old. Lillie planned to go into the Army after high school but was allergic to wasps. That made her ineligible to enter the Army but still eligible for the Navy.

Not everyone starts out eager to work on the flight deck of an aircraft carrier. Lillie hated it at first. She was fascinated by it, but she hadn't envisioned herself as an aviation boatswain, someone who worked on the flight deck all the time. She wasn't looking forward to working in an environment where one small lapse in judgment, such as turning in the wrong direction, could kill her.

She was so terrified of the flight deck that the first time she chocked an aircraft during flight operations, she started crying. Chocks are orange rubber blocks that the crew puts behind each parked aircraft's wheels to keep the jets in place. To chock a jet or helicopter, she had to run out onto the flight deck, oftentimes when an aircraft's rotors were still spinning, and wedge the chocks behind the wheels. Lillie's more experienced co-workers, sensing her fear, would shout directions and urge her on, "Come on, Lillie. We have to chock a bird." She didn't want to.

"Stay low," they shouted. "You have to stay low. Come out the same way you go in. Get lower to the ground. Get lower to the ground."

All sorts of information from training went through her head, and her co-workers kept cramming in more. Lillie was particularly afraid of the E2 Hawkeye because it has two props, one on either side. She had been told about a female sailor who almost got chopped up by the props, which are visible in the daytime, but at night you can't see them spinning. That's one of the reasons why it's important for the sailors to go to and from the aircraft the same way.

The crew on a carrier refers to the aircraft as "birds." Early in the first deployment, Lillie earned the nickname "Little Bird" because she was so small and because at times it appeared she would just fly away. There doesn't have to be much wind on the flight deck to make chocking an aircraft a challenge for a light-weight sailor like Lillie. Just the draft caused by a helicopter's rotors was enough to knock Lillie off her feet. On at least one occasion the wind, and the draft from an aircraft's propellers, nearly carried the "Little Bird" out to sea.

It happened while she was chocking and chaining, a job that preceded her elevators and Ouija board responsibilities. Chains are used to "tie down" the aircraft. During good weather, two chocks and six chains are used for each aircraft. Prior to entering heavy rains or seas, aircraft are tied down with twelve to twenty-four chains.

With the wind gusting at 35 to 40 knots, and the props of a Hawkeye jet spinning, Lillie prepared to sprint twenty feet from the island to the parked aircraft. All she had to do was put one block behind one wheel while someone else did the same to the other wheel.

Normally, because of her light weight, Lillie held onto something or someone or someone held onto her blue jersey to prevent her from blowing away. She was like one of those storm jockeys on the Weather Channel who stands in the middle of howling hurricane winds while yelling into a microphone. She had to plant her feet to maintain her balance.

At this specific moment, however, she didn't have anything to hold onto so she ran to the aircraft as fast as she could

"Chock it! Chock it!" yelled Aviation Boatswain Handler Two Andre Tolbert.

But she couldn't. The wind picked her up and tossed Lillie against the side of the island. She landed on a pile of chocks. After realizing what had happened, Lillie slowly rose and shook off surprise and confusion. Her gaze shifted from herself to the flight deck control room, where her boss, Commander Jones, and others on the crew were peering out a window.

"Are you okay?" they asked, all the while laughing.

"No!" she answered. Lillie had bruised her ribs. She was ordered off the flight deck, but not until after she'd completed her task. She never would figure out exactly how she managed to run back to the Hawkeye, duck behind its spinning prop, and chock it. There would be other close calls and near-death experiences as Lillie's role on the ship changed and she spent less time in the flight control room and more time on the flight deck.

On her second deployment, Lillie went to the Persian Gulf on the *Truman*. To fulfill their mission, the aircraft on the carrier flew fifteen days straight, followed by a no fly day, and then repeated the cycle. This time Lillie had a different job. She was a tractor king, or TK, part of the crew that handled aircraft and directed the planes. She was in charge of the tractors on the flight deck, making sure they had fuel and oil and were operational, and that there were enough drivers to tow the aircraft into position. She wore a yellow jersey with her name on it and the letters TK. Her office: the flight deck.

Before Lillie became a tractor king, she had to learn how to drive the tractors and tow the various aircraft. While the flight deck may appear spacious, with an area of four and a half acres, the amount of available space decreases rapidly when fifty aircraft are parked on it, when aircraft are coming and going, when hundreds of crew members are scattered on the deck, and when other tractors are moving about. The drivers are restricted to when and where they can drive. They work within a limited amount of space using the smallest of angles. They always have to be aware of verbal cues and hand signals from other crew members. They have to know when and how much gas to give the tractor to move it over obstacles such as wires. If Lillie is towing an aircraft and she can't control the tow bar, she can't control the bird. The nose of the tow bar tells her where the bird is heading.

Complicating the driving situation was the horrible weather conditions the carrier encountered. The ship ran into a lot of bad weather at the start of the deployment and up to Switzerland, in the North Atlantic. Sometimes they shut down flight operations during severe weather, but never when Marines and soldiers were in danger and depending on them.

It was cold on the flight deck and the seas were rough. If you weren't protected with gloves and thermal gear, the already hazardous flight deck became even more dangerous. Foul weather slowed everything down. Rough seas could cause a four-degree pitch and roll of the flight deck, making a 60,000-pound aircraft slide. If you were driving a 12,000-pound tractor and towing an aircraft four times the tractor's weight, and the ship took a four-degree pitch and rolled from port to starboard, it could create a tremendous slide, injuring crew and damaging aircraft.

Moving an aircraft onto an elevator with a four-degree pitch was nearly impossible. Add to the four-degree pitch grease from the arresting cables and hydraulic fluid leaking from old jets and the flight deck becomes twice as slippery and dangerous. If the drivers tried to move a bird, the vehicle and aircraft would slide all over the flight deck. They'd have to wait until the weather improved.

One of the most dangerous things that can happen when towing an aircraft is for the bird to jack-knife. Jack-knifing occurs when the tractor is moving forward, and the aircraft slides sideways, its tail whipping toward the tractor. Lillie had been a tractor driver for only about two weeks when she was towing an F-18 to its parking space on the flight deck. It had just stopped raining, so the deck was slick from water and oil, hydraulic fuel and whatever else was leaking from the aircraft, tractors, and other equipment. And the ship was turning. When the aircraft started to jack-knife, and move in the opposite direction of the tractor, the driver is supposed to press on the gas and turn in the opposite direction of the aircraft. Lillie slammed on the brakes and turned into the aircraft. The tractor and jet spun and slid out of control. *Oh my God. What's going on?* She'd seen other people jack-knife an aircraft but when she was going through it she had no idea what was happening or what to do. The flight deck crew yelled and flashed their wands at the captain to get him to press the brake on the aircraft. He missed the signals, presumably because he was sleeping. The plane captain was supposed to watch every move because if the jet jack-knifes, it was his job to put on the brakes.

Equally frightening was the time Lillie towed a jet and the nose of the aircraft hit her in the head and nearly knocked her off the tractor. She was pulling an F-18 at the top of the bow while the flight deck crew was preparing to recover an F-18. She had to move the aircraft quickly. Again, the crew signaled her to hurry up. She pressed on the gas. Then she was directed to stop so she pressed on the brake. The aircraft jack-knifed, and the nose whipped around and smacked her on the head. If she hadn't been wearing her cranial, she probably would have been knocked unconscious.

As Lillie learned more about what it meant to be an aviation boatswain, the challenges she faced also increased. More responsibility meant greater likelihood of being put in a position where she could be seriously injured, and the equipment damaged.

On a typical day, Lillie knew that the H-60 Seahawk helicopter would launch first because it was used to rescue aircraft that fell short on a launch. Next, the early warning aircraft, E2 Hawkeye, took off, followed by Vikings with gas tanks that provide fuel for the aircraft and F-14 Tomcats with longer fuel range.

Lillie isn't certain, but she thinks this next incident occurred during the second event, sometime between ten o'clock in the morning and noon. She had just towed a Hawkeye, an $80 million aircraft that is nearly fifty-eight feet long and has a wingspan of more than eighty feet, from the aft flight deck to the bow of the ship. The Hawkeye was getting ready to launch on catapult two.

Since aircraft carriers have such short flight lines, aircraft are catapulted off the ship and "trapped" when they land, bringing them to a violent stop before they run out of deck. For landing purposes, the tailhook of a jet catches one of four arresting cables and that cable drags the aircraft to a screeching halt. During the second deployment, the crew trapped 2,126 aircraft as they landed on the flight deck. The total traps (recoveries) for the entire deployment was 7,890 during 102 days of flying. The catapult landing is a controlled crash that even the most experienced pilots never get used to, especially when it takes place at night. The aircraft carriers don't like to broadcast who they are and where they are located so they operate with minimum lights. If the pilot doesn't catch that wire, she has to throttle up like she's getting ready to take off. If she doesn't throttle up, she's going off the bow and into the water.

There are four catapults on the flight deck that act like slingshots, shooting aircraft into the air. Each catapult has two rows of slotted cylindrical piping in a trough beneath the flight deck. A bar on the nose gear of the aircraft attaches to a shuttle that protrudes above the deck and is connected to a pair of pistons in the trough. A holdback device is installed on the nose gear to hold the aircraft in place as tension is applied. On a signal from the catapult safety observer on the flight deck, the catapult is fired, which opens the launching valves assembly (the length of time the valves remain open is determined by the weight of the aircraft and the wind over the deck). Steam surges into the cylinders, releasing the holdback and forcing the pistons, shuttle and aircraft forward at an increasing speed.

A 60,000-pound aircraft is accelerated up to 150 miles per hour in two seconds and a distance of 309 feet. The shuttle is stopped when spears on the pistons plunge into water brake cylinders. A cable-and-pulley assembly then pulls the shuttle back down the catapult for the next launch. The sequence of linking an aircraft to the catapult and launching the aircraft takes less than two minutes. From its four catapults, the *Truman* can launch an aircraft every twenty seconds.

Once Lillie arrived at catapult two, a crew tied the Hawkeye down with chains and disconnected Lillie's tow bar from the aircraft. As this was happening, an F-18 jet was preparing to launch nearby. The director and hook runner performed a sweep of the flight deck, looking forward and aft to ensure the flight deck was clear of people and debris. When the deck appeared clear, they gave the signal to put the Hawkeye on tension. The bird was just seconds from launching.

After the signal was given to put the jet on tension, the shooter confirmed that everything was operational and that no one was crossing the foul or shot lines. These lines look like lines you would see on a football field. They are meant to keep the crew safe and out of the way of moving aircraft. The thumbs-up was given to indicate that the flight deck was clear, and the director was getting ready to give the signal to push the button to launch the catapult. As he prepared to give the signal, the crew watched the shot lines to make sure no one crossed them.

Right before the director, Petty Officer 3rd Class Travis Wertz, gave the signal to press the button, Petty Officer 1st Class Malcolm

Worthington saw that Lillie had inadvertently taken a left turn in the direction of catapult two, where the aircraft was on tension.

"Get out of the way!" Worthington shouted. "Get out of the way!"

Lillie looked up and for the first time, saw the jet ready to take off.

Oh my God! He's going to hit me.

She slammed on the brakes.

By now others on the flight deck were signaling Lillie to get out of the way.

With the aircraft on full tension, the pilot was given a signal to suspend the launch. The flight deck crew would have to reset and reconfigure the launch, clear the deck, and repeat the thirty-second launch sequence.

Lillie felt sick to her stomach and wanted to cry. She thought she was going to throw up. She realized she could have died. If the jet had hit her, it could have dragged her and the tractor overboard. Falling into water from a hundred feet up is like landing on concrete, and if that didn't kill her then the ship would have plowed right over her, crushing her, drowning her, maybe chopping her to bits in its giant propellers. Or the leading edge of the aircraft's wing could have sliced her head clean off. Her second thought was that she was going to get into big trouble.

Lillie kept telling herself, Get it together. Get it together. She was shaking so badly she had difficulty parking the tractor. Even though she was scared, she didn't let it control her. She parked the aircraft and retreated to the yellow jersey locker to regroup. She got a drink of water, sat down, and put her head in her lap. She didn't have time to get angry at herself because other yellow shirts were coming and going, and teasing her. As soon as she crossed the shot line, the crew started talking on the radios. Those who saw what happened said, "Lillie just went in the LA (landing area)." Those who missed the action asked, "Who did that?" or "Why did we suspend?"

As Lillie caught her breath and tried to regain her composure, the aircraft handler in the flight deck control room, her former office next door, called her on her radio. He hadn't seen what happened because he had just come on duty. Jones was no longer the handler. He had been replaced on this deployment by Lieutenant Commander George Sharp. Lillie was in big trouble and she knew it—she had almost caused a catastrophe. Never mind her own danger—she could have killed a valuable aviator and sent a heavily armed, fully-fueled, multi-million dollar aircraft careening around the deck out of control. Many things might have happened—all of them bad.

The conversation between the handler and Lillie went something like this:

"What dumb ass went over the shot line like that?"

"It was me, sir."

"I thought it was someone who didn't know how to drive and you are the TK. What were you thinking, TK?"

"I wasn't really thinking. That was the problem."

Clearly, there is so much happening in such a small area on a flight deck that near-death experiences, while they may not be the norm, are not unusual, either. After Lillie described the previous incident to me I asked a couple of her supervisors about the frequency of such mishaps. One said they were common while another said they rarely happen. I guess you'd have to go on a deployment to know for sure.

Looking back on that day, Lillie doesn't know why she made that mistake. She recalled that she was getting impatient because the person directing her was taking a long time and she just wanted to get unhooked from the E2. *Oh my God. Come on. Unhook me.* It had taken about fifteen minutes to get the E2 parked just right, and she was eager to get off the tractor but couldn't until he unhooked her. As soon as he gave her the signal to unhook and pull forward, Lillie shot out of there, right in front of an F-18 getting ready to launch. After a little more thought, Lillie admitted, "I was impatient. I was probably hungry." Not exactly worth dying for—the chow on an aircraft carrier.

It wasn't a very good time for John Dobey, either. As a lead petty officer, he oversaw a flight deck crew of 150, including Lillie. His primary job was to ensure all the aircraft launched on time. "Any time an aircraft doesn't make its launch on time, it's frustrating to me," he said. "It kind of makes me angry."

He wanted to know who had suspended his launch and why. When he found out it was Lillie, he was disappointed because she knew better. "Time after time after time we preach safety and paying attention to your location on the deck. We talk about it all the time in our yellow shirt briefs."

It's important that the flight deck crew have a healthy fear of the flight deck. He always said, "It's best to be scared, because when you're scared you're looking around all the time and aware of your surroundings. Sometimes we take our safety for granted because we're up on the flight deck 24/7. There's so much repetition. But if you get complacent, someone can get killed. You may not realize where you are, that an aircraft is turning and can blow you over the side of the ship. Sometimes you get hurt when you don't pay attention to what's going on."

To reconfigure the jet, the aircraft stays on the catapult while the flight deck crew takes it off and then puts it back on tension. It involves nearly every one on the flight deck, from yellow shirts to the hook runner, the shooter, the coordinators, plane captains, and final checkers. If the aircraft had bombs on it, the aviation ordnance people made sure the bombs were still secure on the plane. It didn't take long for them to reconfigure the launch, only about a minute, but there were a lot of people and steps involved in those sixty seconds.

Despite the near casualties, Lillie does feel as though she's qualified to work on the flight deck. If she didn't feel that way, she wouldn't have taken a test to move up a rank to third-class petty officer. That's not to say she hasn't questioned whether she wants to continue working in that environment. She has tested other jobs below the deck, such as working in the chiefs' mess hall and in security, jobs that aren't as dangerous and don't require her to be exposed to the weather. But when she wasn't on the flight deck, she missed the action. "You get used to it after a while and miss being up there and a part of it," she said. And although she worked longer hours as tractor king and elevator operator than in her other positions, time flew on the flight deck. She'd look at her watch and it would be four o'clock in the afternoon already.

While she knows she is able to work on the flight deck, after close encounters on the catwalk and with a jet on tension, Lillie can't help but wonder if she is cut out to work in surroundings that do not suffer fools—or even errors. One mistake can kill you. Lillie knows she has the discipline. But she's used up a couple of her lives already. How far can she push her luck? "I think I'm a cat," she said. "I think I have nine lives."

Lance Corporal Chrissy DeCaprio, United States Marine Corps.

Little Dee with a Big Gun

*Everyone said **Marine Lance Corporal Chrissy DeCaprio** had a death wish because she had no problem walking up to a potential IED. She was fearless.*

THE FIRST TIME AN IRAQI INSURGENT SHOT AT LANCE CORPORAL Chrissy (Dee) DeCaprio, she was standing in the turret of a scout vehicle. Beside her was a .50-caliber, automatic, belt-fed, recoil-served, air-cooled, crew-operated machine gun. It was a gun that DeCaprio not only knew how to shoot but loved to shoot. It didn't matter that at sixty-one and a half inches, the .50-cal was as long as DeCaprio was tall. Or that with its tripod, the 128-pound gun far outweighed DeCaprio. The saying that the smallest person gets the biggest gun held true.

The petite, brown-eyed, twenty-one-year-old Italian from Brooklyn, New York, with long hair tucked under her Kevlar helmet stood perched in the second of two MP vehicles leading a convoy of fifty seven-ton trucks from Camp TQ to Ramadi. DeCaprio wore a flak jacket, and goggles similar to those worn by swimmers. She chose not to don her night-vision goggles (NVGs) on a regular basis because when she mounted the NVGs on her

Kevlar, they impaired her vision. Occasionally, she pulled them out to scan the black landscape.

As she looked into the darkness of the night, DeCaprio could barely see the first scout vehicle fifty meters ahead of her, and the convoy that she was leading stayed two kilometers behind her. That distance allowed the scout vehicles to stop and start without disrupting the flow of the convoy. It also made DeCaprio and other gunners feel like they were out in the desert night alone because they traveled without lights in certain places (hot zones) and could rarely see the vehicles ahead or behind them. If they didn't encounter problems along the way, the drive would take an hour and a half each way. Unfortunately, they were never that lucky. Something always happened. They made it to the outskirts of Ramadi on a road named Mobile when the firefight started.

DeCaprio, a gunner with 2nd Military Police Battalion, wasn't looking for a firefight that night. Rather, she had shown her spotlight on the ground to find the greatest threat to the convoys, improvised explosive devices (IEDs). All of a sudden she thought she saw tracers—bullets that light up in the dark—fly by her head. But she couldn't ask anyone to confirm she was taking fire because all the other MPs rode inside the vehicle. She ignored the tracers and turned her attention back to finding IEDs. Then another round shot by her. *Oh no.*

Insurgents on the side of the road with AK-47s were targeting DeCaprio's vehicle. Startled but not scared, this female MP was excited to finally fire her .50-cal in combat. There seemed to be a break between each tracer, giving DeCaprio what she thought was plenty of time to duck behind a shield that wrapped around half the turret and to get the .50-cal ready. But then the gunner remembered from her training that between each tracer round, five more bullets were being shot at her. She just couldn't see them. They weren't lit up.

Even though she couldn't see her attackers, DeCaprio knew where the small arms fire was coming from. She turned her gun to face the left and then readied her .50-cal in record time. The gunners carried bullets with the gun but they didn't keep the ammo in the chamber for safety reasons. As soon as she racked—loaded, that is—the .50-cal, she returned fire.

The Humvee was traveling 60 miles-per-hour. With the wind, the noise from the vehicle, and the radio that MPs used for communication, the Marines inside had no way of knowing they were under attack until DeCaprio started firing back. None of the gunners wore headsets to communicate with the Marines in their vehicle. Doing so would have prevented them from hearing the sounds in their environment, and gunners needed to hear and see everything. They're the protectors, the defenders of the vehicle. If something or someone got past them, the convoy could be doomed. The team leader inside the vehicle handled communication. As soon as DeCaprio started firing back with the .50-cal, the Marines in the vehicle knew they were in a firefight. DeCaprio heard them yell up to her, "Hey, what the hell are you doing?" They started pulling on her legs. She didn't have time to respond. Bullets continued to zing past her head.

When the insurgents realized DeCaprio was willing and eager to shoot back without hesitation, enemy fire subsided. During a break in the firefight, DeCaprio looked down at her Marines.

"What?" she yelled.

"What are you doing?" the Marines shouted back.

"We're getting shot at," DeCaprio said.

The convoy behind DeCaprio heard the firefight and radioed her vehicle to find out if it should stop. Her team didn't know how to advise them because it was dark, and DeCaprio couldn't see the enemy. She didn't know if she was firing at five Iraqis or fifteen. She didn't know where they were or how many she had hit. All she knew was that she was shooting at a hostile target.

From the turret, DeCaprio set up security on the side of the road while the convoy continued on its mission. As the vehicles passed by, there were a couple more bursts of fire from the enemy. DeCaprio kept up the heavy fire until they stopped. After about half the convoy passed by, the number of tracer fires decreased even more. The main part of the firefight lasted about ten minutes.

When the convoy finally reached Ramadi, DeCaprio had a hard time containing her excitement. Her adrenaline was flowing. After all, it was her first firefight and she was pretty much out there on her own.

"Did you see that? Did you see that?" she asked the other Marines from her vehicle.

She was trying to get some kind of reaction out of the artillery Marines, but they didn't share her enthusiasm because they weren't involved in the fight. The MPs and Marines on the convoy liked to sleep while they waited for the trucks to deliver their supplies in Ramadi but not DeCaprio. Not this time. She was too pumped up to fall asleep.

As a kid growing up in Brooklyn, DeCaprio was shy. In high school, she was average. But somehow she knew that if she joined the Marine Corps, she could stand out, excel. Being a gunner was a position DeCaprio fought for. She considers it one of the most important roles of an MP because she is responsible for the safety of all the Marines in her vehicle. When the Humvee is moving and a firefight breaks out, it's up to her to keep the Marines in her vehicle alive. Plus, she thinks she's one of the best there is.

Some female Marines had to prove themselves to the male Marines. They had to show they could pull their own weight and wouldn't be a burden to others. DeCaprio was one of those women. First she had to prove herself in training and then at Camp TQ in Iraq. She learned how to shoot the .50-cal at Twentynine Palms in Southern California. DeCaprio shot after the male Marines. When it came her time to shoot, the guys told her it wasn't necessary. But it was to her. She got the feeling they didn't think she'd be able to fire the big gun so they were giving her a free pass. She wouldn't take it. She already knew how to operate it based on her basic military studies. However, she didn't know how hard it would be to rack the gun and how big of a kick it would have. The first time she tried to rack it she didn't pull it back hard enough. The next time she got herself set and threw all of her weight—105 pounds—into it. That time she was able to rack it all the way and fire. The kick was bad, but she was expecting the worst so she wasn't caught off guard.

When DeCaprio first arrived at Camp TQ, a company of field artillery reservists were assigned to Bravo Company because it was short of MPs. DeCaprio, who wasn't assigned to any particular unit, also joined up with Bravo Company. She started as a gunner and later was promoted to team leader. The artillery Marines weren't used to working with women because their military occupational specialty is closed to females. DeCaprio and the artillery men would have to adjust to one another. After working with Marines who were used to working with women, DeCaprio would now have to make an extra effort to earn the reservists' respect. She let them know early on that she expected the Marines in artillery to treat her as a Marine and not their "girl from the block."

One male gunner who was already at Camp TQ when DeCaprio arrived thought he was the best shot on the .50-cal. He may have been—until DeCaprio appeared on the scene and showed him up. The MPs test fired their guns on the range every day. The .50-cals were finicky weapons. They jammed a lot. If the weapon could shoot ten straight rounds without jamming it was doing well. DeCaprio's gun shot smoothly while her challenger's gun jammed. Maybe some of her success came from the loving care she gave her .50-cal. DeCaprio believed in babying her weapon, although she never gave it a name. Marines in her vehicle teased her about her "little friend" in the turret. When she tried to talk over the noise to the Marines in her vehicle, they would jokingly ask her if she was talking to her little friend.

DeCaprio primarily fired the .50-cal during firefights and when Iraqi vehicles got too close to her vehicle. The Marines had prescribed procedures for engaging the enemy. When they saw an Iraqi driving toward their convoy, the Marines would flash their lights. A lot of times the Iraqis liked to see how far they could push the coalition forces. DeCaprio wouldn't let them push her too far because the closer they got to her convoy, the closer she was to jeopardizing the lives of her Marines. She wasn't about to risk everything for a game of Chicken.

During the daytime, the Marines patrolled the cities to establish a military presence. If they pulled over or stopped an Iraqi vehicle that had female passengers, DeCaprio would pat them down. The female MP wasn't needed as much in the evening because she didn't go on house searches and Iraqi women rarely went out at night. But during the day, no matter where she was in the convoy, if the Marines stopped some pedestrians or a vehicle with an Iraqi female, they called for DeCaprio.

"Where's Dee? We need Dee!"

One time DeCaprio had to search an old Iraqi lady. While she patted her down, she detected something out of the ordinary tucked into a shirt beneath her robe. DeCaprio needed to find out what it was. For all she knew, it could have been a weapon or an explosive. When she searched the grandmother a second time, the old lady grabbed DeCaprio's arms. *Oh, I'm going to die.* The MP tried to retrieve the object, but the grandmother wouldn't let her. Through an interpreter, DeCaprio ordered the old lady to put her arms out to the side but she wouldn't listen. Instead, the grand-mother seized DeCaprio's arm. The MP responded by grabbing the old lady and laying her out on the ground. It turned out that the grandmother had a Quran hidden in her shirt. Since then, the Marines have teased DeCaprio for taking down an old lady.

One night DeCaprio's scout vehicle and four other Humvees were patrolling the streets just outside Camp TQ when they ran into trouble. The Marines patrolled the streets in the evenings because that was when insurgents usually rigged and planted IEDs. They hoped their presence would deter the Iraqis from setting up more explosives. During the daytime, the high volume of traffic on the roads prevented the insurgents from going unnoticed.

Two vehicles, DeCaprio's and another, pushed two kilometers ahead of the convoy and then came to a security halt when the lead vehicle reported seeing something suspicious. After further inspection, they determined it wasn't an IED. But to be on the safe side, they set up a perimeter around the vehicles and searched the area. The MPs stayed close to their Humvees because that's where their heavy fire was. If they walked off into the desert, the most they would have was a squad automatic weapon (SAW), or light-weight machine gun. DeCaprio would rather have a .50-cal anyday.

Everybody was talking to one another. DeCaprio danced to the song "BYOB" by System of a Down. Even though she supported the war, she sang this anti-war song. DeCaprio liked to sing the refrain:

"Everybody's going to the party have a real good time.

Dancing in the desert blowing up the sunshine."

DeCaprio kept looking around her because they were in an area identified as having a lot of IEDs. They called these areas "hot spots." Everybody was talking until they heard rounds clicking against DeCaprio's vehicle.

Did someone just shoot at us?

Then they heard another round. DeCaprio didn't have to wonder anymore.

Once everyone realized they were taking fire, they stopped what they were doing, grabbed their NVGs and binoculars (binos), and looked in the direction of the firing.

"I see a car over there," someone yelled.

Everyone started shooting in that direction. The car wasn't driving on the road and it wasn't driving in the perimeter of DeCaprio's convoy, so according to their rules of engagement they couldn't chase it.

The Iraqi never shot back, but the MPs did disable his vehicle.

A few months into her ten-month deployment, DeCaprio was pulled from running convoys to do something that no male Marine or soldier was authorized to do. She was put in charge of guarding a highly valued detainee (HVD)—an Iraqi female—for a month. (The troops did not refer to the detainees as "prisoners" because technically, the United States was not a war. They could be called prisoners only if the U.S. was at war.)

DeCaprio was flown to Al Asad Air Base and then driven to an old hangar that had been converted into a detention facility. In the month ahead, she wasn't privy to any information about the Iraqi woman—her name, why she was there, or when she would be released. She didn't even know why she was considered an HVD, unless all Iraqi women were highly valued detainees.

The first time DeCaprio saw her detainee she was sitting on a bed in her cell. She looked to be about DeCaprio's height, five feet one inches tall, but much heavier. She wore a black robe with sweatpants underneath. Her feet were bare. She appeared to be in her twenties. A quick scan of the cell and the MP saw all there was to see—a small prayer rug, a Quran, and a standard bed and blanket.

Right away DeCaprio got a good feeling about this woman. She looked subdued, like she was "chilling out." *This is going to be easy.* It didn't take long for her to realize just how wrong she was. Over the next month, the prisoner took out her mental anguish on herself and her guard. She controlled every hour, sometimes every half hour, of DeCaprio's days and nights in the detention center. It got to the point where DeCaprio wondered who was incarcerated—her or the detainee.

The detainee was being held until other arrangements could be made for her. Once the Iraqi woman signed papers authorizing her release to a psychiatric hospital, her situation deteriorated to the point where DeCaprio couldn't leave the prisoner even for a minute. She knew she was leaving and didn't want to go. But she didn't want to stay, either. On the days leading up to the prisoner's departure, DeCaprio often found the Iraqi woman banging her head against a wall.

DeCaprio learned how to shoot a .50-cal to protect her and the Marines she traveled with from small-arms fire. But in this war even more important than her training on the .50-cal was the education she received for spotting IEDs. The IEDs have killed and maimed thousands of Marines and soldiers. DeCaprio's convoys dealt with IEDs at least two or three times a week. She and the other MPs usually suppressed the devices before they exploded, but as the Marines got wise to one type of IED, the insurgents would concoct a new and improved variety.

The IEDs came in all shapes and sizes, and in different quantities—ones, twos, stacks, and daisy chains. Oftentimes they were stacked on top of one another to generate a larger explosion, like the ones that wounded Rachelle Spors (the medic) and killed her passenger. A daisy chain was made up of multiple IEDs that were set up about five meters from one another and rigged so that when one went off, it would set off a series of explosions and take out multiple vehicles in a convoy.

First there was the radio-controlled IED. This was limiting because the Iraqis had to stay nearby to detonate them, which increased the user's risk of being discovered. Those IEDs became less effective as Marines and soldiers started to look for and find antennas sticking out of the ground. Then there were the jerry-rigged pressure switches. Those were mostly made by taking a piece of metal, folding it in half, running wires on the inside of the metal, and burying it a little bit so the shiny metal wouldn't give it away. The metal connected to the wires which connected to the explosive. When someone walked or rode over the metal, the two wires connected and sent a charge to the bomb. The pressure point was usually ten to fifteen feet away.

Back in the States, before she deployed, DeCaprio participated in simulations with convoys and fake IEDs to learn about the different explosives and what could go wrong. When she arrived in Iraq, DeCaprio learned where the Iraqis liked to plant the IEDs from the MPs her unit relieved.

Spotting IEDs at night, when the convoy was traveling 60 miles per hour, wasn't as difficult as it might sound. DeCaprio drove the same roads nearly every evening. They always started at TQ and traveled to Ramadi, Fallujah, Al Asad, or Camp KV. She had grown accustomed to spotting strange objects on or beside the road. If there was something different in the road, it could mean only one thing—danger. The leading impediment to a gunner's judgment was the large amount of trash that littered the sides of the road and concealed the IEDs.

During her deployment in Iraq, DeCaprio and the other gunners competed to see who could find the most IEDs. DeCaprio became good at spotting them. Her battalion found eight. She found two and had one assist. She admits to having an advantage because she always drove in the front of the convoy, in the first or second scout vehicle. She was also at a disadvantage because the vehicles in the front were more likely to trigger an undetected IED and become the victim of an explosion. If the rear security found a lot of IEDs that was a problem because it meant three gunners and a whole convoy missed the explosives. Fortunately, that never happened. Riding in the front of convoys, the MPs definitely had their share of casualties. However, DeCaprio thought the Marines in 2d Military Police Battalion had been trained well. They saved a lot of lives. She didn't know of any other battalion that had done what they did and had so few wounded or killed.

On this night, DeCaprio was leading a convoy of fifty vehicles on a four-hour trip to Fallujah. She was standing in the turret of the second scout vehicle. There was another convoy ahead of hers but she didn't know anything about it except that they were escorting third country national (TCN) truck drivers. She had nothing to do with that convoy. She just happened to be driving behind them while leading another convoy.

About a half hour into their drive, the road forked. The convoy in front of her split—the lead vehicles turned where they were supposed to, some trucks from the middle went straight. DeCaprio didn't think this was odd because it wasn't uncommon for drivers to fall asleep at the wheel late at night and veer off the road. At the very least, it was an inconvenience.

DeCaprio's convoy had to stop while the vehicles that had taken the correct route backtracked to find the rest of their convoy. This was taking a long time, too long, so DeCaprio and the lead scout vehicle drove around the convoy and down the road a couple of kilometers. Normally the two scout vehicles kept fifty meters between them, but this time they were a lot closer. From their turrets, DeCaprio and the gunner from the other vehicle searched the ground closely because IEDs had already destroyed a lot of vehicles in this area. As they drove along, DeCaprio caught a glimpse of a divot in the dirt road. But before she could alert anyone, the forward vehicle had driven over it.

DeCaprio's eyes moved from the divot to the first vehicle only to see a cloud of black smoke engulf the two Humvees. When the IED exploded beneath the first truck, the .50-cal shield that protects the gunner was behind DeCaprio, leaving her exposed to fragments flying off the vehicle in front of her. Parts from the truck smacked her in the face. A piece of the truck hit her goggles and broke one side of her protective wear. DeCaprio's rifle was thrown from the turret and hit her in the chest. Oil shot out of the first Humvee and sprayed DeCaprio in the face. She spit black liquid from her mouth.

At first DeCaprio didn't know whether her truck or the truck in front of her had been hit because she felt the explosion but couldn't see anything. A black fog of smoke still surrounded her. She could open her eyes as wide as she wanted but that didn't make it any easier to see. It was like opening her eyes in a pitch black room. She stuck her face down into the turret and shouted to her Marines, "Are you okay?" They couldn't hear her. Voices were muffled, as if her ears needed to pop.

"What's going on?" the Marines in her vehicle yelled. "Is anyone hurt?"

DeCaprio had no idea. Nor did she know if there were other IEDs on the road. She couldn't see and she couldn't get out of her vehicle to check the perimeter. Not yet. It might attract unwanted attention, and Marines don't like to draw attention to themselves. The hazard in checking the perimeter was that insurgents liked to plant secondary IEDs five to ten feet away from the primary IED. Oftentimes the primary IED was just big enough to cripple a truck and stop a convoy in its tracks. Once the convoy stopped, other vehicles and people rallied around the damaged truck to provide medical support and security, and to prepare the vehicle to be towed. The first Humvee was well protected by armor, but if Marines and soldiers were working on the ground, all they had for shields were their flak jackets. All this activity made an ideal location for a secondary IED explosion.

When the IED exploded, it was dusk. Then black smoke made it darker. After what seemed like ten minutes but was really only ten seconds, the veil of smoke lifted and it was nighttime. Nonetheless, DeCaprio could see her vehicle and was able to determine that it was the first truck and not hers that had blown up. The explosion had torn off the whole front end of the other vehicle. After checking the area for insurgents and not seeing any, DeCaprio's thoughts immediately turned to the Marines in the damaged vehicle. If she could be the first one to help a wounded Marine, then by God she was going to be the first one. When a Marine was down, DeCaprio's job instantly shifted from security to buddying until a corpsman relieved her. Besides, what's one less MP in a convoy of armed Marines?

DeCaprio climbed down from the truck and ran to the hit vehicle. First she checked the door on the passenger's side, where the team leader sat. The force of the explosion blew his door off the truck. The team leader was a lot taller and heavier than DeCaprio but she was still able to grab him by his flak jacket and pull him out. She moved fast for fear that the vehicle might catch fire. She was careful not to jerk him because she wasn't sure how badly he was hurt. As she began to drag him, he stood up, limped to DeCaprio's vehicle and sat down. Shrapnel had cut his leg in several places and his hand was bleeding. He said he was okay, so she left him and ran back to his truck to retrieve the others.

Since the gunner was on top of the truck, he was the farthest from the IED and nearly injury free. He crawled out of the turret himself. DeCaprio tried to open the door for a female translator who was sitting in the back of the truck. The door was stuck. She put her hand against the window to push it in. When she removed her hand, she left a clear streak surrounded by dust, dirt, and black soot. DeCaprio forced the door open and removed the translator. She was petite like DeCaprio, so she wasn't heavy, but she was disoriented—dazed and confused. She stumbled, fell to her knees, and tried to get up again. DeCaprio thought that maybe the explosion had affected her equilibrium.

Helicopters monitored the road DeCaprio was traveling because it was one of two roads referred to as IED alley. Pilots responded quickly. As soon as the helicopter landed, DeCaprio put the translator in the aircraft to be medevaced to a hospital at Camp TQ.

Wreckers towed the two damaged vehicles to Camp Fallujah. The vehicles were so fragile that they had to be strapped down so they wouldn't crumble and fall apart on the road. The MPs from the two damaged Humvees, including DeCaprio, were dispersed onto other vehicles. Now the convoy had no scout vehicles and the MPs' guns were inoperable. They had very limited firepower.

Some of the Marines in the convoy looked for the insurgents who set the IED. They knew the militants had to be nearby because the Marines in the helicopters said they saw people on motorcycles driving away. DeCaprio didn't see anyone and that just made her angrier.

The whole time DeCaprio was caring for the wounded and providing security, it never dawned on her that she might be hurt. It wasn't until she arrived in Fallujah and looked in the mirror that she realized she had absorbed some of the effects of the explosions. Reflected back at her was a tough young woman who looked like she had just been in a brawl. She had two black eyes and a puffy red face that had been burned by oil.

After this incident, DeCaprio came to the conclusion that the TCNs had not fallen asleep at the wheel. Instead, she believes the convoy split intentionally. Somehow, the TCN truck drivers knew something about the road that night the Marines didn't know.

A career in the military offers men and women the chance to excel in ways they would not have in the civilian community. Before she even enlisted, DeCaprio had a feeling she was going to have a bright future in the Marine Corps. And contrary to popular belief, size doesn't matter.

What DeCaprio lacks in size she makes up for in gumption. She doesn't need a .50-cal to be confident and courageous. She was that way before she ever became an MP. But the Marine Corps put those traits to the test and exposed her true grit. She passed the test and was eager to return to Iraq and do what she does best—protect her troops.

Captain Vernice "Junk" Armour, United States Marine Corps.

Who Wants to Be Average?

*The Cobra community eats its young—primarily to keep its community strong but also to maintain its reputation. Being a Cobra pilot like **Marine Captain Vernice Armour** requires a strong desire to succeed in an extremely competitive and dangerous environment.*

ON APRIL 3, 2003, A REGIMENTAL COMBAT TEAM WAS ADVANCING northwest along Highway 6 in central Iraq. Up ahead Iraqi armored vehicles and ammunition storage sites littered the road, and squads of Saddam's elite Republican Guard hid in ditches waiting to ambush the intruders. If everything went according to plan, four Cobra attack helicopters would seek out and destroy the enemy before it found the Marines on the ground.

Sitting inside the cockpit of the third Cobra was Marine Captain Vernice Armour, the first African-American female pilot in Marine Corps history and first black female combat pilot in the history of the Department of Defense. This twenty-nine-year-old from Memphis, Tennessee, knew that how she performed in battle would influence how future black women were received in military aviation and more specifically, in the dog-eat-dog Cobra community. Her strengths and weaknesses, accomplishments and disappointments would be watched closely.

On this, one of many night missions that Armour flew in Iraq, she and seven other pilots from Marine Light/Attack Helicopter Squadron 169 out of Camp Pendleton, California, got up while it was still dark at Ali Al Salem Airfield in Kuwait. Armour met the other pilots outside their tents at two o'clock to take a bus to the flight line by 2:30. At the airfield they checked the weather forecast, found out who was getting what aircraft, what was and wasn't working on the Cobras, and were briefed on their upcoming mission by the officer running the flight deck.

Before Armour and the other pilots walked out to their aircraft, they picked up their flight equipment. Armour got her body armor, survival vest, helmet, lumbar rest, night-vision goggles (NVGs), and extra batteries for the goggles. The pockets of the vest were handy for carrying extra water, a mirror, pen, smoke flares, radio, pistol, water dye marker, and survival maps. She carried more maps in her flight bag. As a member of HMLA-169, Armour was used to taking one map with her when she flew around Camp Pendleton and three when she flew to Yuma, about 150 nautical miles away. In Iraq, she had more than seventy-five maps and took most of them with her when she flew. They ranged from maps of the whole country to close ups of different areas of Iraq. Also in her flight bag were the kneeboard she strapped to her leg during the flight to make it easier to read the maps and a six-inch chemical stick that glowed in the dark.

By the time she was ready to walk out to her aircraft for a pre-flight inspection, Armour was loaded down. She held her helmet in one hand and had her flight bag over her shoulder. She lugged a rolled up Therm-a-Rest mattress. When she knew she was going to be gone three to five days, she used the bag for the Therm-a-Rest to carry extra socks, T-shirts, flip flops, M-16 rifle, gas mask, and sleeping bag. She also brought a videotape to record when the pilots engaged in combat.

The increased load didn't bother Armour, who is five feet seven inches tall and has the thick muscular frame of a football player or a weight lifter. Armour became interested in wellness and bodybuilding at a young age. Her older brother's enthusiasm for football and working out with weights rubbed off on her. When she was fourteen or fifteen and the same brother left for college, Armour moved his weights from the garage to her bedroom and made a weight bench. As a freshman in college, she began working out regularly in a gym. Her dedication to fitness paid off. In 2001 and 2002, Armour was named Strongest Warrior at Camp Pendleton. The contest included extraordinary feats such as pulling a jeep and flipping a five-ton truck's tire. Armour also won the base's Female Athlete of the Year Award in 2002, the same year she played running back for the San Diego Sunfire women's professional football team.

When the pilots arrived at their Cobras, the plane captains were waiting for them. The Cobra is a strong, sturdy aircraft. Just its blades span fifty feet. Fully loaded, the aircraft weighs 14,750 pounds. In contrast, a Kiowa scout helicopter weighs about 4,500 pounds. It's like comparing an Escalade with a Mini Cooper. The plane captains opened all the panels in the aircraft that were accessible, and double checked the hoses and fluids, the inside of the cockpit, fuel, guns, weapons systems, and lights. They made sure everything was in working order before the pilots got into their cockpits.

The cockpit in a Cobra has a front and back seat. The pilots choose where they will sit based on the type of mission they are flying and the level of control they want. A Cobra can be flown from either seat, but it's easier to control from the back because that's where the best instruments are located. But if the pilot of the aircraft is leading four Cobras and wants to have the best view of the battlefield, he will choose the front seat. The primary weapon system is controlled from the front, where Armour usually sat as the co-pilot. The aircraft typically carries Hellfire and TOW missiles, rockets, and 20mm guns and rounds. The front seater/gunner targets the laser for the Hellfire, a laser-guided air-to-ground missile used by helicopters to take out heavily armored vehicles. However, the Hellfires and rockets are controlled from the back. Either pilot can shoot the 20mm guns. The TOW missile (tube-launched, optically tracked, wire command-link) is one of the primary anti-tank weapons used by the Marine Corps. It is guided to its target by the front seater who keeps the crosshairs on the target. During the first Gulf War, Cobras destroyed ninety-seven tanks, one hundred and four armored personnel carriers and vehicles, sixteen bunkers and two anti-aircraft artillery sites without the loss of any aircraft.

Before getting into the helicopter, the pilots and co-pilots set up their cockpits. They refer to the setup as "cockpit management." Pilots have to be efficient with their use of the cockpit so they can access what they need when they need it. They can't spend twenty minutes looking for a map. Armour had the same routine every time she went out. She put a lumbar cushion on her seat. The cushion had been handed down to her from another flight school graduate. It helped reduce back pain, scooted her closer to the cyclic stick (used for turning the aircraft left and right), and allowed her to comfortably rest her arm on her thigh. She put her gas mask and NVGs behind her left shoulder and stored her emergency procedures book behind her left elbow. She removed a cushion from where her left arm would rest and replaced it with maps. Armour placed her NVG mount on top of the dash. She stuck extra batteries in the cracks of the padding beside her on the right. On the inside of her body armor behind her right elbow was an inverted M-4 (a smaller version of the M-16 rifle). A Camelback water container hung over her vest.

Armour flew with Major James Ruvalcaba most of the time in Iraq. The thirty-nine-year-old veteran pilot usually chose the back seat because it gave him control of the aircraft and allowed him to put the Cobra exactly where he wanted it at all times. At five feet ten inches tall and 168 pounds, Ruvalcaba looked a lot like he did when he wrestled for the University of Southern California. He was pushing forty and still running three miles in under eighteen minutes and competing in triathalons. At The Basic School (TBS), where all newly commissioned Marine Corps officers go to learn the art and science of being a Marine officer, Ruvalcaba received the "gung ho" award for being the most motivated candidate. He flew Heuys for four years after flight school and then transitioned to Cobras. He believes Cobras have one of the best missions in the Marine Corps. Armour liked flying with Ruvalcaba because of his positive attitude and the ease with which she could ask him questions about anything from aviation to home loans and mortgages. She also got the sense that the senior pilot looked out for her and always had her best interest at heart.

In Iraq, between March and May of 2003, Ruvalcaba and Armour teamed up for nearly twenty-eight missions (each one is 1½ to 2½ hours and can encompass many more sorties), or about sixty hours. Ruvalcaba flew ninety percent of his missions with Armour. Sometimes they were in the cockpit from sunup to sundown. Their longest mission in Iraq lasted about twenty-one hours. They took off at 11:30 in the morning to do a test. Then the rest of the division joined their section and they didn't land for good until 10:30 the next morning. They would fly for two hours, land, refuel, and do it all over again. They didn't shoot anything but they did provide air support for the ground troops throughout the night.

Ruvalcaba rated himself and Armour as average pilots. Armour had been with the squadron less than a year when they deployed to Kuwait. Neither one was a terrible pilot nor were they "shit-hot stick" like the weapons tactics instructors and screaming lieutenants. They held their own.

The plane captains designated a time when all the aircraft would start up and do a "radio check." By five thirty, just as the sun was starting to come up, four Cobras taxied down the flight line and took off. When they were in the air, they moved into formation, with the lead aircraft determining the speed, altitude, route, and tactical formation (position in space) for the others to follow.

Once they crossed the border from Kuwait to Iraq, the co-pilots configured their weapons systems so if they were attacked, all they had to do was flip a switch to arm and shoot. Next they tested their weapons to make sure their guns and flares worked, and that they had good symbology on the Hellfire. Symbology is a term used to describe when the pilot has locked on to a target and is ready to fire. The co-pilots can view their targets through the multi-functional display unit two different ways—by looking at a mini television screen or by looking "heads down" into the telescopic site unit (TSU). Both were like looking at a video of the outside world. When Armour locked on to her target with a Hellfire, a circle with a plus sign inside appeared on an overlay. A steady, non-flashing plus sign inside the circle indicated that she had symbology and was ready to fire her weapon. She put the missile in Lock-On Before Launch (LOBL) mode to squirt out the laser energy and ensure that the seeker head on the Hellfire was moving around and scanning for laser energy. As long as the missiles were looking for their target, they were considered to be in good form. They tested the rockets but didn't shoot them. To test the rockets they went to "arm" to make sure the "select" light came on to show that the rocket pod had been selected. They checked the TOW to see whether the correct symbols came up to indicate the TOW was enabled and ready to fire. And they squirted a burst of 20mm rounds and shot a flare off the side.

The four aircraft flew to a forward arming and refueling point (FARP) in Tallil, 310 kilometers southeast of Baghdad, to load up with fuel and recheck their ammunition. Armour coded up her Hellfires so in the heat of battle all she had to do was find her target, turn on the laser energy, and press a button.

When there were four aircraft, the Cobras flew in a division, and the division was divided into two sections. Armour and Ruvalcaba flew in the first aircraft in the second section, or the third Cobra—Dash-3. The number one aircraft always led the entire division and his section. Dash-3 led his section. Ruvalcaba flew the aircraft; Amour navigated her section of two aircraft, calling out targets and operating the weaponry.

The pilots had a good idea where Regimental Combat Team (RCT) 5 was located on Highway 6 based on information they received from the aircraft they were relieving. With the guidance of Crusty, the regiment's forward air controller (FAC), and sometimes without his direction because he didn't always know what lay ahead, the Cobras were about to engage their weapons in a heated armed reconnaissance mission.

The Cobras were heading northeast when they learned the troops had pushed farther northwest than expected. So they changed their flight pattern to meet the troops where they were heading and not where they had been. As soon as they arrived in the area of the RCT, the pilots spotted a T-55 tank and an ammunition storage site. Having these ammunition dumps along the side of the road posed a threat to the troops by allowing the insurgents to rearm themselves during conflicts. They had to be destroyed. Major James Szepesy (a.k.a. Snoop) called in an attack.

On this attack, Armour and Ruvalcaba provided support for Szepesy just in case his TOW missile went stupid or missed its target. When a missile goes stupid, it leaves the aircraft but doesn't take the guidance signals from the Cobra. So instead of heading toward its target it just dives to the ground about 200 feet in front of the helicopter. A dud doesn't leave the aircraft when the copilot pulls the trigger.

After the aircraft were cleared to fire on the tank and storage site, Armour and Ruvalcaba zeroed in on the targets. Armour looked into her TSU, picked out the targets, pulled the trigger, and fired 20mm rounds while Ruvalcaba maneuvered the aircraft to ensure continuous fire on the tank and storage site and kept the aircraft in formation with the division. Szepesy's missile took out the tank, clearing the way for the RCT to continue forward.

Next Crusty directed the Cobras to fly ahead of the convoy to seek out the enemy, a primary mission of the Cobra. However, the ground troops were taking small-arms fire, which meant there was a good chance the aircraft would be the target of similar fire. The same small-arms fire that bounces off the armored tanks can take down an aircraft. The lead aircraft responded that it was too risky for the Cobras to fly out ahead of the convoy. But just being in the air and having special visual aids allowed the pilots to see much farther than the ground troops. They could scan up ahead, find the enemy, and fire without being on top of the enemy and making themselves vulnerable.

Flying at about the height of a high-tension power line, and varying their speed between seventy and one hundred knots to avoid being shot down, the attack helicopters maneuvered around as they looked for the enemy, their vehicles, and their ammunition sites. At this point the aircraft were shooting "weapons free." If they saw the enemy, they had the authority to shoot him with the appropriate weaponry.

While searching the area the pilots spotted twenty-five abandoned military vehicles with Iraqi blouses, medium machine guns, and ammunition strewn about the area. Some vehicles were dug in with earthen berms to protect them from anti-tank missiles. Others were positioned in such a way that they could support each other from threats coming from multiple directions. Szepesy relayed the information back to Crusty, instructing the troops to hold their ground. "Do not advance. There are armored tanks in front of you."

As the aircraft set up for an easterly attack to destroy two of the armored personnel carriers, Armour began to visualize how she could best support the division. Ruvalcaba would shoot rockets from the back seat and they would both follow up with 20mm on the pull off. All the time they would keep Dash-4 in sight to maintain safety and coverage for the other aircraft in the division. After the success of the easterly attack, the division pulled off to the south and circled to the west for another attack, avoiding Iraqi anti-aircraft artillery. Armour looked around to see where the aircraft and ground troops were in relation to enemy tanks on the ground. She was ready to sight in on the new target. The westerly attack took out more armored personnel carriers facing the ground troops.

During these attacks, the Iraqis tried to channel the Cobras into their line of fire by pouring oil into ditches, starting fires, and temporarily blinding the pilots with heavy smoke. This forced the aircraft to one side of the highway or the battle. When the Cobras flew out of the smoke and regained awareness of their surroundings, the Iraqis aimed small-arms fire and artillery air bursts at the aircraft.

As the enemy came in and out of view, Armour spotted a misty gray cloud in the atmosphere about fifty to one hundred yards away.

"Did you see that?" she asked Ruvalcaba.

He did see it. At first neither one of the pilots knew what had created the cloud. Then they realized they were air bursts from rocket-propelled grenades (RPGs) or something similar and that the Republican Guards were targeting the aircraft. Fortunately, they were able to dodge that rocket.

While they sought out the enemy on both sides of the freeway, Armour looked into her TSU and spotted another armored personnel carrier. She called out her target and heading, and let Ruvalcaba know she was going to take it out with a Hellfire missile. Up until now she had been firing mostly 20mm rounds. She reached forward to the left side of the console to put the weapon selection knob on LOBL in the Hellfire mode so she could squirt the laser energy onto the target. Once it's in LOBL, the missile seeker head starts looking for laser energy and homing in on the target. When she wanted to shoot the 20mm or the TOW missile, Armour had to make a conscious effort to pull up the trigger guard. On the back of the handgrip, where her left thumb rested, was another guard that covered the red button she pressed to launch to Hellfire missiles. She lifted a small flap.

When she determined the symbology was good, she said, "Missile away."

"Missile away," Ruvalcaba responded.

She pressed the red button to fire the missile off the rail, keeping the laser energy active until the missile hit the armored personnel carrier.

If all went well, less than a second later the missile would slide off the rail and head straight for its target. With Ruvalcaba flying the aircraft, Armour destroyed the vehicle.

As the Cobras closed in on the city of Al Aziziyah, they spotted two squads of Saddam's elite Republican Guard sitting in ambush southwest of the city. The Cobras had been taking sporadic fire all along but now the bursts were getting closer and closer, so close the aircraft had to abort one of the attacks. As Szepesy pulled off from another attack, his aircraft received a crippling shot that caused his gauges to fluctuate. In a matter-of-fact tone, he told the other pilots he had been hit. He and his wingman would have to return to the FARP.

Cobras always fly in pairs, so Dash-1 and Dash-2 left together. Armour and Ruvalcaba became the new Dash-1 and the other aircraft, Dash-2. Armour didn't know the extent of damage to Dash-1 and whether they'd make it back to the FARP, even though it was only six miles away. Being hit can be like running out of gas when the gas station is a mile away. If you don't have gas, you don't have gas. If the transmission seizes up in a car, you stop rolling. If it quits in a helicopter, the blades no longer turn even if the engines are still running. Armour couldn't be too concerned about the hit Cobra, though, because her aircraft had just become the lead for the remaining assaults.

Ruvalcaba, hearing that the division leader's aircraft had been hit, immediately turned his section back into the ambush. Circling over the land between the river and the road, Armour was looking for the enemy when she spotted a man in uniform running, jumping, and diving into a ditch along the river. He was trying to take cover while other fedayeen shot heavy small arms and medium-caliber anti-aircraft artillery fire at the helicopters.

"Enemy on the ground, two o'clock. They're running, jumping into a ditch. Guns."

That let Ruvalcaba know that she was getting ready to fire the 20mm guns.

Armour blasted her target with 20mm rounds.

"Rockets," Ruvalcaba said.

"Rockets," Armour repeated.

As soon as Armour heard Ruvalcaba say "Rockets," she stopped shooting and the guns retreated. If she were shooting the guns while he was firing rockets, the guns would go into lockout. The aircraft knows that if the gun is pointing out to the right and the rocket is behind it getting ready to shoot, it could damage the gun. When Ruvalcaba triggered the rocket, the guns would automatically stow. If Armour was still shooting guns, some rounds would drop out as the gun closed. As soon as the rocket came off the rail, Armour could resume shooting the 20mm. Ruvalcaba and Armour took turns firing guns and rockets at the fedayeen. When Ruvalcaba pulled off to the right, Armour kept shooting to the left until they were out of range of anti-aircraft artillery.

They made another pass and Armour could still see the enemy on the ground so she fired flechette rockets. Each of these rockets has 2,200 small nails that are painted red. When the rocket deploys and the nails spray, they give the appearance of a pink cloud that allows the pilots to see where the rockets hit. Armour could see the fedayeen falling to the ground but couldn't tell if they were going down because she had shot them or because they were taking cover. She believes that she killed them and that's okay with her. Each time she destroyed one of her targets—military tank, ammunition site, or insurgent—she felt a great sense of accomplishment. In this situation, in addition to defending herself she was protecting the ground troops who otherwise would have walked into an ambush. Taking out the enemy is what she was trained to do. She wasn't thinking on a personal or emotional level. In the heat of the moment, she was using the tactics she learned in training and applying muscle memory to target, flip switches, and pull triggers.

After taking out the fedayeen, Ruvalcaba returned the focus of the two Cobras to the battalion of armored personnel carriers.

The ground troops were closing in on Al Aziziyah and were vulnerable to the enemy vehicles. Iraqi soldiers hiding in concealed positions could quickly re-man the armored personnel carriers and attack the regiment with deadly fire.

But as soon as the Cobras began firing on the Iraqi vehicles, Armour started to have problems with her weapons' system. She was trying to shoot her 20mm but it wouldn't fire. At the top of the multiple function display unit, the one that resembles a small TV, is a heading tape that senses and indicates the direction the gun is pointing, the direction the aircraft is heading, and the direction of the target. At the time, instead of indicating 360 for north the heading tape was spinning out of control. Armour couldn't accurately target anything because she couldn't get a heading from the TSU that sets up the Hellfire or TOW missiles to fire in a certain direction.

Armour relayed the serious problem to Ruvalcaba. He took her through some troubleshooting steps to get their weapons system back on line but nothing worked.

"Sir, I can't do anything up here," Armour said. "How long are we going to stay out here?"

By now, the other aircraft had run out of ammunition. It appeared that both Cobras were sitting ducks. The aircraft needed to either find a way to fight back or get out of the fight. Since Dash-1 still had Hellfires and Dash-2 had laser, Armour was able to coordinate an attack using her missiles and Dash-2's laser. They call it "buddy lasering."

After launching all of their Hellfires, the aircraft contacted Crusty to let him know they were out of ammunition and were heading back to the FARP. Once they returned to the FARP, landed, and shut down, Ruvalcaba and Armour did a post flight check of their Cobra. This is especially important for pilots who have flown into battle to make sure the aircraft isn't damaged.

They found three holes in the aircraft where they had been hit by enemy fire—one under the cockpit, one in the tail boom (back end of the aircraft), and another in a rotor blade. The round that hit the cockpit is the one that disabled the weapons system.

This was a memorable mission for Armour because it was the first time she fired her weapons for close air support with such intensity, and it was the first time the weapons system went down and she felt helpless. She could see the enemy firing on her and couldn't return fire. Armour felt like sinking back into the protection of the seat, the only armored place in the cockpit.

Deployments, like life, have their ups and downs, highs and lows. A successful mission being a high; a not-so-successful tactics test, a low. Toward the end of Armour's first tour, she dug a hole for herself and had a difficult time climbing out. The pilots in the squadrons take tactics tests to let their leaders know who is "staying in the books" and who isn't. A big tactics test was coming up. The pilots were always notified about the tests a couple of days in advance. Armour had been on a mission in Iraq for a few days and had taken her tactics books with her. She learned ahead of time that there was going to be a test but didn't find out what would be on it. She should have asked around and gotten the information but she didn't. She was one of twenty-five pilots who took the test. Half the pilots failed. Armour got the lowest score. It didn't matter to Armour how many others failed. What mattered was that she failed.

The experience crushed her spirit. She felt she had let herself and her squadron down, not to mention future female Marine aviators. She carried a lot of guilt for her poor performance. She was taken off the flight schedule temporarily and her motivation level dropped. She took full responsibility for putting herself in a position to fail and for not rebounding like she should have.

Armour knows that as a Cobra pilot she has to study all the time because there is so much to know and it's always changing. And when she feels she knows a lot, she has to keep reviewing it to stay sharp because her enemy is studying, too. Ruvalcaba, who had already returned to Camp Pendleton when this test was administered, said that if Armour was taken off the flight schedule, it was serious. But he also said it's just one event.

Armour was in Kuwait and Iraq for eight months, from February 9 to September 22. She arrived home at nine in the evening on her thirtieth birthday. Being home was the best birthday present ever.

Growing up, Armour didn't have a strong feeling one way or the other about pursuing a military career. She was familiar with the military and knew it was an option. Her father was in the Army Reserve, her Marine stepdad completed two tours in Vietnam, and her grandfather was a Montford Point Marine—one of the first black Marines to serve in the United States military. He fought with the 301st Platoon at Guadalcanal during World War II. But it wasn't necessarily her family history that first led her to a military career. Instead, it was her involvement in ROTC.

While Armour was studying physical education and exercise science at Middle Tennessee State University, she read a flyer advertising a free trip to Mardi Gras for anyone who signed up to march in the Army's women's drill team. It sounded like a good opportunity. She didn't have to be part of ROTC to be on the drill team, but a year later (in 1993) Armour joined anyway.

It was during a six-week ROTC advanced camp that Armour first considered her future as a combat pilot. During camp there is a career day when soldiers working in different fields in the Army talk to prospective recruits. Armour kept an open mind. Military aviation was set up in a tree line with camouflage netting. The trees and the netting made it dim inside and hard to see. Once Armour's eyes adjusted, she saw a black woman up front in a flight suit. *Wow, that is cool. Why didn't I think of that?* It took seeing someone who looked like her to get her to think about aviation as a profession. Armour had seen pilots before. She had been flying on airplanes since she was five years old. The sense of awe she felt that day stayed with her and she decided to look into it further. However, when the time came for the cadets to be assigned their jobs, Armour hadn't completed her flight physical to become a student pilot. She was assigned to ordnance but declined the position.

The following year, while walking through the student union at Middle Tennessee State University, Armour saw a Marine recruiter. That sparked her interest enough to visit a recruiting office. A recruiter asked her if she ever considered becoming a pilot. "Absolutely," she said. The recruiter told her that if she made it she would be the first black female pilot. This was news to Armour. She went into the recruiting office with the goal of becoming a pilot. It hadn't dawned on her that she could be making history. She asked the recruiter how it could be that in the mid to late 1990s there were no female African-American Marine pilots. He explained that military aviation had opened up to women only in the past several years.

Armour left the office and did some research on the Internet. She found an article soliciting African-American females to join the Marine Corps as officers on aviation contracts. The article asked,

"Do you have what it takes to be the first?" She e-mailed the site to let them know that she had applied to become a Marine pilot.

The article, "In Search of the Marine Corps' First African-American Female Pilot," was written by Lieutenant Colonel Charles Boyd, USMC. It called attention to the Marine Corps' award-winning recruiting phrase, "We're looking for a few good men" and how it fits into the macho image mystique. Now the Marine Corps' phrase has expanded to "We're looking for a few good men and women." But just as important is its dedicated effort to find a few good minority officer candidates, men and women.

Boyd believed there were probably several reasons why the Marine Corps was having a difficult time finding an African-American woman with the "right stuff." The flow of information may not have been reaching the women or it may not have been presented in a way that would ignite their interest. Or maybe they had to get used to the idea of African-American women being military pilots. The desire to be the first black female pilot called for serious thought. It required discussions with family, close friends, faculty advisors and mentors.

However, once that first black female became a Marine pilot, Boyd believed there would be no limit to the fulfillment of her dreams. She would succeed where no other had dared to go. She would yearn to learn while earning her place in history—Marine Corps history, African-American history, American history.

Armour graduated from college in 1997 and started officer candidate school in the fall of 1998. Her dream was to fly jets or C-130s. She wanted to be a fighter pilot. *Honestly, who doesn't think shooting and dropping bombs is cool? The jets are a lot sexier.*

At the end of flight school in Pensacola, when it was time to match the pilots with their aircraft, there were two slots for jets.

Four of the young officers had earned the high grades necessary
to fly jets but only two would get to fly the aircraft. Armour was
the number three person. She would have to fly a different aircraft. No C-130s were available and the new tilt-rotor aircraft, the
Osprey, was going to go through more testing so her only option
was helicopters.

Armour decided that if she had to fly helicopters, she would
fly the coolest one out there. To her the best helicopter was the
Super Cobra because of its close air reconnaissance missions. She
learned her lesson from the first phase of flight school that being
number three wasn't good enough. If she wanted to fly Cobras,
she would have to be number one in her class. At the end of the
training period, twelve Marine officers stood in the hallway while
a flight instructor wrote the names of twelve aircraft on a black-
board in a classroom. At this point, no one knew who was first in
the class. They called in one Marine at a time, starting at the top.
There was only one Cobra spot and Armour got it. She picked the
West Coast as her training ground.

When Armour decided to become a Cobra pilot, a lot of people tried to talk her out of it. "They eat their young." "They're not
nice as a community." There had been only three other female
Cobra pilots up to that point. Some thought and still think that a
Cobra squadron is no place for a woman. Armour believes it's
important to love and respect yourself and to do what makes you
happy, and to not be guided by fear or what other people think. If
you want something but you fail to try, you've already failed. *If
women don't take the challenge, how is it ever going to change?* Flying
Cobras became a personal challenge. It was something she
wanted to do and she wasn't going to let anyone talk her out of it.

Following flight school in Pensacola and Corpus Christi,
Armour joined Marine Helicopter Training Squadron 303 at

Marine Corps Base Camp Pendleton. She was in HMT-303 when the United States was attacked on 9/11. She joined her operational squadron in March 2002. A Marine light attack helicopter (HMLA) squadron has about nine Hueys and eighteen Cobras. Every Marine Corps pilot is given a call sign that evolves out of a silly or embarrassing situation, or a unique feature or characteristic. The pilots had a hard time coming up with something funny about Armour so they named her "Junk" for "Junk in the Trunk"—or big butt.

It was in the operational squadron that Armour learned first-hand why the Cobra community has earned the reputation for being so harsh. The Cobra pilots claim to "eat their young" to toughen up the new pilots before they fly into battle. If they can't take what their fellow pilots throw at them, how are they going to handle being shot at on the battlefield? "There's no room for error," Armour says. "You don't have time to think when you're out there. You're reacting or even better, on the offense. To just do it, you have to know what to do. It has to be ground into your muscle memory."

Each squadron has its own personality and its own way of breaking down and building up its pilots. Armour compared the squadrons to fraternities. Many fraternities have a common goal of service and education, but they develop different reputations and vary on how they welcome and initiate new recruits into the brotherhood. Like fraternity pledges, new Cobra pilots pay their dues by sitting at the duty desk, keeping track of the flight schedule, answering the phones, and washing the engines. Washing the engines meant running soapy water through the inside of the engine to clean the internal blades that had been exposed to excess sand or saltwater atmosphere (Iraq and the coast of California, i.e. Camp Pendleton). The whole process takes about an

hour to an hour and a half. It wasn't a big deal. It was just something the pilots didn't like getting picked for, especially when it
was really hot outside.

Another reason Cobra pilots are so tough on their young
is because every eighteen months the squadron splits and the
pilots go in three different directions for six months. Then they
reintegrate for eighteen months and start the process over again.
When the members of the squadron integrate with other units,
they are expected to represent the high standards of the Cobra
community.

Ruvalcaba, who has spent sixteen years in a tactical squadron,
four as a Huey pilot and twelve as a Cobra pilot, says it takes a very
aggressive personality to go looking for a fight, which is exactly
what the Cobras do when they are flying armed reconnaissance
missions. Armour isn't necessarily one to go looking for a fight,
but she's tough and can definitely hold her own. She's no
pushover. She was in the fifth grade when she stood up for her
brother who is sixteen months younger than her. After school,
the students could buy popcorn or slushies on the school ground
as they left for the day. One time a boy came up to her brother
and took his popcorn. Armour's brother cried as he told his big
sis what had happened and pointed out the culprit. Armour
didn't waste any time retrieving the popcorn, pushing the boy
down, and telling him, "Don't mess with my brother!" Then she
returned the popcorn to her brother.

She began riding horses when she was about six years old and
quickly realized that her sweet little pony couldn't compete with
the bigger and faster horses in the same category. One time
Armour was walking home with her dad after coming in second
or third in a barrel race. She looked at her small ribbon, and
then she looked up at her dad and said, "Daddy, I need a big

horse." For Armour, it's all about rising to the challenge. And when the gauntlet is thrown down, she knows it's the strongest and the fittest who come out on top.

Armour loved flight school and the training squadron. She didn't have the same fondness for her operational squadron but doesn't want to make an issue out of it, either. She shrugs it off, as if it to say let bygones be bygones. After all, she says, some of it was just a matter of women being new to aviation. It's not as if every woman who comes after her will face the same hardships. Ninety-seven percent of the guys she flew with had never flown with a woman before. The sense of exclusion she felt was no different from what similar women went through when they entered other male dominated fields—whether they were the first female students at the Citadel or the first female lawyer trying to make partner.

"You're a woman," she says. "You'll always be a woman. You'll never be one of the guys. But you can be part of the team, and that's where the difference is. Some squadrons make you feel like you're part of the team and some don't."

Armour, who had participated in many team sports growing up, never got used to the feeling of being left out of the squadron.

"Hey, Bob, Joe, want to go to lunch?" one pilot would say to the others in front of Armour.

"What about me?" she'd ask.

"Oh Armour, you know you're always invited," came the familiar response.

"Yeah, but you said Bob and Joe. You didn't say Vernice."

Neither Armour nor Ruvalcaba thought the response of the male pilots was personal. And to Ruvalcaba's knowledge, no one picked on Armour or gave her anything that was unfair. Some guys are just close. He compared the squadron to an office. There are always some coworkers who are going to be closer than others, regardless of whether someone is male or female. You pick your friends in a squadron, but this may be easier said than done when you're the only female pilot. Armour says a woman on a male football team is alienated and left out because she can't go into the locker room with her teammates. The same holds true for the squadron. "It's not personal, but you'll never be one of the guys."

Fitting into the squadron was one of several distinct challenges Armour would face. Being the first black female combat pilot meant having to handle media distractions in the middle of a war when she was supposed to be preparing for a mission. A day or two prior to a mission, the squadron commander usually talked by phone to headquarters and to the ground troops. Then the commander passed along the information to his pilots to let them know what was expected of them. One of the co-pilot's duties during this period was to prepare the maps and record as many details as possible about the upcoming flight on to the kneeboard, i.e. which radio frequencies they would use, where they would be flying, and what their call sign would be. All this information had to be readily available prior to take off.

On at least one occasion Ruvalcaba observed that Armour was tied up with a media interview during a pre-mission planning session and was not able to build her situational awareness like the other lieutenants. She was still able to hold her own in terms of flying but her situational awareness of where they were going and who they were supporting wasn't as strong as if she had been in on the pre-mission planning. "I don't fault her," Ruvalcaba said.

Armour doesn't think anything was briefed that the other pilots couldn't bring her up to speed on. "I doubt very seriously that it negatively impacted the mission that we eventually went out on. And if it did, he (Ruvalcaba) would have told me."

Being the "first" black female combat pilot added to the likelihood that Armour would be alienated from some of her peers. It's true she got the spotlight because she was the first and not the best at something. But ultimately the reason for being in the spotlight didn't matter. Attention is attention is attention. Being in a squadron is like being on a team and anytime one member gets more attention than the others she risks being alienated. Armour could have told the media to go away but that wasn't what she wanted. Hers was a story of optimism during a time when good news was hard to come by. She also believes in being a positive role model and giving back to her community. The more people who know about her the greater impact she can have on the nation's youth no matter their gender, race, or ethnicity. But of course Armour holds a special place in her heart for young African-American girls. Was there a lot of pressure? "Absolutely." Was she alienated for that? "Yes, I was."

She thought the added pressure was unfair, but if she could help pave the way for others the way it had been paved for her, then the sacrifices were worth it. She believes in the Bible verse, "To whom much is given much is required." She says, "It would be the most selfish act I could do not to give back from the many blessings that have been given to me."

Armour couldn't believe it when she learned she was going back to Iraq. When she left the country in September 2003, she thought she was leaving for good. She didn't know the deployments were going to be so often, a revolving door. A month passed after arriving in Iraq before it really hit her that she was back in the Middle East. This time having combat experience helped. Not that flying missions was old hat, but she definitely knew the lay of the land better than the first time.

On her second tour, Armour, the squadron, and the 11th Marine Expeditionary Unit from Camp Pendleton were stationed at forward operating base (FOB) Duke, twelve miles northwest of Najaf. Armour flew mostly with Captain James Grogan, a pilot she described as five feet ten inches tall, medium build, brown hair, and an on-again off-again moustache. He was a pilot who wanted to go out, do a good job, and represent the squadron well. She enjoyed flying with Grogan because, like Ruvalcaba, he would help her out if she had any questions. They shared an interest in weight lifting. Grogan ordered kettle bells and had them shipped to Iraq. The other pilots made fun of him for going to such lengths to work out.

Armour's second deployment was much more dangerous than the first time she was in Iraq because the insurgents had been honing their skills with surface-to-air missiles and small-arms fire. During her first tour, Armour could fly directly over a city without too much concern of being shot down. On her second deployment she spent less time flying over urban areas because the enemy was targeting the aircraft more. This wasn't as apparent in the daytime as it was in the evening when the pilots could see the red tracer rounds heading their way. Identifying the rounds meant the Cobra pilots were going on the offensive to defend themselves.

During the Battle of Fallujah in April 2004, Armour helped provide security for medevac aircraft that were transporting the wounded and dead to the nearest available hospitals. The tempo was high. The pilots spent most of their twelve-hour shifts either flying or doing mission planning. The casualty collection points were on the outskirts of the city, where it was safer for the medevacs to land and pick up the wounded. The Cobras stayed airborne, flying about a thousand meters from the pickup area and ready to employ their weapons if they or the ground troops were attacked. If she was looking through her TSU during a pickup,

Armour could see a huddle of Marines and medics transporting casualties to the aircraft.

Four months after Fallujah, another battle raged in and around the city of Najaf. Armour and Grogan were on thirty-minute strip alert at the forward operating base. This meant that no matter where they were—ready room, chow hall, computer lab—they had to be able to get their gear, get in their aircraft, do radio checks, and get off the flight deck within thirty minutes of the first call. A thirty-minute strip alert was the standard. If they were on a fifteen-minute strip alert they couldn't leave the ready room. So the section was ready when they learned that troops had made contact with the enemy. They were airborne within fifteen minutes.

They took off at 6 A.M. Armour and Grogan were flying with one other aircraft, a Huey flown by Major Glen Butler and his co-pilot, Captain Keith Thorkelson. Putting these two aircraft together was a new technique used to give the Cobras better coverage. The Cobras would fly in first with their superior missiles, rockets, and 20mm guns and would be able to pull off safely because of the coverage of the Huey door gunners. The Huey has door gunners on the side whereas the Cobra has only a gun off the nose. As the Cobra pulls off to the left or to the right, the Huey can cover its pull-off much more effectively than a Cobra.

When they arrived at Najaf they linked up with the aircraft already on the scene that had been targeting a building on the fringe of the city. The enemy was using the building as a hiding place and as a point of attack. An arms cache had started to burn, but it hadn't been destroyed. The previous section had run out of ordnance and was returning to base. Armour and her section would destroy the cache, but they would have to do it from a distance because of the heavy fire coming from the area. Armour fired several Hellfire missiles into the target, keeping it burning and denying the enemy access to the weapons cache.

Next the pilots turned their attention to an enormous cemetery nearby. Soldiers were sweeping the cemetery and battalions had the enemy forces trapped in several areas. The Cobras were to advance into the cemetery to an area that contained the Imam Ali mosque, an Islamic holy site that housed and was surrounded by enemy ground forces. The mosque was surrounded by thousands and thousands of above-ground graves, and catacombs that the insurgents hid in. Finding the enemy was a nightmare for the soldiers because there were countless places to hide. The ground troops had to go through the cemetery and catacombs systematically. Flying in this environment was extremely hazardous because of the enemy's capabilities and willingness to fire at the aircraft. This threat, coupled with the inherent dangers of urban flight, demanded from the pilots an immense amount of precision, situational awareness, and flight leadership to effectively accomplish the mission.

The pilots had taken off with maps and digital imagery of the cemetery, and stayed in constant communication with the forward air controller (FAC). When they first got out there, they made runs toward the cemetery but were careful not to fly directly over it. They turned right or left about 600 to 700 meters from the cemetery. The Cobras could hit their targets by flying up to the cemetery and while they were pulling off. They didn't have to fly over their target, which would have increased their risk of being shot down. The insurgents on the ground would certainly target them. The pilots never wanted to fly within range of the enemy. They just wanted to hit their targets and pull off before they could be hit. They especially didn't want to fly over a target that they were blowing up.

The aircraft learned that the 1-5 Cavalry Battalion, which had been taking fire from an enemy mortar position in the middle of the cemetery for most of the morning, was pinned down. The FAC wanted the aircraft to make a run on the Imam Ali mosque, which was where they believed most of the firing was coming from. But the FAC would have to give the pilots a "talk on" to the target because they were either too far away to see the target or something was obstructing their view. The cemetery was so congested and the firing was coming from so many locations that the aircraft couldn't fly close enough to identify the target. However, 1-5 Cavalry was still taking mortar fire and was determined to find and destroy the enemy position.

After several minutes, Armour located what she thought to be the target. Due to the lack of a mark and the fact that several buildings had the same description, the section was not yet able to make positive target identification. Then they observed muzzle flashes coming from the mosque and decided to destroy it.

The section repositioned to attack from the west, using a ridgeline near the cemetery as cover. Starting the attack from below the ridge provided protection during ingress but obscured the target for a proper lineup. Armour had used all her Hellfires on other buildings and had only one TOW missile left. There was nothing wrong with firing a TOW in this situation. In fact, she could shoot a TOW in a little closer to the target than she could a Hellfire. If she was too close to the target with a Hellfire, it wouldn't have time to arm.

As the section climbed to attack, Armour had only seconds to reacquire the target and fire her last missile. Due to the tight constraints of the cemetery, Armour's aircraft had to close within a few hundred meters of the heavily defended mortars to fire her weapons. As soon as the aircraft was above the ridgeline, Armour located muzzle flashes directed at her aircraft and quickly determined that the firing was coming from the mosque. She had her target. Still under intense fire from small arms and RPGs, the aircraft stopped climbing and flew nose first toward the building. Armour lowered her head to look into her TSU.

"Target in sight. TOW ," she said.

"TOW," Grogan repeated.

She pulled the trigger.

"TOW on the wire," she said.

Nothing.

Nothing.

Nothing.

All the while they were flying farther and farther into the engagement zone. Hoping the TOW wasn't a dud, Armour pulled the trigger again and to her relief the TOW motor fired up and the missile slid off the rail. Seconds later the TOW hit its target.

Immediately following the TOW launch, Grogan shot six or seven rockets into the mosque. The entire time Armour kept her head down and looked through the TSU to keep the target in sight so that she could follow up with 20mm as the aircraft flew out of the target area. They had successfully hit and destroyed a Mahdi Army position. The troops on the ground reported no further mortar fire during the day.

The battle damage assessment reports confirmed the building had been destroyed, several insurgents killed, and no further mortar fire during that day. The Cobra and Huey received only light battle damage despite the high volume of small-arms fire they encountered during the engagement. The Cobra fired twenty-six rockets, 200 20mm high-explosive incendiary rounds, a TOW, and three Hellfire missiles.

For Armour, being a Marine Corps pilot was never about being first. It was about not wanting to be average. And because she didn't want to be average, she ended up being first. "Do what average people do; have what average people have," Armour says. "Who wants to be average? I don't. Do you?"

Lieutenant Colonel Polly Montgomery, United States Air Force.

Taking Command of the Herk

"My first impression, before she even came to the squadron, was that we were getting a commander who had never flown C-130 planes and was coming off a staff tour as some general's aide. Some of us thought she just got this position because she was a general's aide. Now we're getting this C-141 female commander—this is going to be a nightmare. That was the general feeling in the squadron. Of course, she's not that person. Day one of her being there we realized that thought process was completely wrong. . . . Within a week of being in the squadron it was evident that she was going to be great."

—*Major Mike Frame speaking about his new boss,*
Air Force Lieutenant Colonel Polly Montgomery

SEPTEMBER 2004

It was one of Lieutenant Colonel Polly Montgomery's first flights in combat. The forty-one-year-old Air Force pilot and her crew of five had spent the day transporting troops and cargo into cities and air bases in and around the Sunni Triangle—a great location if you were looking to get killed.

Montgomery's C-130 aircraft was climbing out of Baghdad at about ten o'clock in the evening. They had one leg left, north to

185

the city of Balad, to pick up troops before turning south to their home base in Qatar.

Montgomery, five feet seven inches tall and weighing 138 pounds, sat in the pilot's seat on the left. She had a thin face, short black hair, dark eyes, and freckles. She was solid muscle from running, swimming, bike riding, and yoga. When asked how long she had been in the Air Force, she liked to say, half-jokingly, "All my life." Her father, Tim Padden, is a retired Air Force two-star general. Montgomery was commissioned a second lieutenant after graduating from the Air Force Academy.

Beside her, in the co-pilot's seat, sat her instructor, thirty-eight-year-old Major Mike Frame. He stood five feet eight inches tall and was heavyset. He was balding, had a mustache, and was some-what slovenly in appearance—not exactly a poster boy for the Air Force. But first impressions can be deceiving, and in many ways this father of four set the standard for professionalism. Frame had about sixteen years in the Air Force when he and Montgomery began flying together. They barely knew each other. He would soon become one of her closest friends and one of her favorite co-pilots. He was honest, spoke his mind, and was one of the few air-men not intimidated by Montgomery.

Normally, the commander of a combat squadron knows how to fly an aircraft before taking responsibility for up to twenty planes and 200 airmen. But during wartime, odd things can and do happen. For fifteen years Montgomery had flown the C-141, a long-haul aircraft whose work was much like that of a commercial jet. But that airplane was being scrapped. The war began while Montgomery was working as the executive officer to the vice com-mander of Air Mobility Command Staff, Company Headquarters, at Scott Air Force Base in Illinois. As her tour wound down, it was recommended she take command of a squadron of C-130s preparing to go to Al Udied Air Base in Qatar in support of the war. Unlike the C-141, the C-130 "Hercules" was meant to fly troops and cargo into less developed locations with short runways. So the work was more seat-of-the pants flying, landing in rugged conditions under dicey circumstances and hoping there was enough runway to take off again and no soft spots to trip your wheels.

Montgomery started training on the C-130 in April 2004. Three months later, she cut her schooling short to take command of the 41st Airlift Squadron at Pope Air Force Base in Fayetteville, North Carolina. In the process, she became the first female commander of a combat squadron in the Air Force. There was no time to rest on her laurels, though, because by the time she arrived at Pope, most of her squadron had already left for Qatar and was transporting troops in and out of combat.

Montgomery wasn't the type of commander to sit around Pope for two months, wait for her airmen to return, and then say, "Hey guys, let me give you some advice." They would have looked at her as if to say, "Who the hell are you? You haven't even been there. You don't even know what we do. You're a 'T-tailer.'" A T-tailer is someone who flies a C-141, C-5, or C-17. If you look at the tail of any of these aircraft, it has a horizontal and vertical piece that looks like a T. A C-130 only has a vertical piece (no crossing "T"). The people in the C-130 community are not T-tailers; they're tactical (combat) airlifters. When a C-130 person calls someone a T-tailer, it isn't a term of endearment.

Montgomery knew, as did her airmen, that if she didn't go to Qatar she'd never live it down, never really be a member of their exclusive club—a tight-knit cadre of blue-collar rough-and-ready fliers who can take off under fire and land on a postage stamp of dirt and not even work up a sweat. She'd have to go to the war to earn her air cred. Montgomery resolved to go to Qatar, meet her airmen, and earn some "real" flying experience. Little did she know her baptism of fire would occur within a week of arriving in the Middle East. Fortunately, the former T-tailer had about 4,000 hours of experience in her old aircraft to fall back on.

The most unnerving time for the crew of a C-130 is when the aircraft is climbing or descending because that's when they are sitting ducks. Herk crews are accustomed to taking fire during the war because the 155,000-pound metal aircraft is such a low and slow moving target and obviously full of Americans and their expensive gear. Once the plane is in the air and leveled out, it becomes a more difficult target, capable of swerving and swooping and otherwise taking evasive action. The crew especially likes to fly at night because the weapon that poses the greatest threat to their aircraft is a shoulder-fired, low altitude surface-to-air missile known as an SA-7. The SA-7's effectiveness depends on its ability to lock on to the heat source of low-flying aircraft. For that missile to hit a C-130, the person on the ground firing it has to be able to see the Herk. This is difficult since the Herk, like most aircraft in a combat zone, flies without lights.

Every time they took off the crew anticipated being shot down. It was every airman's nightmare. This was especially true for Montgomery, who was still unqualified to fly the C-130 when she landed in Qatar. Although she had had an auspicious career to date, she remained untested in the Herk. She had a lot to learn, and under more ideal circumstances, she would have gone through that training on friendly territory back in the States.

As the aircraft climbed into the sky above Baghdad, Montgomery heard a monotone voice say—

Break left.

SAM (surface-to-air-missile).

Seven o'clock.

Flares.

Loadmaster Brandon Touchon, stationed in the belly of the plane, had just issued a threat call, alerting everyone on the airplane that one or more hostile forces had targeted the aircraft. Touchon was one of two loadmasters who stood on either side of the aircraft, looked through a porthole window on the top of a door, and notified the crew when they spotted an incoming missile. It was a critical job because the C-130E model they were flying didn't carry weapons. Their minimal self-defense was Kevlar installed to reinforce the doors and the area around the cockpit, and the personal weapons the crew carried onboard with them in case they were shot down and had to fight their way to friendly ground.

The Herk is a reactive and not a defensive aircraft, which sounds kind of odd on first reflection. At the time it was built, during the Vietnam era, there wasn't a great need for an elaborate defense system. The Viet Cong didn't have anti-aircraft guns, let alone missiles. At best, some ground troops might have taken pot shots at the airplane with an old French carbine. Newer models of the C-130 come with defensive systems.

Loadmasters have gotten good at having sharp eyes and have kept many a C-130 in the sky by spotting missiles in time to take evasive action. When Touchon made the threat call, his manner was so blasé that Montgomery wasn't sure if he was serious. Then the Weapons Missile System (WMS) went off, emitting a loud tone in the headsets that could be heard whether or not the crew was wearing them, and more importantly, confirming the threat call.

The WMS detects the type of missile that is targeting the aircraft based on the signal the rocket puts out and determines the direction it originated. Then it launches flares from the back of the aircraft to distract the rocket. The missiles are looking for infrared signals and heat from the plane. The flares emit a hotter signal than the plane to draw the rocket or missile away from the aircraft.

HOLY SHIT!

That was the initial reaction of a crew that never knew when it was going to be the target of a missile. It was always a complete surprise—the ultimate HOLY SHIT. Montgomery's first thought was, *This is not goddamn happening to me!* Then she thought, *Goddamn it—this is happening to me!* as she maneuvered to avoid one or more missiles.

Moments later, Touchon's threat call was validated as flares started popping out of the Herk. It sounded like when you're sitting in a car and someone pounds on it. Visually, the flares look like lightning shooting from the Herk.

One of the biggest fears for any pilot is that he or she responds to a threat call by turning the aircraft in the wrong direction. Pilots can alleviate some of their worries by attending pre-mission briefings and finding out who their loadmasters are going to be and who will be standing at which door. Montgomery knew in advance where Touchon was standing. So when she heard him say "break," she automatically knew which direction she needed to turn. "That's Brandon. He's in the left door." Making a threat call is so crucial that the airmen did as much as they could to idiot proof the process, including putting a big "L" by the left window and a big "R" by the right window so there wouldn't be any confusion when it came time to tell the pilot which way to turn the aircraft. A seemingly small act such as flip-flopping the loadmasters could lead to confusion and prove fatal for the crew.

The missile tracks on the heat of the aircraft's engine and usually comes up from the back side of the plane because that's the hottest side. If it's coming up the left side of the plane, Montgomery wants to turn into the missile to shield the engine. It's a completely unnatural move, but that's how you defeat a heat-seeking missile. If she accidentally turned away from the missile, and broke right, she would make herself twice as big a target as before, and she and her crew would probably die. Normally, loadmasters won't flip flop. In fact, many will stand in the same door for an entire 120-day rotation for that reason.

By now, the slightly agitated crew was expecting an incoming missile. Montgomery immediately maneuvered to evade it. She reacted before her instructor could follow her on the yoke and throttles. In this type of a crisis situation, if Montgomery hadn't responded fast, the more experienced instructor or co-pilot would have taken control of the airplane and executed the defensive maneuver. Both the threat warning and her quick reaction startled Montgomery. Halfway through the maneuver she wondered, *Damn, am I turning the right way? Is that what he said?* She had a fifty-fifty shot at getting it right.

The loadmasters continued looking out their windows to see if a missile was tracking them, and the navigator and the engineer in the cockpit did the same to try to find the source that had set off the flares.

Typically after a missile was shot at the Herk from one direction, the Iraqis knew that the maneuvering made the aircraft vulnerable in the opposite direction. So more often than not the Iraqis fired something that wasn't too dangerous, like a rocket-propelled grenade, to get the pilots to maneuver, and then they shot a missile with higher probability from the other side. That happened all the time. But the pilots knew that strategy and were expecting it.

After she maneuvered, Montgomery and her co-pilot started talking on the radio to air traffic control, other aircraft, and the joint service command center—telling them where the Herk was located and what the crew saw, if anything. Montgomery gave as many specifics as possible about the threat. If there were helicopters or ground troops nearby, they might haul ass to the site of the rocket launch and nail some insurgents. It was especially important that no other aircraft fly over the spot where they had been a target. There could be a van on the ground filled with missiles and insurgents waiting for an opportunity to fire them at the next aircraft that flew by.

Less than a minute had passed since the WMS went off when it sensed another missile and started popping out more flares. Montgomery's crew didn't see anything so no one knew where the missile was coming from and where it was headed. After hearing the system go off a second time, the crew aborted its final mission of the evening and flew back to Kuwait.

Since that night, Montgomery, speaking in a quiet, monotone voice, has gained a certain amount of pleasure poking fun at Touchon's less than animated threat call.

"Break left. SAM. Seven o'clock. Flares."

"Afterwards, I'm like, 'Brandon, HEYYYY, HEYYYYY . . . Is that your first time you've called?'" Montgomery said.

"Yeah," he said.

But that was Brandon. He didn't get excited about anything. And from then on, they laughed about it. Break left, SAM . . . Touchon was considering a career in the ministry.

From the moment she arrived at Pope, and then Qatar, Montgomery was under the microscope. It was as though the airmen of the squadron were determined *not* to accept her. However, she knew what she was getting into and was up to the challenge. Montgomery is a high-energy individual who in addition to being a wife, mother of three children, and commander, also found time to train for marathons and triathlons. At Pope and in the desert, she often arrived at work before her airmen and left after them. Giving her an extra boost was the Pleasant Morning Buzz java from Whole Foods, mailed to her in abundance by her husband, Todd.

The airmen became intensely dedicated to Montgomery, but it was an allegiance she had to earn. They knew when she chose to go to Qatar that she had left her family behind. This action alone helped her establish credibility in a squadron where more than half of the airmen were married and had children. The commander couldn't speak with authority on how tough it was to deploy if she hadn't done the same.

The airmen also noticed that when there weren't enough loadmasters to go around, their commander would volunteer to fill in. In Qatar, the loadmaster was the most undermanned position in the aircraft crew. It was also the most physically demanding role. When it was hot, the airmen got sick and couldn't fly, so there were a lot of loadmaster holes. During combat, there always have to be two loadmasters, one in each door, but one doesn't have to be a loadmaster as long as he or she has been through training and knows how to respond to a threat call.

Filling in for other people when positions were understaffed came naturally for Montgomery, who has watched her dad do the same since she was in grade school and he was the installation commander at Scott Air Force Base. Montgomery remembers one time when it was snowing. Her dad went out to the flight line, stopped the driver of the snowplow, gave him a thermos of hot coffee, and told him to sit in his staff car while the general drove the plow for a while. Airmen who have been in the Air Force for nearly two decades said they had never seen the likes of Montgomery before.

Airmen who worked and flew with Montgomery likened their female commander to the C-130. Montgomery and the Herk are about the same age, work tirelessly, and expect a lot from their crews while giving much in return. And they have similar personalities. However, Montgomery can claim significantly better health than the dilapidated aircraft, which has grown weary over the years. Although they were both born around the same time, in the early 1960s, the C-130E went to work a lot sooner than Montgomery. The aircraft began earning its valiant reputation as early as the Vietnam War, when it first transported cargo in and out of the jungle. Montgomery didn't start flying until after she graduated from the Air Force Academy in 1986. Another decade would pass before she could fly in combat.

Sometimes, when the airmen talk about their aircraft and their commander, it's hard to determine which one they're talking about. They'll say things like, "It's her personality that wins you over," or "It has such a personality. It asks a lot of you but it gives a lot back." Oftentimes, airmen will hear the Herk or Montgomery before they see them. In the case of the plane, the Herk's engine has a unique sound that enables the airmen to distinguish it from other aircraft. Likewise, their commander has an unusual laugh that sets her apart. If Montgomery is walking down the hallway, airmen will recognize her laughter before they see her.

Those in the 41st Airlift Squadron looked forward to flying with their commander because she was a hands-on boss who didn't mind getting dirty. She liked to kid around and tell stories, both of which were good for morale. To some of her crew she was a stand-up comic, a regular Ellen DeGeneres. She'd poke fun at people, play practical jokes on her airmen, and do just plain silly things. She has a goofy picture of herself in a flak vest that she printed on labels and made into stickers. The photo was about the size of a nickel. She'd stick it to her co-pilot's headset so when she was flying and looked at the pilot seated beside her, she'd see a funny picture of herself.

Montgomery and the Herk are similar in dependability. Everyone jokes about the Herk because it always breaks down. But when the airmen were on a mission and it malfunctioned, it still brought them back. You could shoot it, hit it, lob missiles into it, and smash it into the ground. For the past forty years the Herk has flown in combat and very few C-130s have been lost. It was going to bring you home. Montgomery was the same way.

When you're flying in combat and the temperature is 140 degrees and the sand is blowing, the airmen have one purpose and that is to get in, get the troops, and get them out safely. And the C-130 did that every time. But for the aircraft to do that, it needed someone special at the control. That person had to understand that if you let it, the plane would bring you home. Montgomery understood that. When she stepped into the plane, she wasn't the squadron commander; she was the aircraft commander. One airman said he would fly to hell and back with Montgomery and do it with a smile because she understands the true mentality of flying, the mission, and ensuring that the crew comes home.

In Iraq, eight out of every ten missions performed by Montgomery and her squadron were "packs," meaning they were carrying troops—their most precious cargo. While the crews of the Herk loved to fly the Marines and soldiers out of combat, they hated to bring them in. They'd fly in fresh troops who had never been to Iraq before or not-so-fresh troops who had been away for a couple of weeks for some R&R. Or they relocated troops to another area of Iraq. For Montgomery, it was hard flying troops into combat zones because when she looked at the young men and women, she knew that some wouldn't make it back alive and even those who did would be changed forever. They weren't going to be the same people when they returned to the United States.

Montgomery didn't transport many wounded troops during her first deployment, but she did move some non-American soldiers who had been killed in the war. She picked up an Iraqi who had died in a prison in southern Iraq. He was lying in a big case used to transfer the dead. She knew it was an Iraqi insurgent body because the handlers told her so. Montgomery was used to seeing transfer cases waiting to be moved. Whenever she saw them, she stopped what she was doing to pay her respects to the deceased. But what caught her off guard this day was a silver case used to stow an Iraqi body.

In contrast, two nights later Montgomery traveled to Mosul to pick up a Turkish civilian truck driver who had been beheaded by Iraqi insurgents. The airmen joked a little about whether he was going to come out in a transfer case or a body bag. The difference between the two is huge. The body bag is dark brown and made of heavy plastic, like a thick lawn bag. It's obvious when there is a body inside because it pokes out in all the right places and there is a tag with the individual's name on it. Montgomery made everyone bet—bag or case. It may sound irreverent to joke and bet during such a somber occasion, but the airmen knew they were picking up an HR, human remains. And their intentions were meant to be anything but disrespectful. If anything, they were overly emotional. Whenever they transferred a body, whether it was an ally or an enemy, it affected Montgomery and the airmen. Montgomery tried to lighten the mood the only way she knew how, through humor, if she thought her airmen would respond well to it.

A truck backed up as close as possible to the C-130. The ramp between the truck and plane was dark. A big tarp, when lifted, exposed a series of bodies still on stretchers. Montgomery was disheartened to see an American ally in a two-bit body bag when the Iraqi insurgent was in a transfer case. Later, she learned that there weren't any transfer cases in the area. One by one the bodies were put into body bags like you would put a sandwich into a plastic bag, and then carried up the ramp and onto the C-130. All this was eerie and reminded the commander of the opening scene of the 1986 movie *Platoon* when the new guys walked out of the back of a plane only to be replaced by body bags being transported back home. It was no longer just a scene in a movie. It was chilling and personal.

Montgomery traveled to Qatar as a commander but not to oversee her squadron. At the time, her airmen were under some-one else's authority. She just wanted to see what and how they were doing, and to get some real-life combat experience so she would be ready the next time her squadron deployed. The follow-ing year, in 2005, she and her airmen returned to the Middle East. This time, Montgomery was based out of Ali Al Salem Air Base in Kuwait. Expectations were higher, as she now took on the dual role of aircraft commander and commander of a squadron of 200 airmen. Both jobs would challenge her in unexpected ways.

On the ground in Kuwait, Montgomery's job may not have been life threatening but it could be as intense and as stressful as dodging incoming missiles. Early in her first full deployment with the 41st Airlift Squadron, a thirty-three-year-old female staff ser-geant charged Montgomery's senior master sergeant, one of the highest positions an enlisted person can hold, with sexual harass-ment. The staff sergeant and the senior master sergeant had been communicating through e-mail in the desert. The content of the e-mails became progressively more personal and emotionally revealing, more so than one would expect between supervisor and worker. The master sergeant grew more and more enamored with the young enlisted woman and was accused of making unwanted advances. It was a difficult case for Montgomery because it didn't appear to be black and white. She wasn't sure who was at fault but she also realized it wasn't her place to make that decision.

The accusations affected Montgomery on a personal and professional level because in addition to their working relationship, the master sergeant and the commander were longtime friends. They had flown C-141s together, and she had brought him to the squadron to supervise her loadmasters. He was prosecuted, found guilty, and sent home.

Prior to the charges against her master sergeant, Montgomery had heard in workshops that sexual harassment cases distracted from the mission, but she wasn't convinced of that until the accusations surfaced in her squadron. Then she became a true believer as the episode took the focus off the war and gave everyone something else to think and talk about. As commander, she had to move the squadron beyond what had happened. She held a meeting and addressed the situation. When there is a lot of gray area in a case it makes matters much more difficult. For a while, the loadmasters and enlisted personnel were split.

Montgomery also had to be able to help her young pilots through the stress of combat. It wasn't unusual for crews to fly multiple missions in one day. Between flights, one pilot/navigator was having a panic attack and wanted to take an anti-anxiety pill. He thought he was having a nervous breakdown. Airmen can't fly if they're taking anti-anxiety pills. They're not supposed to take anything that can affect their faculties, not even Motrin. If they did, they could be taken off flight status. If a pilot took Actifed and had an accident, the Air Force would require a urinalysis right away to see if there was anything unusual in the airman's system. Frequently when crew members started requesting anti-anxiety medicine it simply meant they needed some time off.

Montgomery's command referred several airmen to the psychiatrist and they were fine afterward.

One of Montgomery's greatest challenges during this deployment had to do with how well she handled the grief that came from missing her children. All three of her children were in their formative years, five and under, which meant Mom missed some critical moments she'll never be able to recapture. Five-year-old Molly lost her first tooth. Charlie, four, made the switch from drinking out of a bottle to drinking from a glass. And Betsy ("Booboo"), just under two years old, spoke her first words when her mom was gone.

Two of Montgomery's children were born a year apart but within one day of each other, and those days fell right before Mother's Day. May 8, 2005—Mother's Day—was not one of the lieutenant colonel's better days.

By mid-morning, Montgomery still hadn't left her room. She was living in a metal corrugated building that had four separate entrances for four different rooms. She had fairly nice furniture but couldn't keep the room clean because of the desert sand and dust. She had a double bed that she covered with embroidered sheets from home and used monogrammed towels that her mother had sent to her.

It was a Sunday, so technically Montgomery didn't have to work. But that didn't stop First Sergeant Dan Beasley, the commander's right-hand man, from calling his boss on her cell phone. She didn't answer, which was strange because Montgomery always took his calls. While they were in Kuwait, day in, day out, Beasley was the most important person in her life. This easy-going and likeable guy, with twenty-four years in the Air Force, was charged with protecting Montgomery and seeing that she found time between flights and administrative duties to rejuvenate. He accepted his role with a strong sense of loyalty and vigilance. In the process, Beasley became Montgomery's closest confidant.

Before deploying to Kuwait, Montgomery told Beasley she would need him to pull her out of difficult times and vice versa. And that she would need him more than he would need her. Mother's Day was one of those times.

When Montgomery didn't answer her phone, Beasley went to her room. He climbed the temporary metal stairs that led to her door, and stood there and knocked until she answered.

"Time to come to work," he told her through the closed door. Since it was Sunday, Beasley didn't mean it literally. He just wanted Montgomery to come out of her room and get some fresh air. That way he could take a good look at her and see for himself that she was okay. He wanted her to come out and play, take her mind off things, but there are some days when you just don't want to do that.

"I'm not leaving," she said, while thinking to herself, *Okay, there is a legitimate reason why I feel like shit today. I'm thousands of miles from my family.*

There was the distance, and there was the package she received the previous day from her children that included pictures they had drawn. Seeing the pictures made the commander ache even more for her children. She needed some time alone.

"Get your ass out here," Beasley said, as he continued to bang on the door.

While flying in the Herk, a lot of times the airmen who were also parents talked about their children. One question came up repeatedly: What's the best age for you to be away from your kids? The father of an infant might express regret over missing a child's first steps while the parent of a teenager had just missed seeing his daughter on prom night or his son score his first soccer goal. By

Marine Lance Corporal Chrissy DeCaprio and a provisional MP wait in the staging area of Al Taqaddum for a convoy to begin.

DeCaprio and her fire team prepare for a patrol.

DeCaprio during an unusually long 28-hour convoy to and from Al Asad. At one point they found an IED and had to wait for EOD to clear it. Then they had issues with some of the trucks in the convoy. It was a long day. One of DeCaprio's Marines was joking around and said, "Smile, D!" This expression was the best she could come up with.

DeCaprio on a dismounted patrol of an Iraqi road outside Al Taqaddum. She was looking for IEDs and possible triggers—making sure her patrol was able to pass safely. DeCaprio's Marines liked to make fun of her, saying that all her gear made her look even smaller than she was and that she was "playing" Marine.

DeCaprio as a turret gunner manning the 50-cal.

The results of an IED attack on the lead vehicle in one of DeCaprio's convoys. It was estimated that the vehicle was hit with at least triple-stacked rounds. There were no casualties, but nearly everyone on the convoy was wounded. DeCaprio's vehicle was very close to the damaged vehicle, so she and her Marines were the first to respond.

Sergeant Bobi Severyn and Sergeant Cassie Lucero serving in Camp Fallujah, Iraq, 2006.

First Lieutenants Deb Turley (CH-53D pilot), Natalie Moore (CH-53E pilot) and Amy Roznowski (AH-1W pilot) at the Marine Corps Ball in Pensacola, Florida, one month prior to their "Winging" in November 2003.

Natalie Moore inside a CH-53E.

First Lieutenant Lindsay Mathwick stands in front of the Hands of Victory monument in Baghdad, Iraq.

Corporal Lynn Murillo, the late Major Megan McClung, and Staff Sergeant Amy Forsythe served on the public affairs team for I MEF in Camp Fallujah, Iraq.

Army Specialist Janet Sutter of the 18th Military Police Brigade provides security during a mission in Baghdad in December 2003. PHOTO BY STAFF SERGEANT MARVIN L. DANIELS / COURTESY OF U.S. ARMY

Army Specialist Jennie Baez of the 47th Forward Support Battalion provides security during an operation in Al Anbar Province, October 2006. PHOTO BY LANCE CORPORAL CLIFTON D. SAMS / COURTESY OF U.S. ARMY

the time these conversations had ended, everyone agreed that there was no good age.

For the first fifteen years she served in the Air Force, Montgomery was single. Then she married and started a family. When the fathers, especially the new parents, talk about missing birthdays, Montgomery knows their heartache. She also knows what it is like to move into a new house and two years later still smell its newness because she has spent so little time there. She knows what it feels like to live in a town for two years and still get lost driving to the store. She knows what it feels like to not know things about her children that 99.9 percent of moms take for granted. Montgomery recalls a day when she bought Molly and Charlie hot dogs at the golf course. She had to ask them what they wanted on their hot dogs. The woman in the restaurant preparing the food gave her a look as if to ask what kind of mom doesn't know what her children take on their hot dogs?

Because she is a mom, Montgomery can also be tough on someone who, after several deployments, hasn't learned to cope with being away from his children. By that time, Montgomery is thinking, *I've been out here a lot longer than you have. Get over it.* Now if a male commander said that to an airman, the airman might think to himself, *Fuck you!* If a female says that to one of her airmen, the airman is more likely to believe that if she's a woman and can get over it, then he sure as heck can.

One airman, with tears in his eyes, visited Montgomery in her office one day. His one-year-old back home had pneumonia. His child wasn't in the hospital. Montgomery reassured him that lots of babies get pneumonia. It's normal. The fact that his child wasn't in the hospital was a good sign. It probably meant the illness wasn't a life-or-death situation. She was able to talk him through it because she had been through similar illnesses with her children. She knew how he felt and as a woman, Montgomery was willing to take the extra time needed to talk to him through it. That would become important when it was time for that airman to fly again. He would be able to focus because she had helped to ease his mind. If a male commander had been in a similar situation, he may have been more direct about the child's condition. Where Montgomery completely transformed to the role of mother, the male commander probably wouldn't have put on his father hat.

It may sound like Montgomery had it all together, but in wartime there's no such thing. No one is exempt from feeling out of control when something happens back home and they are helpless because they are thousands of miles away. No one is immune from feeling sad when they miss a child's birthday, an anniversary, or the memorial service of a grandparent. In some situations, experience doesn't matter. You are going to be affected by what's happening back in the States and what's going on in the desert no matter what—because you are human.

When Beasley went looking for Montgomery, he couldn't blame her for being sad. But in combat, her role as commander took precedence. After Beasley had spent several minutes banging on her door, Montgomery emerged from her room wearing her black Rayban sunglasses. Although they covered her tear-stained eyes, Beasley knew what was going on. Montgomery was fairly transparent when it came to her moods. She was always so full of positive energy that he knew immediately when something was wrong. Her energy level dropped; she smiled less.

Together, they walked to the back of the chow hall and found an empty table. She talked about her children; he listened. Later in the day, she flew to keep herself busy. It might sound like a bad idea, but flying gave Montgomery something other than her children to focus on. Instead of wallowing in self-pity, she reminded herself why she was in Iraq in the first place. She told herself, *I've got fifty Army soldiers I need to transport so that Molly, Charlie or Betsy don't have to come back here fifteen years from now and do the same job I'm doing.*

When the deployment began, Montgomery and Beasley would sit in the back of the chow hall and talk comfortably, but eventually their meals became less private. The airmen began to see mealtime as an opportunity to talk with the commander. Back home, Montgomery was able to separate herself from her work by going home at the end of each day. In the desert, there was no going home. And while she appreciated that the airmen wanted to talk and bounce ideas off her, sometimes she just needed a break. There was no end to the questions and comments. Some young airmen wanted to know about their next assignment. They were eager to learn about their future. Some thanked her for the e-mails she sent to family members—including parents—back home informing them about the squadron's activities. Others came to her with suggestions. And still others sought her out to request a new roommate or to ask to fly with another aircraft commander.

Montgomery, and especially Beasley, came up with some creative ways to avoid interruptions. On one or two occasions, Beasley snuck Montgomery off their base and to another military installation. When they reached their destination, usually within an hour's drive of their airfield, the lieutenant colonel would relinquish her cell phone to Beasley. If it rang, he'd step away and answer it. One time Montgomery spent the day swimming in and relaxing by a pool on another base. Then she and Beasley drove to the PX, where they purchased cigars and Near beer, a non-alcoholic malt beverage. They drove back to their base in a small pick up truck, windows down, smoking cigars, and drinking beer. When the day was over, Montgomery felt refreshed, as though she had spent a day at the lake.

Walking the seven-mile perimeter of the air base also helped Montgomery put some distance between herself and her airmen. It's not that the commander wanted to get away from her airmen. It's that she wanted to get closer to herself. She described it as a "delicate balance between distancing yourself from your airmen enough for your own self preservation, but being in them enough that they know it and you understand what is happening. There's a point in a commander where you have to find the perfect balance—I'm one of my guys and I empathize and sympathize with them, but on the other end of the spectrum, I'm the commander. I have to get them combat ready to perform their mission."

She likened her position to that of Gregory Peck's in the classic World War II movie *Twelve O'Clock High.* In the film, a squadron commander has reached his breaking point, and tough guy Peck steps in to replace him only to face the same fate. Peck tries to maintain emotional distance between himself and his airmen, but it's hard. Just like it was nearly impossible for Montgomery to sit back at Pope and wait for her squadron to return, or to stay on the ground when her airmen were flying missions. She chose to fly a lot in Iraq because she wanted to know what the airmen were going through on their flights and experience it firsthand.

Peck explained in the movie that it always comes down to the group commander. "He's going to bust open. Why? Because he's a first rate guy and he's thinking about them instead of missions." It's called over-identification with your men.

Montgomery wasn't exactly sending her fliers into swarms of fighters and fields of flak, but she faced a similar challenge: "I think when you care about people it's more bothersome that you can't take care of every little problem they have."

Commanders have the luxury of determining how much they will fly. Some fly very little while others fly a lot. Montgomery could have said that she wasn't going to fly, but that wasn't her style. She wasn't a desk jockey who just sat there and said, "I've done my time. I don't want to go anywhere. Or I have three children at home and don't want to risk my life by flying in combat." When she did something, she put her whole self into it. She put too much into it sometimes.

Her attitude made all the difference to the airmen under her command thousands of miles from home. Airmen say they can tell which commanders care about their people and she genuinely cares. When she says something, she means it. She doesn't hold back.

A soft spoken pilot named Jim McCall summed it up this way, "It really, really makes a difference when you're there with someone who cares, is passionate about it, and is capable of making good decisions and analyzing things. Unlike any other commander we've ever had, she's unique. She knows the names of not only every person in the squadron but also their families. She actually knows what's going on in their families."

James Schram, a technical sergeant who flew with Montgomery in Iraq, experienced her exceptional leadership early on, even before he began working for her. He met Montgomery in the hallway of a building at Little Rock Air Force Base. Because they were both wearing Black Cat patches, they stopped and acknowledged one another. Montgomery introduced herself. Two months later Schram ran into Montgomery at Pope. He was dressed in civilian clothes. She said, "Hey, James. We met in Little Rock." He couldn't believe that she not only recognized him but that she remembered his name.

McCall grew more and more animated when he talked about flying with Montgomery. "It's a blast. She's a good pilot. She engages in a million conversations, is quick witted, and keeps morale up. I'm amazed at how she can leave her desk, compartmentalize what's going on there, and then fly a combat mission."

Remarkably, the female lieutenant colonel and first commander of a combat squadron in the Air Force still lacks self confidence. She attributes it to being a woman and to the Air Force.
She has spent a good part of her life growing into the roles and
the positions she has held. "The Air Force does that." But Schram
sees it another way: what Montgomery calls a lack of confidence
anyone else would recognize as an extremely competitive attitude. "She wants to be the best at whatever she does. If she were
digging ditches in Macon, Georgia, she would be the best ditch-
digger the state of Georgia has ever seen. She will do and work
and sweat and cry and bleed until she can be the best but she will
never recognize it as being the best. She could do a great job on
something but her self-critiquing wouldn't let her recognize it as
a great job."

When you work for someone like that it does nothing but
bring out the best in everyone else. "It's not even a matter of liking her—it's just working for her that makes you want to be better
than anyone else," Schram said. "She brings that out. She doesn't
expect it or ask for it."

March 22, 2005, was an unusual day all around. In the hours
leading up to an afternoon flight, Montgomery volunteered to fill
in for another pilot and fly to Balad Air Base to pick up troops.
The plane was having rudder problems, so the maintenance crew
replaced the Herk with a spare aircraft. This was hardly cause for
alarm. The Herks were always breaking down. When she made
the switch from the C-141 to the C-130, Montgomery got used to
Herk mechanics fixing or jerry-rigging something on the aircraft
to keep it going. She also learned that she could beat the crap out
of the Herk and it would still do what she wanted it to do. While

her allegiance was at one time to the C-141, to hear her talk you would think Montgomery had been flying Herks all her life. She speaks fondly of her new (old) aircraft and wouldn't think of trading it for a slicker model. Granted, the newer models don't have as many maintenance problems because they are highly computerized. But when they do break down it can take days or weeks to repair, whereas on the Herk, the engineers just put some duct tape over a hole and the crew is on its way.

Pilots like Montgomery, who were fairly new to flying C-130s, tended to have more patience with the ailing aircraft than a veteran C-130 pilot. Pilots who had been flying the C-130s for a long period of time became easily frustrated when the aircraft broke down because they knew the Herk during its glory days and knew its capabilities. Before Montgomery climbed the ladder into the Herk on that morning in March, she walked around the aircraft to make sure nothing had fallen off and to see that the windows were clean.

When the crew took off, it was running several hours behind schedule. The afternoon mission turned into an evening flight as the C-130 began its climb out of Kuwait. Since they were only about twenty miles from the border and the combat zone, they had to reach a certain altitude in a short time to be safe from missiles. To make the fast climb, they "spiraled up," making circles during their ascent instead of flying in a straight line or on a particular route.

Sitting beside Montgomery was a young pilot, Lieutenant Tim Houston. Also in the cockpit were the navigator, Steve Morris, and the engineer, Schram. In the back were two loadmasters, Airmen Ken Hardwick and Stuart Hopson.

While they climbed toward the border, each crew member performed a series of flight checks. In the cockpit, Schram made sure all four engines, two on each wing, were functioning normally. Immediately, he determined that the number four engine had an abnormally excessive vibration. It was malfunctioning.

"Pilot," Schram said into his helmet mike. "Eng. We've got a problem with number four."

"What do you got, eng?"

"We've got a really bad vibration in number four. Take a feel."

They weren't going to make a decision as significant as shutting down an engine based on one person's opinion. As the pilot, Montgomery had final authority. She touched the throttle. As an aircraft commander, one of her responsibilities was to respect each person's knowledge of the plane. That deference helped keep the crew combat effective. She didn't always have to take their suggestions, but she did have to be able to weigh their input before making an informed decision. The throttle vibrates to begin with. Montgomery didn't feel any additional vibration, but it was possible the throttle was shaking more than usual and it was so subtle only the engineer could detect it. She wanted to trust the expert, her engineer. Montgomery had to decide between letting the engine run and telling the engineer he was wrong, shutting down the engine and continuing their mission, or heading back to their airfield. She decided that since they were so close to their airfield, they would shut down the engine and head back.

A tough break. There had been a lot of tough breaks lately— too many. In combat, a pilot needs luck, and no doubt about it, Montgomery had hit a streak of bad luck. This was the third time in three flights that she had lost an engine and had to abort a mission. It happened, but you didn't want to make a habit of it. You'd start to feel jinxed. Your crew would begin fretting that you were jinxed.

When Schram told her an engine was out, Montgomery's first thought was, *Are you kidding? You're killing me here. Everyone is making fun of me. They're saying, 'I'm not flying with the boss anymore.'*

The crew in the cockpit had memorized the emergency procedure for shutting down an engine. They knew it by heart, verbatim,
including words that were in quotation marks, words that were
hyphenated, and the location of periods and exclamation points.
They had to have it memorized because in an emergency situation,
they wouldn't have time to take out the manual and read it.

Once they put themselves on a good heading back to base,
Montgomery instructed her co-pilot to shut down engine four.
They declared an in-flight emergency with Mahallah, the control
center they were in touch with prior to switching over to the air
base tower. Mahallah directed them to a location about twelve
miles off the southern end of the runway. They trained on three
engines so technically this wasn't a big deal. As long as nothing
else went wrong.

The air traffic controller notified Montgomery that there was
another C-130 in their airspace. That wasn't necessarily cause for
alarm. It wasn't unusual for more than one Herk to be flying in
the same airspace. But Montgomery needed more information
than that: Where is it? How close is it to her aircraft? She was
already flying under less than ideal circumstances and now this? It
was night time. She could see ground lights but would she be able
to see the lights of another Herk? Her aircraft was crippled. She
didn't have time to be screwing around. Since the altitude and
clock position of the other plane were unknown, Montgomery's
crew didn't know where the hell to look. When they scanned the
sky outside the aircraft, they couldn't see any other planes. They
had to be able to see it to prevent themselves from turning, climbing, or descending into it.

Air traffic control in Kuwait was still antiquated but it was getting better. There was a lot of, "Hey, I'm here. Where's the other
guy?" And it was crowded. There were airplanes coming and going
at night and you couldn't see them. But it wasn't like Chicago's

O'Hare. The airspace was very controlled. The controllers basically cut a swath of airspace for the Herks, along with a way in and out of all these airfields and pilots had to adhere to the rules.

Putting two planes on the same altitude was the worst possible scenario because it would have been so easy for one to turn into the other. Everyone in the aircraft, except for Montgomery and her co-pilot, Houston, manned a window. They were all asking the same questions, Okay, where are they? Are we aft of them? Are we on the same heading?

As each second passed, Montgomery got closer and closer to the runway, which meant she had to configure the aircraft to land. Her crew couldn't spend the next five minutes looking for a plane because by that time they would be over the airfield. Yet if they didn't remain in the windows there could be a mid-air collision. Montgomery's first priority was to get rid of the extra stress and get the aircraft on the ground. She got on the radio.

"Back off!" she told the other aircraft. "Turn outbound." She let them know which way her aircraft was heading, its altitude, and that she was preparing to land.

"Get out of the way."

Montgomery had to be firm. It would be a lot easier to talk about what had happened on the ground after the fact than it was to argue about it in the air. The other aircraft was from her squadron.

They were at 3,500 feet and on a straight course for landing. The other aircraft was still nowhere in sight. Montgomery and her crew had already talked about how they were going to land the plane. If they couldn't get the aircraft on the ground on their first try, they would perform a go-around procedure on three engines.

Knowing the other plane was out there troubled Montgomery. She flew into the airfield tighter than usual, a decision that hurried everything up, but according to the flight engineer, it was the right course of action. By the time the other C-130 backed off, because of the position of Montgomery's aircraft and the short distance from the runway, she couldn't land the plane on the first attempt. Her aircraft was too high and she couldn't get it down fast enough. When Montgomery realized she wasn't going to make a neat landing, she decided not to rush it. She leveled off the plane, closed the pattern, and went back to land nice and normal.

Nine times out of ten it's not what happens to the plane that kills you; it's your bad reaction that kills you. You don't want to compound the problem. Montgomery came back around in the Herk and made a decent approach to the runway. The last thing she wanted to do was to make a bad landing and close the airfield, because then she would be the big show. Montgomery didn't want to be a big show.

All this time, the pilot, co-pilot, and engineer were talking to each other about how the airplane would handle without an engine, the location of the other aircraft, and what to expect from the aircraft when they landed the Herk. The crew was trying to "get ahead" of the airplane and anticipate its next move instead of being caught off guard, which could be deadly. If Montgomery thought aloud about doing something dangerous, the rest of the crew would have a chance to voice their opinions. Or if Montgomery wasn't considering a particular option, the engineer or navigator could clue her in. On a C-130, a crew airplane, it's all about backing up one another. As the aircraft commander, it was Montgomery's responsibility to take everyone's comments into consideration. History has shown that some plane crashes could have been avoided if the crew had thought the captain would listen and spoken up. It's called crew resource management. Billions of dollars are spent on finding the most effective way for a crew to work together and the resources they need to be successful. Each crew member brings his or her skills and abilities to the fight, and hopefully the aircraft commander can sift through the information quickly and make the best decision.

As the aircraft came across the front of the runway, different scenarios played out in Montgomery's mind. Without four engines, the aircraft was less symmetrical. Am I going to have difficulty landing this aircraft and controlling it once it's on the ground? How much will it pull in one direction when she lands, and when she puts the props in reverse, how much will it pull in the other direction?

Twenty feet from touching down, a critical time when landing an aircraft, the Herk lost another engine. This time it was the number three engine—on the same side as the number four engine. So they had two engines working on one side of the aircraft and no engines on the other side. It was the equivalent of having two flat tires on the same side of a truck traveling more than 100 miles per hour. Also, the aircraft hadn't been flying long so it still had a full combat fuel load. The crew was landing with a heavier plane that would sink faster to the ground. The aircraft was traveling at 118 knots when it hit the ground, shot to the left, and headed off the runway. It seemed to be the worse possible scenario, but it wasn't over yet.

When Montgomery attempted to put engines one and two into reverse to slow the plane, this action only aggravated her ability to control the aircraft. She grabbed hold of the nose wheel, a small steering wheel, to swing the aircraft around while she simultaneously kicked the rudder to help push the plane back to the center line. But the heavy aircraft was moving too fast for the nose wheel to react. For a few terrifying seconds it was like driving a truck—without tires on one side and with very little brakes—at a high speed on black ice. Montgomery should have remained terrified, but by now she was just plain mad. *Goddamn it, why isn't the airplane reacting the way it's supposed to?*

She got excited. At one point she was "standing on the brakes"—an expression that means she was pushing the brakes to the ground. The action is similar to when you think you are going to rear end another car and you slam on the brakes. However, she had to be careful not to push too hard. Otherwise, she could blow out all her tires and then she'd have no control. Soon, the aircraft came to a dry skid. Montgomery regained some control of the plane and basically dragged it off the runway and onto the taxiway. But by this time nothing she did caused the plane to react in a normal way.

The runway was approximately 9,800 feet long and 150 feet wide. On a normal landing, with three engines, they would be able to stop within 5,000 feet. It would take less distance than that with four engines. With only two engines, they used 8,500 feet—not because it wouldn't stop but because they were trying to control it. The control tower instructed Montgomery to turn the aircraft 180 degrees and exit to the taxiway which was narrower than the runway. They had slowed to twenty miles per hour but the C-130 still only wanted to go in one direction—opposite the taxiway. The aircraft commander didn't want to drive off the runway, into the grass, and over lights. It was a "pilot thing"—she so badly wanted the airplane to follow her lead.

"Boss," Schram finally said. "We've gotta shut her down."

When the aircraft finally came to a stop, there was an audible and collective sigh of relief among the crew. No one talked. They couldn't believe what had just happened. About fifteen minutes had passed from the time they shut down the first engine to the time they shut down the plane. Crew members said landing the Herk that evening was as scary if not more terrifying than the times they took enemy fire.

September 30, 2005

Three weeks before she left for her third deployment to the Middle East, Lieutenant Colonel Polly Montgomery was scheduled to make some remarks at the 317th Veterans Group memorial wreath dedication ceremony at Pope Air Force Base. She wasn't the keynote speaker, but as the commander of the 41st Airlift Squadron and host of the ceremony, she was expected to say a few words to an audience of World War II veterans and their spouses. Montgomery had been out of town on military business for ten days, returning the night before the ceremony. The morning of the dedication, I rode with her from her office to the site of the ceremony, Air Park at Pope. Montgomery did not appear stressed but she was noticeably distracted as she thought about what she was going to say to the veterans who had traveled from all over the country to participate in this ceremony. She obviously wanted to say something meaningful and profound, yet with work, family, and travel, she hadn't had the opportunity to write anything down.

When we arrived at the park, Montgomery eased her way into clusters of veterans as if she had known them her entire life. And in some respects, as the daughter of an Air Force general, maybe she had. At times, Montgomery stepped back from one of the groups and took in the big picture. It wasn't easy for her to fade into the background, though, because these veterans weren't used to seeing a female commander of a combat squadron. She was one of the main attractions.

During the ceremony, she stood in formation with some of the airmen from her squadron. When it came time for her to speak, Montgomery's comments were brief, thoughtful, and right on target. She told the veterans that they were heroes and that they had provided big shoulders for her airmen to stand on. She wanted her young airmen to take a good look at those who came before them and to realize that the airmen of today were part of something much bigger than themselves.

"You're standing on the shoulders of giants," Montgomery told her airmen. "You're where you are today because there were people just like you, before you, who endured the strain of war. You're taking their place. You're the next greatest generation."

A man who later stood and read the names of the deceased wept as Montgomery spoke.

Gunnery Sergeant Yolanda Mayo,
United States Marine Corps.

Live from Iraq

*By the time the war started in Iraq, the total number of National Guard and reserve troops on active duty was 188,592. It was the largest reserve call-up since the 1991 Gulf War. These weekend warriors had planned on giving up a weekend a month and two weeks a year for war games in exchange for pay and help getting a college education. But for many the part-time commitment had become a full-time job. A decade ago, the Pentagon required 2 million days of work from its reservists. In 2003 the total climbed to 15 million. Active-duty Marines and soldiers are doing their jobs when they deploy, but reservists, including **Marine Gunnery Sergeant Yolanda Mayo**, are leaving their jobs behind.*

MARCH 17, 2003—THE DAY U.S. PRESIDENT GEORGE W. BUSH GAVE Iraqi leader Saddam Hussein and his sons forty-eight hours to leave Iraq or face "military conflict," Gunnery Sergeant Yolanda Mayo was in Kuwait. As part of the 2nd Marine Expeditionary Brigade (MEB), which later became Task Force Tarawa, Mayo was one of 600 Marines preparing to cross the Line of Departure into Iraq. The trucks and Humvees were lined up, and the Marines were loading their gear onto the vehicles when the sirens sounded to warn of an incoming Scud missile.

At first Mayo, a thirty-five-year-old public affairs chief, and the Marines around her just stood there, stunned. This was the first time—to their knowledge—that the Iraqis had targeted them and they were frightened. When Mayo left North America on a ship headed for the Middle East, she and the other Marines and sailors were under the impression that Saddam had weapons of mass destruction. They had no way of knowing for certain whether Saddam had chemical weapons, so they had to assume the worst. Adding to their anxiety were the two syringes issued to each Marine and sailor. If a Scud landed nearby and released a harmful chemical, the troops were to take one or more of these injections—2-PAM chloride and atropine—to counteract the lethal effects of nerve gas. They were to store the syringes in a pouch in their pants pocket. The troops were especially fearful of Scuds that were armed with VX, the deadliest known nerve agent. As little as 200 micrograms can kill a person. Once they were in Kuwait, Marines in each truck were also given a cage with two pigeons. These birds would ride with them on the convoy. If the pigeons died, the troops were to immediately put on their gas masks because that meant there were hazardous chemicals in the air. The troops in Mayo's truck named their pigeons Anthrax and VX.

After the sirens sounded, almost simultaneously Mayo and the other Marines realized the significance of the alarms.

"Take cover!" they shouted. "Take cover!"

Where? They didn't want to stay near the trucks and Humvees because the vehicles were sitting targets. They ran for the berms—manmade sand dunes—and cement Scud bunkers.

Sweat dripped down Mayo's skin. She covered her brown eyes with a gas mask and adjusted her Kevlar helmet over a mane of long brown hair that she had twisted into a French braid. As she huddled in a berm, waiting for the next explosion, Mayo and the other Marines looked around for their buddies and made sure everyone was accounted for. After a lot of waiting and anticipation, someone finally gave the all clear. The mood remained tense and serious until a Marine across from Mayo said, "So I guess we rate that extra pay now?" His tongue-in-cheek comment referred to the additional pay the military offers for hazardous duty or for being in combat. Mayo burst out laughing. Others laughed so hard they had to take off their gas masks before rolling around in the desert sand. That marked the start of the war for Mayo.

Mayo, a veteran of the first Gulf War, and Captain Kelly Frushour were about to become one of the first female public affairs teams in combat. Mayo, a native of Kawkawlin, Michigan, is five feet seven inches tall and has a medium build. Frushour was born in Ipswich, England. Her mother is British and her father is a retired Air Force colonel. She has lived in Norway, the Azores, and throughout the United States. Frushour is five feet six inches tall, pale, with freckles and light brown hair. She reminds Mayo of the cartoon character Strawberry Shortcake. The two Marines got along well in Iraq because of their ability to find humor in most situations.

In the months ahead, Mayo and Frushour had the critical job of telling stories of the overall war, the battles, and most importantly, of the individual Marines. America can be against the war and still support the Marines in large part because of the personal stories generated by public affairs. Mayo likened these stories to the photo "Raising the Flag on Iwo Jima" by former AP photographer Joe Rosenthal. It's a piece of art that tells the story of the individual Marines and a sailor. That's what public affairs seeks to do. They're trying to capture moments in pictures and in words, and send the photos and stories to the hometowns of Marines and sailors. They wrote or edited the stories of riflemen who fought the insurgents, who trained Iraqi soldiers, and who repaired Iraqi schools and hospitals. But before they could concentrate on reporting the news, the public affairs team had to get over some rough patches.

One of the challenges they faced was the influx of embedded media. The civilian media weren't new to war but how they received and reported the news was different in Iraq. In Vietnam, for the most part reporters attended media pools to get their stories and everyone was given the same information. In Iraq, the reporters, photographers, and TV cameramen traveled with individual units. At the onset of the war, public affairs had so many people in the media to manage that they were unable to fulfill their own mission of telling the Marine Corps story.

There were other challenges, too, such as transmitting news from the battlefield to the United States. The Marine Corps had the video cameras, tapes, and editing systems to capture and produce the stories, but none of that mattered without a satellite phone plan and a large enough bandwidth to transmit the news and pictures back to the States. As soon as the embedded media sent a report to the States, the whole world knew what was happening in Iraq. But Internet access was in high demand in Iraq, and public affairs had to share it with everyone in their unit. And the bandwidth was so small that sending one high resolution photo took forever. They were better off staying up late at night and sending the photos or stories when no one else was using the computers. Other factors impeding the correspondents' ability to get their job done were the heat, sand, and the constant movement of their equipment.

Mayo and Frushour traveled with the main body of the 2nd MEB convoy. Their final destination—Al Kut. Before leaving Kuwait, Frushour gave her Humvee to the correspondents who were traveling ahead with the regiment because they didn't have a vehicle, and she knew she and Mayo could find a ride with the main body. Find a ride they did with none other than 4th Recon, a reserve unit from San Antonio, Texas. The only problem was that everyone knew women didn't travel with recon. It just didn't happen. Recon Marines are the eyes and the ears of the units they serve, and their operations are often marked by close combat, extraordinary bravery, and nearly unbelievable survival despite overwhelming odds. They venture into the backyard of the enemy. They're the elite of the elite in the Marine Corps and their job is closed to women. To let an outsider in is one thing. To let a female outsider in is quite another thing.

Since Mayo knew she would be joining recon and not the other way around, she went out of her way to introduce herself. A young female enlisted Marine would have trembled in her boots at the mere thought. But if any female Marine could get away with introducing herself to recon without being consumed with fear, it was Mayo. She wasn't timid. If anything, she was quite the opposite—daring and bold. She would have to be to have started a television news show at Marine Corps Base Camp Lejeune, where she interacted with male Marines at all levels, from privates to generals, and from different units, on a regular basis. She was also familiar with the art of persuasion, having sold ads for a radio station and worked in marketing and advertising for Camp Lejeune.

Through her years in the Marine Corps, Mayo had gained enough knowledge about recon to know that she was "trespassing" into male territory and going where few if any women had gone before. Even if she was just sharing the same truck, she knew recon was off limits to women and that she would not be welcomed. She had been in the Marine Corps eighteen years and served in the first Gulf War as a mechanic. She knew that a female traveling with recon in 1991 never would have happened. But war had changed and not just women's roles in it. American Marines and soldiers were fighting on so many different fronts that to prevent women from being on the front line would have meant taking them completely out of the war. The front line was everywhere—from Ramadi and Fallujah to Baghdad and Al Asad, and every road and village in between.

Recon had been told that public affairs would be traveling with them. They had been given ranks and names, Gunny Mayo and Captain Frushour, but that was all. Naturally, recon assumed that their new passengers were male Marines. Imagine their surprise . . .

Mayo checked in with a recon gunny. He reminded her of every television show or movie she had seen with a gung-ho Marine. He was a big guy, with a moustache, a farmer's tan, and a bandana tied around his head. If she'd met him in a dark alley, Mayo would have turned and run in the other direction.

She told him who she was and that she was checking in. He looked at her as if to say, You're kidding, right?

"You're Gunny Mayo?" he asked.

Mayo, standing there with all her gear, said, "Yeah, that's me."

She told the gunny that her captain was coming, too.

As if on cue, Mayo turned to see Frushour walking toward her with her gear on her back. The captain was hunched forward from the weight of the pack and her typically pale face had turned bright red from the exertion. However, this color change was no cause for alarm. Frushour says that because she has British blood, she turns red from something as simple as a sneeze.

Before the convoy even left Kuwait, it was obvious to recon that the women were Marines first. On one occasion, the recon gunny grabbed Mayo's pack and noticed she was still using the old style pack, an ALICE (all-purpose lightweight individual carrying equipment). The ALICEs had been replaced by MOLLEs (modular lightweight loadcarrying equipment) but a lot of the old timers still favored the ALICE pack.

He was surprised Mayo was still using an ALICE pack. Maybe he thought that because she was female, she would have gone shopping for the latest style, the newest fashion in packs.

"I'm not carrying that stuff—MOLLE pack," Mayo said, indignantly. The recon gunny said he didn't carry it either.

On another occasion, the recon gunny was getting something out of Mayo's pack for her. As he hunted for it, he was amazed at how neatly everything was rolled and tucked. "Wow," he said. "You really are a gunny, aren't you?"

Mayo thought about how the male Marines sometimes forgot that all Marines—male and female—are trained the same way. When they realized that Mayo was just as much a Marine as they were, they were fine with her.

Once the convoy headed out, Mayo and Frushour did their best to fit in with recon, but it wasn't always easy. The convoys stopped on a regular basis to let everyone go to the bathroom; however, if a recon guy had to go between stops, he had the option of just whipping it out and relieving himself off the side of the truck. The women, on the other hand, were at the mercy of the convoy. If they requested that their vehicle stop so they could go to the bathroom, they would be holding up the whole convoy. Mayo didn't want to slow down or delay the convoy so she limited her intake of food and water, and chewed gum to quench her thirst. On at least one occasion Mayo made herself sick from a lack of food and drink. When the convoy stopped, she was so weak that a corpsman had to treat her for dehydration and other symptoms related to malnourishment.

When the convoy did stop, the men were much quicker than the women at going to the bathroom. They didn't have to take off all their gear. They just had a few buttons to undo. They would be finished in a few seconds whereas the women had to take off their flak jackets and vests, and pull their pants down. The whole process took a lot longer for women.

The women also had to deal with any issues they had relating to modesty and discretion. Marines train to go to the bathroom in the field but when Frushour went to the field, there were always hills and trees, or some manmade structure that she could either use or hide behind. She never went through desert training in southern California. When she crossed into Iraq, Frushour looked out at the vast flat land in front of her and for a fleeting moment she wondered where she was going to go to the bathroom. She couldn't see anything she would be able to duck behind. When she actually had to go to the bathroom, the thought of where she could and would go consumed her.

On one occasion the convoy had stopped, and one of the female Marines couldn't go to the bathroom. But as soon as she got in the truck and the vehicles started rolling again, she had to go. Instead of asking the convoy to stop, she removed the contents of a plastic MRE bag, went to the bathroom in the bag, and threw it overboard. It's like the old Marine slogan, "Improvise, adapt and overcome."

A female major improvised by bringing along a small contraption that allowed her to go to the bathroom like a guy. It looked like a funnel with a tube. The major would stand up, press the funnel against her, and urine would squirt out in front of her. From the back, she looked exactly like a man going to the bathroom. Recon also had a portable tent so a female, or anyone for that matter, could go to the bathroom in privacy. The tent came with disposal bags and toilet paper.

Just deciding what kind of tampons to take to the desert was an ordeal. Their hands were always dirty so some chose not to use the OB brand, even though they were wrapped in plastic. Tampons wrapped in paper got sweaty and expanded in the women's pockets. Some medical professionals encouraged female Marines to take birth control pills and skip the last week so they wouldn't have to deal with their periods while in Iraq.

☆ ☆ ☆

The higher your rank in the military, the more you know about the mission ahead. Mayo was a little more in the know as a public affairs chief in this war than she was as a mechanic for 2nd Force Service Support Group (FSSG) in Saudi Arabia in the first Gulf War. In Desert Storm, she felt sheltered. She wasn't told a whole lot about what was going on. And in some ways, that made her job a lot easier. Mayo just went to work and did what she was told to do. She had no control over what happened. This time around, Mayo got a good look at a map of the battlefield. Red dots represented the enemy; green dots were friendly forces. The green dots were moving closer and closer to the red dots. Mayo knew what was happening but she didn't know how it was all going to play out. *Am I going to respond right? Am I going to know what to do?* Knots formed in her stomach.

As the convoy headed toward the battlefield, Mayo's greatest fear was that she would never see her children again. She didn't have this fear during the first Gulf War, when she was a twenty-three-year-old corporal, married but without children. Now she knew exactly where she was, that there was a possibility she could be wounded, even killed. She envisioned a white government vehicle pulling up to her house, Marines walking up to her front door, and her unsuspecting children answering their knock. Her children were nine and ten when she left for Iraq. Her daughter, Sydney, turned ten two days before the war started. Mayo kept seeing their expressions the day she left home. Sydney's lips trembled. Her son, Tony, tried to be a young man as he fought back his tears.

The convoy passed vehicles on the side of the road that looked like they had been attacked or burned. It was obvious that something had recently happened there. When the trucks stopped for the night, some Marines dug holes, laid down in them, threw sand over themselves, and fell asleep. This was dangerous. There were reports of Marines getting run over by Humvees and tanks because the drivers didn't see them. Mayo, sweaty and dirty, rode in the back of a seven-ton truck, which doubled as her bed. Sandbags covered the bed of the truck for extra protection against improvised explosive devices (IEDs). On top of the bags were boxes of supplies. Unknowingly, Mayo had chosen a huge box of C-4—a high quality, powerful plastic explosive—as her mattress.

She began making preparations to bed down by unrolling her sleeping bag when another Marine shouted, "Hey, look at that." Mayo looked up and saw explosions in the distance.

Their initial reaction was, "Wow! Cool!"

Then a sergeant from 4th Recon broke the spell.

"Hey, those are coming at us," he shouted, referring to the missiles and rockets causing the blasts.

The horns in the vehicles started going off—*beep, beep, beep.* Already dressed in full chemical and biological warfare gear, the Marines tugged on their gas masks.

They stood for a second looking at the rockets.

One Marine still didn't understand the gravity of the situation.

"Those are cool," he said.

"They're firing at us, idiot," Mayo said.

"Oh shit!"

It turned out to be the biggest Fourth of July celebration Mayo had ever seen. Only it wasn't the Fourth of July, and they weren't in the United States. It was war. And the fireworks were missiles, tracers, and rockets. Although none of the enemy's weapons landed near Mayo, the half-hour show reminded her that she was driving into and not away from the war.

"Is that where we're headed?" a Marine asked, looking in the direction of the "fireworks."

"Yeah, that's where we're headed," another answered.

In the early 1980s, while Mayo studied broadcasting and theater at Central Michigan University, her high school sweetheart, Matt Balenda, enlisted in the Marine Corps. Mayo attended his graduation from boot camp in San Diego and six months later her first Marine Corps Ball. Young and in love, Mayo decided to join Matt. She enlisted in the Marine Corps. She also wanted to serve her country. Mayo had visions of "saving the world." Matt was behind her all the way, writing to her and encouraging her to be strong as she went through boot camp. He accompanied Mayo's parents to Parris Island for their daughter's graduation. Mayo was sworn in on Christmas Eve 1985.

After the first Gulf War, Mayo became a reservist and turned her attention to starting a family and to selling ads for a radio station in Jacksonville, North Carolina. She was working full-time as a civilian in marketing and advertising on Marine Corps Base Camp Lejeune in Jacksonville in January 2002 when she was recalled to active duty.

A thespian since elementary school and a natural communicator, one of Mayo's hobbies was performing in community theater productions. Her favorite role on stage was the wicked witch in *The Wizard of Oz*. She finds playing mean characters fun and challenging. She is especially fond of this classic because of its theme, "There's no place like home." It was a message she told herself over and over again in Iraq.

Before the Marines left Kuwait, Mayo was put in charge of an embedded reporter, Andrew North of the BBC. But early into their journey she had reached her limit with him. During one of the convoy's pit stops, North grabbed his gear and took off into a field to make a call via satellite phone. This action was discouraged because it could give away the convoy's location. The recon Marines weren't going to go after him, though, because North wasn't their responsibility. And, for all they knew, he could have been walking into a minefield. One of them let Mayo know what was happening.

"What are you talking about?" she asked. "Where is he? "Where did he go?"

She couldn't believe it. She wondered why he didn't just draw a target on himself with the pink and black jacket he was wearing. He should have known better. He went through training to be embedded. Mayo had to stop him.

She walked to the edge of the road and told him he could either get in the truck now, or she was going to leave him there to wait for the next convoy. Visibly upset because he wasn't being allowed to do his job, North packed his equipment and returned to the truck.

"Well," Mayo told him, "you can't do your job if you're dead, either."

That evening, when the convoy stopped for the night, North decided to do a live broadcast. Mayo was just lying down to get some sleep in the back of a seven-ton truck. All of North's gear was in the same truck. He made several trips onto the truck to get his equipment. Each time he stepped on Mayo, who was camouflaged among all the packs and duffle bags.

The last time North stepped on the truck—because Mayo made it his last time—the broadcaster caught his gas mask on the gunny's MOPP (Military Operational Protective Posture) suit. A clip on the mask caught on the MOPP. In layman's terms, MOPP stands for "WEAR OR DIE." The suit is designed to protect troops from biological and chemical agents. If you tear it, it's useless.

North grabbed his gas mask and pulled it.

If Mayo wasn't awake before, she certainly was now. Her life depended on it. She yelled at North to stop. He kept pulling and she kept telling him to stop.

Finally, she reached up and grabbed him by the jacket. The troops were behind her, watching. She shouted, "This is the last time. Get off, or I'm throwing you off on your head. Do you understand? You're caught on my MOPP suit. Rip it, and you're going to wish we left you back at the camp."

He got off the truck.

Mayo was trying to be nice to him, but it was getting harder and harder. Here she was traveling in a convoy in the war zone. They didn't know what they were heading into. It was all new. And this reporter was taking unnecessary risks.

That same night, the Marines got word of another possible gas attack. Mayo had just fallen asleep and was all covered up when one of the Marines woke her.

"Gunny! Gunny! Gunny!"

"What do you want?" she snapped back.

"Um, gas," he replied, sheepishly.

"Fine," she said. She put her mask on and fell back asleep. She woke up two hours later still wearing her mask. Everyone else had already taken theirs off.

She woke one of the sergeants and asked him why he hadn't woken her up to take off her mask.

"We were scared," he said. They were afraid she was going to react to them the way she responded to North.

"We looked over and saw you were breathing and were okay," he said.

That night, North didn't dare try to get back on the truck after his encounter with Mayo. But while retrieving his gear from the back of his truck he hadn't grabbed his sleeping bag.

The next morning, when Mayo woke up, her Marines said, "Gunny, you killed him."

"What are you talking about?" she said.

North had cuddled up, as if he had been freezing, next to one of the truck's tires and had dirt piled over himself for an added layer of insulation.

Oh my God, I killed the reporter.

"Is he okay? Somebody wake him up. Is he okay?"

In late March, the convoy stopped just thirty miles shy of An Nasiriyah. A powerful sandstorm was headed their way. They were close enough to the city that they had good communication but not so close that they would be directly affected by the battle. The main body was made up of mostly staff Marines—riflemen but not grunts.

Just as the main body was stopping, regiment started getting reports that an Army unit had been ambushed and soldiers were missing. They began running into remnants of Army Private First Class Jessica Lynch's unit coming out of An Nasiriyah. Regiment was going in. Their mission grew from securing the bridges to also performing a rescue mission. That evening, eighteen Marines from Task Force Tarawa were killed.

Engineers pushed up sand to make berms around the main body. This was the first time they had stopped long enough for the troops to set up their two-man tents and to establish a command center. They were planning to stay in that location for more than one night. They got the command center up and running, the computers started, and established communication. Inside the command center were two rows of tables with phones and computers, and a center aisle where Marines, including Major General Richard Natonski, conducted the business of war. It was loud, with lots of activity and noise, and one big-screen TV that showed the news.

During the next twenty-four hours, Mayo and Frushour were eager to find and connect with two of their correspondents who were with regiment. Mayo called Staff Sergeants Dan Jones and Matthew Orr from a field (tactical) phone in the command center. Just getting through was a feat. When Mayo explained who she was, she was told to call another line and then another line. It took a couple of hours to reach the correspondents. In the meantime, she could hear the battle in the background.

She finally got through to someone who told her that the correspondents were at the aid station. Her first thought was that they had been wounded.

"What? Oh my God, what happened? Are they okay?"

"I don't know," the Marine on the other end of the line said. "You're going to have to call."

Mayo got through to the aid station and was told they weren't there.

"They come on at . . ."

"What do you mean they 'come on?'"

"They're guarding EPWs [enemy prisoners of war]."

"They're what?"

Public affairs is typically set up in a peacetime manner, which means that even though Mayo technically belonged to II MEF, Frushour to division, and others to group, they all worked together in one office back at Camp Lejeune. For the most part, they weren't identified with their individual units during peacetime. So when they deployed with their units, no one knew what to do with them. They were just seen as extra Marines. Hence, the correspondents were told to guard the EPWs when they were supposed to be at the battalion level like the embedded media. (Public affairs is no longer set up like this because of the problems experienced during the war. Mayo calls it MCLL—Marine Corps Lessons Learned.)

Mayo said she needed to talk to her Marines. "Go find them. I'll call back."

When Jones, one of the correspondents, got on the phone, he said to Mayo, "Gunny, come get us."

By this time, Mayo was ready to jump into a Humvee and go to her correspondents.

Jones said he, Orr, and the combat cameraman had been on guard duty.

"Who's taking pictures?" Mayo asked.

"Who's taking pictures?" Jones asked, unbelievingly. "We're just trying to stay alive."

"I understand that," Mayo said, "but you have a job to do, too."

Mayo was livid. She and Frushour needed to get the correspondents away from the regiment so they could regroup and report the news.

Adding fuel to the fire, the 2nd MEB (Camp Lejeune Marines) fell under I MEF from Marine Corps Base Camp Pendleton. When

Camp Lejeune learned that Marines from I MEF had been killed at An Nasiriyah, they assumed the Marines were from the West Coast. Then the casualty reports started to come in and all the Marines were from Camp Lejeune. Yet no one from Camp Lejeune had heard from their public affairs team.

On March 26, a small convoy of seven trucks that included Natonski and his operations officer jumped ahead to be closer to An Nasiriyah and the ongoing battle. Frushour was part of that convoy. At the time, Frushour thought there was a lull in the battle so fear wasn't her overriding emotion. She was riding in the back of a truck and the only intelligence she was getting was what the Marines in the front passed back. When you're in the back of the truck you just go where the truck goes. They drove thirty-five kilometers and it took forever. They had to drive slowly over the rough roads, and they stopped often while recon drove ahead and made sure the area was clear.

Once when the convoy stopped, the truck with the general and operations officer sped past Frushour's vehicle heading in the opposite direction. Later, Frushour found out regiment was about to be attacked and there were reports that Saddam's Republican Guard had taken the train station and regiment was planning a big counterattack. The general and operations officer were heading back to the command center where they had good communication. The rest of the convoy waited awhile and then continued north.

It was dark when they reached their destination. Frushour assumed they had stopped just south of An Nasiriyah. When she got out of her truck, she saw lots of tents, Marines, and sailors. She walked up to one of the Marines and asked him what unit he was with. He said he was with Combat Service Support Battalion 22. Oh, Frushour thought, they belong to regiment. They must have set up south of An Nasiriyah while regiment went on to the city. Turns out she was *in* An Nasiriyah with the regiment but she wouldn't find this out until later.

Mayo, still thirty miles south of An Nasiriyah, usually treated intelligence briefs as just words until she heard weapons firing and felt the ground shake, which was exactly what started to happen. They could feel the fighting thirty miles away but in the desert night, it may as well have been five miles away. It was too dark outside to see anything—they were maintaining light discipline—but Mayo could hear it. Not seeing the weaponry but hearing the explosions made the situation scarier. All Marines with M-16s were ordered to the berm. They ran with their rifles locked and loaded. The rest of the troops, those such as Mayo who carried 9mm pistols, held vigil and prayed to God that they didn't have to fire their weapons because if they did it meant they were looking into the eyes of the enemy.

A staff sergeant ran past Mayo with his pistol pulled out.

"Staff sergeant, where are you going?" she yelled.

"To the berm!" he said.

"No," Mayo said, looking at him and trying to appear composed. "You need to calm down. We have Marines up there with M-16s. We need to stay out of their way. We have jobs to do, too. Let them do theirs."

While she did her best to appear unruffled, Mayo's heart was beating much faster than normal. She jumped in a foxhole, and looked up over the hole and into the one next to hers to make sure one of her Marines was okay.

"Neely," she whispered. "Are you there?"

Lance Corporal Bryan Neely had been assigned to Mayo just before they left Kuwait. Neely had dark hair and wore glasses, and was constantly smoking Newport or Marlboro Light cigarettes, two favorite brands of the Marines. Mayo was protective of Neely because of his youth. He reminded Mayo of her son, Tony.

When he answered, Mayo said, "Don't go too far from me. I want you in my sight at all times."

After spending time with male and female Marines, Mayo discovered that the emotions and dialogue were the same between the genders. Just because she was a female and the person in the next foxhole was a male didn't mean he was any less scared. They all feared for their lives. The anticipation was the same. They were all wondering, What's going to happen next? Am I going to get out of this alive? Mayo was seriously thinking that she was in that foxhole with a buddy and that this could be it.

Later, Mayo walked by some Marines who had hunkered down in foxholes. All of a sudden one of them popped his head out of the hole.

"Hey," he said, "you're the gunny from TV."

"Yes, I am," said Mayo, who was instrumental in establishing the Marine Corps' first live daily television news broadcast at Camp Lejeune. There was a time, leading up to the war, that if you lived in the Jacksonville and turned to channel 10 on your TV, you would find Mayo interviewing Marines.

"What are you doing here?" the Marine asked. All the guys started laughing.

"Fighting a war," she said. "What are you doing here?"

Having met up with Combat Service Support Battalion 22 in An Nasiriyah, Frushour walked around in the dark, shaking hands and greeting Marines she hadn't seen since they left Kuwait. She went into the shock trauma platoon tent where Navy medical was treating wounded Iraqis who had been caught in a firefight. The general's interpreter, who traveled in the back of the truck with Frushour, was also in the tent. In talking to an Iraqi family, the interpreter learned that their little girl was cold and needed blankets. Frushour gave her the liner from her poncho.

Frushour was still in the shock trauma tent when a Marine dashed in and shouted that the Fedeyeen had surrounded their position and they needed to go to the berms. They immediately shut off all the lights. Frushour had just arrived and had no idea where anything was, including the berms, so she followed the others. They all had their weapons drawn; Frushour carried a 9mm. As she crouched behind the berm, she saw what looked like sparklers but were actually RPGs. She could hear them exploding nearby.

It was dark, foggy, and muddy. People were running back and forth. Frushour was having a hard time determining whether the people were Marines or Iraqis. At one point she saw tracer rounds shooting from behind her and the other Marines and sailors. "Shouldn't the dirt be between us and the enemy?" someone asked. They slid over the berm to the correct side. During a frightening moment, those within reach grabbed one another's hands for a second or two. Then someone pointed out that a doctor's weapon was aimed at Frushour's head. Everyone was scared.

A vehicle showed up with wounded Marines and all the Navy medics snapped to. They put their weapons away, got up, and immediately started taking care of the Marines. A second earlier they were looking at each other wide-eyed and full of fear. Now they were full of purpose. Frushour learned later that when the young Marine ran into the tent and said they were surrounded, he was talking about the regiment and not the support battalion. But she hadn't known at the time that the battalion was co-located with the regiment. Frushour wishes she had known that earlier.

She would have felt a lot better knowing she was behind a Marine regiment because as far as she's concerned, there is no safer place to be than at the back of a Marine regiment.

Mayo returned to Camp Ryan in Kuwait to set up a news bureau. Frushour found Orr and Jones in An Nasiriyah, and gave them Mayo's camera and laptop so they could e-mail stories to Mayo. It was obvious to the public affairs team that they needed a central clearinghouse to filter their information. Mayo would set up a relay from Point A (the field) to B (news bureau) to C (the United States). They would spread things out and get stories from the front to her and her team of correspondents—Sergeant David Drafton and Corporal Sean Rhodes—in Kuwait. Mayo would proofread and edit the stories and send them to the States. When Sergeant Rob Henderson joined her, he researched hometowns and high schools on the Internet so stories could be sent to the Marines' hometowns. Mayo was supposed to send the information to Camp Lejeune but that wasn't always possible because of transmission problems. So she created what she believes was a more effective method—she started calling in favors from her media contacts throughout the United States and going directly through them.

Between communication breaking down and correspondents being sent off to guard EPWs, this public affairs team was unable to generate any stories about An Nasiriyah. The American public found out what was going on before Mayo did because she wasn't with her correspondents and she didn't have a TV in front of her. When Mayo returned to the States and people asked her if she had any pictures from the battle of An Nasiriyah, she had to tell them no. The only pictures she had were from embedded media. Mayo and her staff missed the first two weeks of the war. CNN got it. MSNBC, NBC, ABC, CBS, Fox—they all got it. Her staff missed it.

They missed the first two weeks of the war but were able to get everything after that. From January 2003 to May 2003, the public affairs team led by Frushour in Iraq and Mayo in Kuwait produced more than 130 internal public affairs stories and photos, and coordinated the reception and combat embedding of more than fifty members of the national media. In the end, Mayo received the best compliment when James Conway, commanding general of I MEF, said Task Force Tarawa was the voice of I MEF during the war. Conway became commandant of the Marine Corps on November 13, 2006.

Frushour and her correspondents stayed in An Nasiriyah for about a month. The entire main body eventually moved up to where Frushour was located and set up camp. When headquarters sent teams out to check damage or to fix something, Frushour would put her correspondents on the convoy. Sometimes they knew what they would be covering before they left; other times, she sent them out to find stories.

After about a month in An Nasiriyah, they headed to Ad Diwaniyah. Public affairs set up camp in what looked like an abandoned television station. It had a huge antenna and fenced-in yard. There was a small village nearby. Regiment spread out. Here and in An Nasiriyah the correspondents wrote a lot of stories about rebuilding the cities and about what the Iraqis needed.

One night Frushour had just taken a baby-wipe bath and was lying down in her T-shirt and shorts on her sleeping bag. She was reading when the light outside revealed the silhouette of what looked like a giant man approaching her tent. The chief of staff tapped on the tent. Frushour unzipped the door. A situation had come up and she was needed. She dressed and met the chief of staff, lawyer, and a couple of upset embedded Polish reporters. It turns out the reporters had been embedded with another Marine unit on the other side of Iraq. Nothing was happening there, so they decided to drive to Karbala, fifty kilometers southeast of Baghdad, for more action. They wrote "TV" in duct tape on the side of their vehicles and drove across Iraq. Along the way, they were ambushed at a fake police check point. Two of their people had been kidnapped. They wanted the Marines to rescue their reporters. Somehow, the reporters who had been kidnapped got away and eventually they were all reunited.

Frushour stayed in Ad Diwaniyah for about a month before crossing over to Al Kut. There, she stayed in a hangar at the airport close to but not in the city of Al Kut. The airport had obviously been bombed because there were huge, gaping holes in the runways to prevent Iraqi aircraft from taking off. Both Ad Diwaniyah and Al Kut were cities on the major supply route from Kuwait to Baghdad. The Marines were keeping the supply routes open.

While in Al Kut, the Marines from Task Force Tarawa found a patch of land overgrown with weeds and littered with trash. Soon, Marines would learn that this area was the final resting place for soldiers who fought in World War I as British troops sought an alternative route to the center of the Ottoman Empire. With Gallipoli a failing battle, the British decided to approach via Mesopotamia, now modern day Iraq.

The troops landed in Umm Quasr and moved north to Baghdad through the Tigris River valley. North of Al Kut but south of the capital, the British troops found they could push no further. They fell back to Al Kut where they were besieged for approximately six months. Many found their final resting place there.

Along with the weeds and trash, the headstones had been weathered and damaged; some were not visible due to the dense vegetation, some had toppled over and were broken. The Marines were appalled by the condition of the cemetery and decided to do something about it. They cleaned it up by replacing the headstones, pulling the weeds, and picking up the trash. The Iraqis saw what they were doing and joined in. When they were finished, they invited the British soldiers and vicar and held a solemn rededication ceremony.

The cemetery was bordered on three sides by buildings. During the ceremony Iraqis stood in the windows and watched. At the end of the solemn ceremony, everyone bowed their heads as the vicar said a final prayer. When they were finished, the Iraqis wanted to contribute to the ceremony and sing, but knew only one American song. They sang "Happy Birthday."

Mayo knew when she left Iraq that she would be going back. She was frustrated because the Army was relieving the Marines and the ethos of the two branches is so different. The soldiers are peacekeepers. The Marines go in, kick down doors, take names, and drive people away. They do what they have to do and get out. This time they left before finishing their job. They'd be back.

Lights, Camera, Action

In January 2004, Mayo returned to Iraq. This deployment would differ vastly from her first tour a year earlier. She was still a correspondent, but this time Mayo was the news bureau chief in Baghdad for the American Forces Network (AFN), which falls under the office of the Assistant Secretary of Defense for Public Affairs. AFN is the brand name used by the United States Armed Forces Radio and Television Service (AFRTS) for its entertainment and command internal information networks worldwide. It is the one broadcast around the world and to the ships at sea that carries bowl games on New Year's Day and the Daytona 500 to deployed troops. Mayo's job was still to find and report stories that showed the human side of the war only this time she transmitted the stories to the Pentagon. Also, in 2003 the emphasis was on print media. This time she was either standing in front of the camera reporting the news or standing behind the camera directing her crew and cameras. Her office was located in the convention center in the Green Zone.

On the outside, the convention center looks like a building you would see in an American city. It's made of glass and brick. Inside, the building appears pristine with its marble floors and a wide stairwell that leads to meeting rooms and auditoriums on the second and third floors. But if the rooms could talk, they would not seem so unspoiled. Saddam had used one auditorium to publicly execute people. The blood was so heavy on the floor that Marines couldn't scrub it out.

On the first level, Iraqis would line up outside the door to borrow money or get information about a missing relative at the Iraqi assistance center. The Coalition Press Information Center (CPIC) was located on the second floor. Every member of the civilian media in Iraq had to go through CPIC. Mayo's press room was next to CPIC. Between the assistance center downstairs and CPIC upstairs, hundreds of people passed through the building daily.

Bombings and explosions were such an everyday occurrence in the Green Zone that Mayo and the other service members laughed at the Green Zone's description as the safe zone. They thought a more appropriate title would have been the "impact zone" because they were shot at nearly every day. When Mayo told people that she worked in the Green Zone, she got the sense that they thought she was safer than everyone else in Iraq. Ironically, she felt more secure in cities such as Ramadi and Fallujah, actual battlegrounds at the time, partly because she would be with Marines in those areas and she always felt safest when she was surrounded by leathernecks. In the Green Zone, Mayo worked with the joint command, and had twenty Marines, soldiers, and airmen working for her. Those from the other branches of the armed services were a different breed than the Marines. She'd give a soldier or an airman an order and they would question it. Tell Marines what to do and they do it without question.

One reason the insurgents targeted the Green Zone was because the Iraqi Governing Council met in a building that adjoined the convention center where Mayo's press operations were set up. Since members of the Governing Council often passed between the two structures, both buildings were heavily guarded. While Mayo worked in the Green Zone, her press crew filmed numerous conferences involving Ambassador Paul Bremer, administrator for the U.S.-led occupation government, and Iraqi Prime Minister Iyad Allawi.

When they reported on air, Mayo and her service members always stated that they were broadcasting from an undisclosed location in Iraq. Mayo couldn't help but think this was unnecessary since numerous satellites dishes stood exposed on top of the building. She joked with other service members, "Don't you think people know where we are?"

Mayo traded the shelter of a seven-ton truck and a tent from her first deployment for a trailer on the grounds of a presidential palace in Baghdad. It was in that trailer that Mayo fought a most unusual personal battle. Someone had bought the wrong knob for the bathroom door. Every time Mayo shut the door, she got locked in. One time she wasn't alone. Moths entered the compact room and their numbers multiplied by the second. Mayo frantically swatted them and each time she hit one, five more materialized. She turned on the water, thinking that if she sprayed them they would lie down in defeat. That was hardly the case. The water just stirred things up and made the situation even messier. Mayo screamed as she tried to shake the door open. A male Marine passing by pulled the door open, only to find Mayo standing there, dripping wet, with a towel wrapped around her, and dead moths everywhere.

"Oohrah," Mayo said rather matter-of-factly to her rescuer. "Thank you very much."

Following that incident, Mayo never closed the door all the way for fear she would be trapped again. Soon, it wouldn't matter because she relocated to what had once been a Baath Party house.

Moths were hardly her biggest problem or scare in Baghdad. There were many other challenges, including transportation. Sometimes Mayo rode to work in a Humvee or SUV. Other times, she took a bus. One morning as she boarded the bus the driver told her not to stand at the bus stop anymore. It was blown up that evening.

One day Mayo walked up to the third floor of the convention center to negotiate a contract with an Army major. She wanted more space for her reporters who had to cram into small rooms to edit their film.

She heard a loud explosion.

The convention center shook.

Before Mayo could react, the major sitting across from her jumped up, grabbed her, and threw her to the floor.

"Get down! Get down!" he shouted.

Mayo lay face down on the floor. Experience had taught her that this was the safest place to be in the building during an explosion.

But her first thought when she hit the floor was, *I have to go.*

"I've got troops," she told the major. "I've got to check on my troops."

The major looked at her, surprised perhaps by Mayo's composure and immediate sense of duty. Before he could say anything, Mayo pushed herself up and ran through the hallway of the third floor to the stairs.

Once on the second floor, Mayo yelled, "Get out! Get out!" She wasn't ordering her troops to get out of the building. She was ordering them to congregate. Sometimes when her staff was working in the interior rooms of the center they couldn't hear an explosion on the outside. Under the circumstances, she didn't have to yell because the blast was strong enough for everyone in the building to hear and feel. Her troops had already begun to gather outside their offices.

The initial explosion came from mortars that landed near the guards who protected the entrance to the Green Zone, less than the length of a football field from the building. A second explosion rattled the building as Mayo ran down the steps. That tremor came from a suicide bomber who had driven his vehicle into the security gate that separated the Green Zone from the rest of the world.

As Mayo converged with other troops, she spotted a female airman who had been working at the reception desk. This airman, a brand new staff sergeant, stood frozen, looking straight ahead. Mayo saw the airman watching the window in front of her. The convention center had been built as a showpiece and its windows were enormous, taking up whole walls. They were reinforced so the glass wouldn't come crashing down on the building's occupants. Everyone watched as the window blew inward like a bubble and then bounced back out. Mayo had never seen anything like it. The airman's expression indicated that she never had either. Her stunned expression reminded Mayo of the little girl from the movie *Poltergeist* after she saw an apparition.

But this was no time to be standing around, dazed. Small shards of glass flew from the window.

"Let's go," Mayo shouted.

She and her troops pulled the airman into the press room, an interior office and one of the safest places in the building. Having lived and worked in the Green Zone for a while, troops knew that when they heard one explosion, there was a good chance it would be followed by others. So they stayed put until they were given the all clear. During this time, the airman remained speechless. When she got her voice back, she said she didn't know what to do when she saw the window coming at her. So intense were the explosions that morning that they caused every window in a building next door to shatter.

Mayo knew a news story had landed in her lap, but it wasn't her role to report the bombings. However, on this occasion the other networks were nowhere to be found. Her boss, Admiral Gregory Slovitch, was standing nearby and reading Mayo's mind. "Gunny," he said, "I want it covered right now."

"Yes sir," Mayo said.

Mayo's staff was still trembling from the explosions, but Gunny Sal Cardella stepped up and said he'd go. Mayo needed one other person. She had an airman, Rachel Jarrett, but she was so new.

"I don't know about this," Jarrett said.

"I'm not sending you alone," Mayo said. "We're going together."

They threw on their flak jackets and helmets, and grabbed their cameras, microphones, tapes, and tripod.

Jarrett was shaking so badly she couldn't load her pistol. Mayo took it from her and loaded it.

"Have you shot this before?" Mayo asked.

"No," she said. She had fired it only to familiarize herself with the weapon. She had never qualified with it.

"Jarrett," Mayo said, "I love you but don't stand behind me."

Mayo and her staff were accustomed to traveling in and out of the Green Zone, but passage shut down immediately following a bombing. The admiral would have to escort them. Mayo was not prepared for what she saw. As a veteran of the first and second Gulf War, one might think that the gunny had grown accustomed to the sights and smells of war, but that wasn't the case. She could imagine herself becoming partially numb to the death and destruction that surrounded her, but never one hundred percent. There was nothing familiar about seeing a Marine who had lost limbs from an IED or had his face blown off. Every wound and death hit a new or untouched nerve and emotion.

The explosion had catapulted vehicle parts in every direction. Human remains were scattered on the ground. Mayo saw a leg in one area, still attached to a shoe, and the rest of the body was lying somewhere else. In her mind, she found the scattered body parts and put them back together again. Blood was splattered everywhere. Rivaling the horrifying sight were the odors of charred flesh and burning oil.

The scene reminded Mayo of an even worse suicide bombing that happened when she and her crew were in Babylon four months earlier. They had been sent to a Polish camp, where more than thirty nations were represented, to set up a press room and a live remote. The coalition forces were hopeful that they would capture Abbas al-Massawi. His arrest would be a big deal, and they wanted to publicize it to the world, but the Polish military didn't have its own press room.

The morning after she arrived, Mayo and several other female service members walked to the shower trailers. After showering, they were dressing and putting their hair up when they heard a *boom*, followed by another *boom*. The generators quit, and the power went out. Mayo fumbled in the dark for her flashlight. Once she found it, she and the others threw their belongings in their bags. A major ran to the trailer and yelled, "Grab all your stuff. They need a favor from us."

The explosion they had heard came from a suicide bomber who had driven his car into the wall of a housing project, causing buildings to collapse on top of residents. The Army asked Mayo and her crew to document the aftermath of the incident. Mayo agreed, even though her crew was more accustomed to shooting news stories—twenty seconds here and twenty seconds there— rather than recording every detail of an event. Her crew watched and taped as dead children were pulled from beneath the debris. While they were taping, Iraqi civilians threw rocks at Mayo's young staff and shouted, "Go home, Americans." Mayo urged her crew on. "Keep going," she said. "Keep going."

The Army major pulled her aside. Mayo had scheduled an interview for later in the day with officers from the Iraqi Civilian Defense. The major let her know that over the past twenty-four hours, one of the officers had been assassinated and another's daughter had been killed. He still wanted her to interview some of the captains. They needed to send a message that they would not let the bombings intimidate them. Mayo and her crew spent a week in Babylon, and every day was filled with violence and death.

Back at the suicide bombing in Baghdad, Mayo, who had grown accustomed to putting a positive spin on her stories, turned the explosion that rocked the convention center into a feature about the success of the Iraqi cleanup effort. The multinational forces had trained the Iraqis in emergency services such as fire and medical. So even though American service members responded because the incident occurred outside their gate, the Iraqis handled the situation themselves. Mayo saw the cleanup as a testament to the training, and that was her focus.

Colonel Musab al-Awadi, prime minister of Iraq at the time, stepped outside the conference center to speak about the bombing. Mayo looked around and realized that she and Jarrett were the only media present. Suicide bombings had become so common that they no longer attracted media attention the way they once did. Not only did she interview al-Awadi, but Mayo also was in Baghdad when al-Awadi was elected and sworn in, and when the interim constitution was written. For someone who loves history, Mayo had now become a part of it. She witnessed it, filmed it, and sent it back to the Pentagon channel to be viewed by military and government officials.

On March 19, 2004, Secretary of State Colin Powell held a news conference in Mayo's convention center press room. Prior to the conference, Iraqi journalists made it known that they would stage a walkout to protest the killing of two Iraqi journalists by U.S. troops. Mayo and her staff scrambled ahead of time to figure out how they would handle the situation.

After Powell was introduced, he stood and walked to the lectern. As soon as he began to speak, a reporter rose to his feet and started speaking Arabic. Mayo had her headset on and the cameras were rolling when about thirty other Iraqi journalists stood up and left the hall.

"Camera 1," she said.

"I don't have a shot."

"Camera 2"

"I don't have a shot."

The cameramen tried to zoom in on Powell but their only shot was of the back of people's heads. After the Iraqis walked

out, Powell said that ensuring the freedom of speech and the ability of individuals to stand up and walk out of a press conference
was the very reason why coalition forces were in Iraq. Mayo was
impressed with Powell's poise and thought that if she were ever to
become a politician, this was the kind she'd want to be.

In her headset, the Pentagon was saying, "What's going on?
What's going on?"

When the story first broke that prisoners were being abused at
Abu Ghraib and then when the trials got underway, Mayo was
charged with escorting the media to the prison. She described
Abu Ghraib as a "pit from hell" and "hell on earth" but wouldn't
elaborate. She said she couldn't speak about what happened
there. During those trips, she befriended journalists from CNN
and MSNBC, but she also grew increasingly frustrated at the press
for its single focus on Abu Ghraib and its lack of interest in troops
who worked around the clock to get the schools open, to find
equipment for the hospitals, and to protect the dams and bridges.
Mayo was trying to show them the positive work that the troops
were doing but they weren't listening.

Through her reporting, Mayo interacted with many women
from other countries. Those experiences often left her with a
greater appreciation for her life back in the States. One time she
traveled outside the Green Zone to an inner-city school in Baghdad to interview female Iraqi high school students for a video she
was helping to produce for USAID. During Mayo's visit, the
school principal told her the girls didn't have much of a chance
for advancement. They hadn't known anything but war their
entire lives. Most wouldn't graduate. Some would become pregnant at a young age. Many would be abused by male Iraqis. This

new information left Mayo reflecting on the fragile childhoods around the world, but especially in war-torn Iraq.

On another occasion, Mayo flew to Jordan to help produce an historic documentary on the first female soldiers in the Iraqi armed forces. Female American soldiers, Marines, airmen, and sailors are dedicated to their country, but the female Iraqi soldiers take commitment to another level. Unlike Mayo, who continued to maintain her roles as wife and mother while serving her country, Iraqi women who joined the armed forces had to give up their personal lives because the insurgents and the old Iraqi government didn't want them in the military. When they joined the Iraqi Armed Forces, these women were surrounded by dissension and chaos yet they were willing to carry on and risk their lives and the lives of their families to serve. They went so far as to keep their military service a secret. If they were discovered, their families could be killed. The new government is more supportive. There were twenty female soldiers in the first graduating class. Many of them were college educated and familiar with computer technology. Nearly all of them hoped to become commissioned as officers. And all of them expressed an immense love for their country and an intense desire to see the Iraqi government evolve into a democracy.

Mayo left Iraq knowing that the United States military and coalition forces were helping the Iraqi people, especially the women. She knew they were changing lives and giving Iraqi women opportunities which up until now they had only dreamed about. As a mother, Mayo looked into the eyes of the young women and saw her own daughter. She realized the reason she was in Iraq in the first place was to build a better future for her daughter, son, and all children. She doesn't want them to have to endure the terror that has become so familiar to young Iraqi women.

Mayo's hope is that the Iraqi women learned something from her, too. She hopes she helped them understand they can be whatever they want to be. The principal of one of the schools told Mayo that one of the girls wanted to be a reporter. Mayo talked with that female student for an hour and let her use her video camera. The student was overjoyed. Her teacher said the girl would never forget Mayo or the U.S. Marines.

*Lieutenant Estella Salinas (center), United States Navy,
with two friends.*

A Healer of the Guardians of Peace

*As a child, **Navy Lieutenant Estella Salinas** didn't know what she wanted to be when she grew up. She only knew what she didn't want to be—poor.*

LIEUTENANT ESTELLA SALINAS SQUATTED BESIDE A YOUNG MARINE whose fingers had been mangled when a mis-timed grenade detonated in his left hand. The docs had amputated two of his fingers, and he was lying on a cot in the tent of a mobile surgical company—a *M*A*S*H*-type outfit—in southern Iraq.

He wanted to know which fingers he had lost.

With a slight Spanish accent, the thirty-seven-year-old Navy nurse whispered: "The index and middle fingers on your left hand."

Salinas held the young Marine's bandaged hand and gently patted his forehead with a damp gauze. They both cried—he for his lost fingers, she because . . . well, just because. Because that was who she was. You could try to stay aloof from the suffering, but it never really worked, not if you cared.

Earlier in the day, the patient had been part of a unit of Marines disposing of ammunition left behind by Iraqi soldiers, and the operation had turned messy. The ordnance was old, unstable. Just handling a grenade or a mortar round could make it go off in your hand. The explosions had ripped through the disposal detail, turning a routine duty into disaster. Some had already died from their wounds. Others had survived surgery and been carried to the holding ward to recover.

The young Marine looked up at Salinas and asked her a question. What he saw was a nurse of medium build, with dark brown eyes, short black hair, and light brown skin. "What will my girlfriend think of me now?" he wanted to know. "Can my girlfriend love me if I'm deformed?" Salinas understood that the patient was crying not so much for his physical wound as for the uncertainty that lay ahead. The fear that life as he had known it, the future as he had imagined it, was gone.

As Salinas focused on her patient, she also had to be aware of what was happening around her. She was the division officer of three busy holding wards for Bravo Surgical Company, a makeshift hospital that followed Marines as they headed into combat. She and her staff of twelve nurses and more than seventy corpsmen—the Navy equivalent of battlefield paramedics—worked round the clock to stabilize their patients and move them out within twenty-four to forty-eight hours to make room for the newly wounded. Each patient's condition determined where he or she went next. Some were sent to a higher care facility and others returned to their units.

Salinas tended to the patient while medics weaved between the cots, equipment, and supplies that had been crammed into the tents that make up the hospital. Each tent held twenty cots in two rows of ten. The desert sand served for a floor. Stacked at one end of each tent were containers the size of footlockers used to store and transport crucial medical supplies such as IV fluids and tubing, irrigation fluid, emesis basins (kidney shaped bowls to capture vomit), water for drinking and cleaning, needles, gauze, alcohol pads, tape, Band Aids, and medication. Everything but the tent, stakes, and pegs fit into the containers. Each tent also had a portable sink hooked up to a water system so the staff could wash their hands.

Nearby, in the operating and emergency rooms, doctors listened as severely wounded Marines ignored their critical condition to check on their buddies. This was common. Sometimes their buddies were lying on the next gurney; other times, no one knew where they were. Maybe a medic had already taken their buddies to one of Salinas's holding wards. This is when a wounded Marine, bravado still intact, could be overheard saying "Don't worry about me. Take care of my buddy. He got it really bad." Not realizing that he got it a lot worse than his buddy did.

By the time patients arrived in Salinas's holding wards, they had most likely been anesthetized and operated on. Some had limbs amputated and shards of shrapnel plucked from their skin. Then they were stabilized, at least physically. The same couldn't always be said for their emotions. They were usually wounded in a sudden flash of pain and noise, rushed to a medical team that could save their lives, drugged or unconscious, everything happening so fast. But in Salinas's wards time slowed, the drugs wore off, and reality set in. Here grief began to supercede physical pain. Grief for lost buddies, grief for their own mangled lives. Grief for the person they used to be, now gone.

In the holding wards, Marines and soldiers awoke to the emotional reality of war. This was where they faced lives lost, lives ruined, lives changed forever—for the worse. Here, limbs were not cut off. That had already happened. This was where they realized that they were no longer physically whole, and their emotions started to fray. The emotions in the holding ward would oftentimes mark the beginning of a long, painful, and bitter personal battle.

This was where, for instance, a wounded gunny or chief warrant officer who had been in the Marine Corps for twenty or so years, gathered the strength to get off his cot and roam the ward.

Still groggy from the anesthesia, he'd manage to do a head count. Soon, he would realize he had arrived at the surgical company with seven men and now there were only five. Where was so and so? he'd ask. If those Marines weren't in the holding ward, they were most likely in the expectant ward (where they were expected to die), or the morgue.

Salinas would sit down with the Marine and explain: His best friend had died, or some unlucky nineteen-year-old Marine wasn't going to make it. She didn't sugarcoat the truth. Not only was she a straight shooter, but she also knew better. She let the Marine know that she was sorry about the ones who didn't make it but there was nothing she could do for them now. That didn't mean she didn't care about the ones who died. She wanted to cry her eyes out every time this happened, but that wasn't what the Marines needed. She would redirect the experienced Marine to the ones who were going to survive—those were the guys who desperately needed him. He was the one with the strength and confidence, the one who could help pull them through because they always counted on him. Then she'd watch as the Marine stood up and walked to his men.

In combat, caring for the wounded required a pound of tough love and an ounce of empathy. Salinas had to be stern with her patients, forcing them to fight through their pain and to be optimistic. But she also sat at their bedsides by the hour holding their hands, looking them in the eyes, and saying, "You have more in you than this." She forced them to go through the hard times, like a mother helping a child through a difficult situation. Helped them come out whole—in spirit if not in body—on the other side.

On a personal level, Salinas identified with the patient who had lost two fingers and with his fearful questions. He was mourning the life he felt he'd lost when the grenade exploded in his hand. When he asked her what his girlfriend would think of him now, it was the kind of question Salinas could handle. She happened to know firsthand how cruel people could be about deformities and handicaps. So she did exactly what she had been trained *not* to do. She opened up to him.

Why not? He opened up to me. Sometimes being human means there's no damn way to relate to a person objectively. At this point, the wounded Marine didn't want to hear about the months he would spend in rehabilitation, the boring, painful hours of repetition to re-learn simple tasks he had mastered as an infant. He yearned for a connection—to know that Salinas was human and that she understood his sorrow.

"I'd be lying if I said looks aren't important," she told him. "They are." But then she was able to reveal something she had learned some years back. When you are with someone who truly loves you, missing some fingers is a reason to care for a person more and not less. It's the individuals and not their appearances that keep a mature relationship functioning.

Salinas confided her own experience. She'd been born with a deformed rib cage—what they called a "pigeon chest"—and had required difficult surgery to correct it. The result was an ugly scar stretching across her chest. She'd agonized over how her fiancé would regard her—could she still seem attractive, sexy, alluring, with that purple ridge of flesh across her breasts? Most men she knew loved looking at a woman's bare breasts, and there she was with a huge scar between hers.

Her fiancé was able to look past that scar. She told the Marine, "Now he loves me for who I am as a person, not how I look. When someone really loves you, they will not see that you have fingers missing. They'll see you as a whole individual."

During this exchange, the nurse broke two of her cardinal rules—she got emotionally involved, and she cried. But Salinas knew even then that both of them were better off because she had broken the rules, taken a chance and left herself exposed to comfort a young man and remind him of the healing power of love.

This young Marine was hardly the most seriously wounded of the parade of maimed patients carried into Salinas's ward during the war in Iraq. She saw Marines who had lost arms and legs, an Iraqi boy who had his face blown off, men and women so peppered with shrapnel it had to be removed one painful shard at a time, bullet and motor vehicle wounds, and first- and second-degree burns. But when you have been a nurse for more than ten years, like Salinas has been, you have seen many of these wounds before. Sometimes it was the more intimate moments between nurse and patient that left the most lasting impressions. For Salinas, the young Marine who had lost two fingers represented the hundreds of patients who passed through her holding wards.

Salinas's first destination in Iraq was a remote strip of desert named Camp Anderson. She and the surgical company arrived hot and exhausted at two in the morning. After four hours of restless sleep, they began setting up their tents and equipment to make the camp operational. They arranged the tents for optimum efficiency, starting with triage (ER), then surgical (OR), the holding wards (ICU or med surge), and ancillary services (lab, X-ray, pharmacy).

Because sniper fire and chemical and biological warfare were a real threat, they all were required to wear their chemical gear, which weighed about eleven pounds and made the 120-degree heat even more unbearable.

For protection, the medics had been issued 9mm pistols and bullets, but as far as Salinas was concerned it would have been just as effective if she had been given one or the other. She didn't expect to ever shoot the weapon. Navy medical wasn't what you would call warfare savvy. They took care of other people, not themselves. While the Marines cleaned their weapons daily, Salinas's staff checked medical supplies.

But just because you were in the medical corps didn't mean you could always count on protection. There was a famous incident in the first Persian Gulf War in which Iraqi wounded were sent back to a surgical company to be treated. They took their weapons inside the tents and shot at the nurses and doctors. Unfortunately, this war wasn't like previous wars when provisional rifle companies provided protection and security for medical battalions. With the downsizing of the Marine Corps from 245,000 in 1982 to 175,000 in 2004, and with the military performing triple the missions of only a few years ago with far fewer troops, the surgical battalion was vulnerable to attacks by the enemy. It didn't have the luxury of a provisional rifle company. Every infantry battalion in the Marine Corps, except one, was fighting in Iraq.

Salinas and the rest of Bravo Surgical Company were still setting up tents when their first patients arrived. But they weren't Marines. They were Iraqis—three women (a mother, sister, and daughter) and the daughter's three little sons. Salinas and her staff had expected Iraqi patients at some point but not this soon. This Iraqi family hadn't stopped at a checkpoint after repeated attempts to make them halt, so American troops opened fire on them. While the daughter and one of the boys were taken to surgery, the mother, sister, and two other boys (both under the age of one) waited in the holding ward.

Salinas watched, unbelieving, as the children's grandmother and aunt sat side by side on a cot, facing away from the boys who were now in the care of the medical staff. Salinas was fairly certain these Iraqi children had never seen Americans before, and she couldn't believe their relatives weren't sitting by their sides, providing comfort. She thought about her own son and daughter back home, and the emotional support that she would have given them.

While the two Iraqi women waited in the holding ward, Salinas noticed that one of the women had human tissue on the back of her *hijab*—the headscarf worn by Muslim women. The temperature outside was over one hundred degrees. It was even hotter in the tent. The combination of heat and human tissue attracted flies and mosquitoes that carried disease. Salinas, responsible for maintaining infection control standards in her wards, didn't care how the tissue came off the hijab. She just wanted it off.

Only one person on the medical staff of more than two hundred spoke Arabic. That was a doctor who worked in another tent and her Arabic was shaky at best. Since they didn't have translators, Salinas had to rely on her own version of international sign language and eventually her staff was able to remove the tissue. This was Salinas's first introduction to the Iraqi culture.

Camp Anderson was isolated, and they hadn't been there long. When Salinas stood on the perimeter of the camp and looked around, all she could see was sand and a long row of Patriot missiles to intercept incoming Scud missiles. That view would change over the next few days as Iraqis began arriving by foot, bus, and truck for medical attention. Since they were so familiar with the desert and always seemed to know where the surgical companies were located, the Iraqis ended up guiding the Marines to their own medical facilities.

The Iraqi female patients posed the greatest challenges for the medical staff because their long black robes veiled their wounds. If the patient were a female Marine, Salinas could start her assessment while the woman was walking toward her. If Salinas was sitting on a cot beside a female Marine, the nurse might take her patient's hand to see if she was hot or cold to the touch. If there was a wound to the stomach, she could just lift the patient's shirt and look at it. She couldn't tell anything from looking at an Iraqi woman because she was covered from head to toe. She couldn't put her male nurses with female Iraqi patients. Even walking down the street an Iraqi woman doesn't want a man looking at her, never mind performing a medical assessment of her.

This was a great source of frustration for Salinas. She couldn't be bothered with cultural differences and wondering whether she was going to offend an Iraqi woman because she looked straight into her eyes or because she looked at her body during an assessment. Salinas had three wards to run and a lot of people were depending on her. These cultural matters seemed frivolous to her. She was far more concerned with tending to the wounded and to her staff.

Fortunately for the Iraqis, the medical corps doesn't turn away patients, even if they were considered the enemy and their problems had nothing to do with combat, which was often the case. The Geneva Convention requires that all wounded and sick be cared for during wartime, regardless of the injury or illness. Finding the surgical company was a great opportunity for the Iraqis to obtain free health care, and Salinas couldn't blame them for that.

Salinas and her staff also had to be prepared for the occasional Iraqi national and prisoner, and had to give the Iraqi patient the same consideration their Marines received. This was hard for the nurses and medics. Some Iraqis were as seriously wounded as the Marines and there wasn't an endless supply of provisions, so the staff had to prioritize. The surgical companies didn't automatically treat Marines first. They had to go by wound.

There was at least one unsettling incident in which an Iraqi received preferential treatment. An uncle brought his nephew for medical treatment for a wound unrelated to combat. The uncle claimed to be a religious leader helping to keep peace between the Iraqis and the Marines. He threatened the medics, saying that

if his nephew didn't get immediate medical attention he didn't
know how much longer he would be able to pacify the Iraqi people. The staff had to choose between treating this man or jeopardizing the safety of U.S. military personnel in the area. So they
treated him.

Each of the three holding wards served a separate purpose—
one for ICU, a second for Marines, and another for non-American patients. As new patients arrived, the staff had to be diligent
about keeping the Iraqi and Marine patients in separate holding
wards. The last thing they wanted was for a wounded Marine to
wake up beside an Iraqi soldier.

This was not as much a concern in the ER and OR, where
patients often were in excruciating pain and barely conscious. But
even in those rooms tempers flared when there were two conscious fighters from opposite sides of the battle. Early one morning, an Iraqi soldier and a Marine were lying on gurneys in close
proximity to one another in the ER. The Iraqi had a shoulder
wound. He was screaming and combative. A Marine with an open
lower leg fracture was short on compassion. He kept saying, "Just
shoot him. Just shoot him." The doctors adjusted the morphine
until the Iraqi prisoner quieted down and they were able to move
the Marine out of the triage area.

Salinas had to rotate her nurses and corpsmen between the
wards because if they had it their way, they would all choose to
treat the American patients. Everyone wanted to take care of the
Marines. When they were assigned to the non-American ward, the
medical staff had to put personal feelings aside, provide the
patients with the same level of care they would give a Marine, and
use common sense. They couldn't let their guard down or be
careless. Any object could be used against them, including something as simple as a stethoscope hanging over a shoulder or a pen
left lying around.

During war, danger crept into the least expected places. Salinas thought the medical staff would be safe from their Marine patients, but that wasn't always the case. Before they were allowed to enter the triage area, all patients—Iraqis, Marines, and sailors—were supposedly stripped of their gear by security. The Marines often arrived with their pockets loaded with knives, guns, and grenades. Not having weapons on them was especially important when they were coming out of anesthesia and were disoriented. If they had weapons with them, there was no telling what would happen. One Marine had tucked a grenade in his gas mask carrier and it wasn't detected when he entered triage. In the holding ward, all his gear, including the grenade, was stored under his cot. The cots were narrow and the gear plentiful. Each Marine had a helmet, flak jacket, pants, boots, and more. The ward was so crowded that the staff was constantly pushing and kicking gear back under the cots. When the Marine got ready to leave, he pulled out his grenade. All this time Salinas had been concerned about the threats from the Iraqi patients and she had been kicking a grenade.

Estella Salinas is the daughter of Constancia and Florentino Salinas, migrant workers who struggled daily to feed their fifteen children. They moved the family numerous times during Salinas's childhood, with Dad traveling ahead to find fields to work and a house to live in. They journeyed from Texas to the onion fields in California, to Tennessee, Missouri, and Minnesota, finally settling in Nebraska. As soon as Salinas was old enough to handle a hoe and a machete, she joined her siblings in the fields. She doesn't remember her exact age because her family didn't celebrate birthdays. "Why draw attention to something you couldn't afford?"

In the summertime, before sunrise, the children piled into the back of a truck. The family spent their days picking up what the combines left behind and removing weeds, row by row, until it was too dark to see. The lifestyle didn't seem unfair or difficult to Salinas because it was all she knew. Despite their hard work, the income from working ten- to twelve-hour days in the fields was barely enough to keep this large family going. To supplement their earnings, the children rummaged through the city dump for aluminum cans to sell while their dad searched for wire, hoping to make money from the copper.

In her Hispanic community, everyone was expected to fend for themselves but they also looked after one another. They lived by the motto that actions speak louder than words. Salinas's parents seldom told her they loved her, yet she never doubted their affection. It was love through action.

During her three days at Camp Anderson, Salinas and her staff worked around the clock to treat more than one hundred patients. In the evenings, they were required to work in no-light conditions, which presented a variety of inconveniences and hazards. Since most of the fighting occurred at night, that's also when the majority of casualties arrived. The medical staff had to close all the flaps in the tents before they could turn on lights to treat the patients. This prevented air circulation and forced the temperature to rise even higher.

Working in no-light conditions made something as routine as walking outside the tents hazardous. To transport recovering or dead troops to ambulances and aircraft, the medical staff carried stretchers outside and past several tents in the dark. The medics couldn't see and often stumbled over tent stakes and lines. The no-light conditions also meant convoys had to drive through the desert with their lights off. This led to a number of crashes and mishaps. If the Marines were convoying and hadn't quite reached their destination, they'd pull over for the night. Some slept inside their vehicles while others slumbered outside. One Marine was dropped off at the surgical company because his feet hurt. He had fallen asleep by a vehicle. When the driver of a seven-ton vehicle prepared to drive off in the dark, he didn't see the Marine and ran over his feet. Amazingly, the Marine's feet were bruised but he didn't have any broken bones.

Most of the patients who arrived in the holding wards had wounds that were not life-threatening but still needed immediate attention. Salinas and her staff worked hard to control the environment and make their patients comfortable. They improvised, raising the flaps of the tent during the daytime to let the air flow through. But that also meant that the sun could beat down on a patient, so they hung blankets to block the rays.

Salinas went into the war with two goals—to ensure that her holding wards operated smoothly and that her staff returned home alive. During their first several days in Iraq, she and her staff worked as many as twenty hours at a stretch. Since it was busiest in the evenings, even when she did lie down on her cot Salinas rarely got a good night's sleep. Her mind stayed preoccupied with thoughts of her staff and patients. Salinas didn't meet her mostly young and green staff until a few weeks before they arrived in Kuwait, their initial destination in the Middle East. In a short amount of time she had to determine their level of expertise so she could figure out who to match up with whom. She didn't want to have all experienced nurses and medics in one tent and all inexperienced ones in another. She had a nurse who had just graduated from college and had volunteered at a summer camp handing out Band Aids, and labor and delivery nurses. None had bedside combat skills.

She constantly asked herself, "Are they okay? Who is taking care of what patients? Is a strong staff member paired up with a weak staff member? Do they require more assistance?" Also keeping her awake at night were the frightening and unexpected sounds of war. Some people could get a good night's sleep, but she wasn't one of them.

At home, Salinas wound down by cooking for her fiancé and children, and reading. Sometimes she tried out new recipes from magazines. If she was too busy, she put the recipe aside for a day when she wasn't so rushed. In Iraq, she didn't cook or read. When she did have a moment to relax, she wrote letters to her children, fifteen-year-old Nick and thirteen-year-old Carmen, other family members, and friends. She wouldn't have access to e-mail until two days before she returned home. When she couldn't sleep, she'd flip through a small photo album that she carried in a pocket of her cargo pants.

After three days and more than one hundred patients, Bravo Surgical Company broke camp and moved deeper into Iraq. They followed Marines to the Euphrates and Tigris rivers, and up to Camp Chesty, in central Iraq.

These Marines, including Sergeant Major Harmon Meeker, Salinas's fiancé, were participating in some of the war's fiercest fights, including the battle for An Nasariyah, where eighteen were killed and many more were wounded. The battlefield had moved so fast that Meeker was one hundred miles ahead of the surgical company, his primary provider.

If anything happened to Meeker, a senior enlisted officer, or the one thousand men who reported to him, they would go through Salinas's surgical camp. Salinas wasn't the only one in Bravo Surgical Company who had a Marine fighting. She and others relied on nightly briefings to learn the whereabouts and well-being of husbands and fiancés. They hoped that if they did see their loved ones it was because they walked into the tent and not because they were carried in on a stretcher.

Meeker had been a Marine for twenty-two and a half years, twenty-one as a non-commissioned officer. Salinas was certain he would never be wounded because if Meeker was hurt he wouldn't be able to lead his troops and he wouldn't let that happen. Yet as confident as she was, she still looked up each time the tent flaps opened and a Marine was carried in on a stretcher.

At Camp Chesty, which was larger than Camp Anderson and serviced a variety of helicopter units and POWs, the no-light condition was lifted. Finally, the medical staff could shed its cumbersome chemical gear for lighter, cooler uniforms. Here, the staff still treated an increasing number of Marines with shrapnel wounds. They also received Iraqi patients who had been suffering from a stomach virus before the war. One of the patients was a child. Unfortunately, the medical staff hadn't anticipated the need for pediatric nursing in combat care and didn't have the supplies to treat small throats, airways, and veins. They couldn't use an adult IV on a one-year-old. However, one of the hospital ships did have a specialty provider on it.

The ordeal became not in treating the child but in medevacing the young patient and a parent to the ship. There was only enough space in the helicopter for one parent to go with the child. But neither parent wanted to go. The father said he was staying behind. The mother refused to go because her place was beside her husband. Salinas was indignant. She knew that if her children were sick, there was no question where she would be. She would have stayed by the child's side from start to finish. *We're the enemy, and you're going to leave your child in my care?*

It took a lot of coaxing before the mother finally agreed to travel with her son, but she didn't go because she thought it was the best thing to do. She went because the medical staff convinced her.

Thirty days into her deployment, Salinas was allowed to make one call. She phoned her children. It was one of the toughest calls she has ever made because although she trusted that they were in good hands, she missed them. Making the decision to leave them and fulfill her military obligation by heading off to war was the hardest choice she ever made. Salinas was well aware she could be killed and her children could be left motherless.

If you're a single parent, or if both parents are in the armed services, the military requires a short-term and a long-term "plan of care" for your dependents before you head off to war. Salinas had lined up a brother and a sister-in-law to provide long-term care, and her father-in-law as a short-term care provider. But because of illnesses in the family, none of them was available.

By this time, Salinas had been divorced for nearly a decade. She was the one constant in her children's lives. She never wanted to leave Nick and Carmen to go to Iraq. She asked herself, "How could a woman who prided herself on providing a stable environment for her children agree to go to war?"

On the other hand, Salinas had made a commitment to the military, so how could she not go? Unlike some, Salinas didn't look at her role in the Navy as a choice. While protesting her orders was an option, it wasn't something she felt someone with integrity would do. There were a lot of things she didn't want to do but she did them anyway because they were the right things to do. She told herself that it all came down to standing up for the life she wanted for her children and for their offspring.

She wondered what would happen if everybody who didn't want to go to war found a way to get out of their deployments.

While Salinas labored to find a caretaker for her children in the days leading up to the war, others with arguably less at stake went to great lengths to avoid a trip overseas. A forty-plus-year-old woman got pregnant. The last time she was pregnant was with her fifteen-year-old daughter. A Marine asked his girlfriend to shoot him in the knee. Having never shot a gun before, she didn't expect it to recoil. She shot him in the head, instead, and killed him. Another Marine jumped out of a building to purposely injure his legs.

Navy medical personnel are known as "the healers of the guardians of peace." Salinas knows that may sound hokey, but it's the truth. The Marines are the guardians of peace and it is the surgical company's job to heal them. For the sacrifices that the Marines make, Salinas could make the sacrifice to go to Iraq and take care of them.

After careful consideration, Salinas accepted the offer of a young, single woman to watch Nick and Carmen. The woman worked at the same hospital as Salinas, Camp Lejeune Naval Hospital, and colleagues spoke well of her. But just a few days before Salinas was scheduled to depart, the caretaker backed out.

With no one lined up to watch the kids, Meeker on a ship headed for the Persian Gulf, and her mother and brother seriously ill, Salinas scrambled to get her affairs in order. At the eleventh hour, she arranged for her good friend and co-worker, Lieutenant Commander Lovette Robinson, to stay with Nick and Carmen. On the weekends when Robinson worked at the hospital, another nurse colleague, Pat Hearst, stayed with the children. Robinson and Salinas had been best friends since they met in San Diego in the mid 1990s. They were co-workers at Balboa Naval Hospital before transferring to Camp Lejeune.

Nick and Carmen have known Robinson most of their lives. She is like an aunt to them. Salinas could have approached her friend sooner to watch the children but she didn't want to impose on their friendship and on Robinson's demanding job as the division officer for Camp Lejeune Naval Hospital's multi-service ward. However, Robinson was an appealing choice because she was single and wasn't tied down with children of her own. Plus, she understood from a military standpoint why Salinas felt she had to fulfill her wartime obligation.

Deploying is considered a job equalizer. When a woman is able to deploy, she becomes as desirable and capable as a male Marine, soldier, or sailor. Although some men, like women, make excuses to avoid serving during wartime, there are distinct, female-related reasons (i.e., getting pregnant) that add fuel to the argument that women shouldn't be allowed to serve in the military or in combat. Robinson understood that women have to be willing to do what men are willing to do.

Bravo Surgical Company's final destination was Al Kut. To get there, the surgical staff rode by wired off areas of unexploded Iraqi ordnance that would have to be cleaned up. They didn't encounter firefights, but there was a lot of security with this convoy, including Cobra helicopters keeping watch above the trucks.

The surgical company set up tents during a sandstorm near an Iraqi Air Force Base outside Al Kut. There was still a lot of resistance in the area. The medical staff stayed up all night treating incoming casualties from a firing accident with the Marines. Three died, but the doctors managed to medevac five alive after surgery. It was a rough night.

To care for the mortally wounded and the dead, Bravo Surgical Company always set up an expectant ward and a morgue at the end of the row of tents, away from recovering Marines. The dental staff ran the expectant ward because they were in the least demand of all the doctors. There wasn't a huge need for teeth extractions in Iraq so the dentists, who are physicians first, supported the medical staff and filled in where they were needed. The surgical company had all sorts of doctors with them, including podiatrists and gynecologists, but that didn't mean they were expecting to deliver babies during the war. They're all doctors who have branched out into their specialties.

One of the highest levels of care was performed in the expectant ward. Even though those patients weren't expected to survive, the staff valued their lives as much as someone who was going to make it. The medic who attended to an expectant patient was the last human that patient saw on earth, the last voice heard, and the last hand held. It was a role that all the medical staff took seriously and that some took personally. Salinas treated these patients as if they were a family member, a fiancé or a child. When Mom and Dad couldn't be there, Bravo Surgical Company was going to do everything it could do to make that patient comfortable.

All of the medical supplies used to treat recovering patients in the holding ward could also be found in the expectant ward. The medics were determined to make these patients' last hours as comfortable as humanly possible.

Salinas, who occasionally crossed over into the expectant ward, had great difficulty with these patients. She made a special effort *not* to concentrate on the faces of dying Marines. She would sit beside a Marine, hold his hand, and listen to him talk about Mom and Dad, brother, sister, girlfriend, or wife and kids. She looked into their eyes and listened but tried not to take every single one of those stories to heart.

Salinas had a particularly difficult time accepting the deaths of the nineteen- and twenty-year-old Marines who died early in the war. It broke her heart to see the Marine who had lost his fingers and thought his life was over. His life had changed, but it hadn't ended. It was harder for Salinas to see a Marine carried back to the morgue because that was it. There was nothing left to say. They were just kids and they were killed right off the bat. They didn't even have a chance to see what was accomplished.

As shocking as wounds could be, people heal. But there were some things from which people never recovered. People don't come back from the dead. You can't replace an entire body. When Salinas was working in the holding ward and a Marine who had died was carried through on a stretcher, Salinas looked away because her emotions were raw and on the edge. She told herself to concentrate on helping the Marines who were alive because she couldn't do anything else for those who had died.

One night when Salinas stepped outside the tent for a breath of fresh air, she saw a young Marine who had died being carried out on a stretcher. The sight flooded her mind with questions: Who is he? Who will remember him and the sacrifice of his life? Who did he leave behind? Will anyone miss him? What was he planning to do in life? How will this country honor him? Will our country honor him? She feared he would be lost in the politics of war.

He gave his life so other people could be free to live. Again and again in her mind, she saw him being carried away. She will always remember him. He was all those men and women who did not come home.

As a child, Salinas didn't know what she wanted to be when she grew up. She only knew what she didn't want to be—poor. She recognized the cycle of poverty that existed in her family. If Salinas stayed home, she would repeat the cycle. Her solution was to join the military after high school. She embarked on a ten-year career as an Air Force mechanic. This trade appealed to her because it meant she wouldn't have to depend on a man to fix her car.

By choosing a career in the armed services, she had job security, benefits, and retirement—three things her parents never had. In selecting the Air Force, Salinas could also be stationed at Offutt Air Force Base in Omaha, Nebraska, which was close to her parents' home yet far enough away that she could establish some independence.

Early in her enlistment, the Air Force sent Salinas to England where she met a man, married, and started a family of her own. Her marriage started off rocky and stayed that way. She was twenty-one and naïve. When she and her husband divorced, Salinas still owed the Air Force four years. In that short period of time, she needed to devise and implement a plan that would enable her to support herself and her children. Her mom has no formal education and her dad's schooling topped off at the seventh grade in Mexico. In high school, Salinas hadn't considered college as an option. It seemed like too slow a route for her to achieve the security she craved.

But by her mid-twenties, Salinas discovered that education was the ticket to escaping the cycle of poverty. She wouldn't have to go back to the fields if she could learn a trade. After returning to Nebraska from England, Salinas enrolled in a college nursing program, not because she had a strong desire to work in the medical profession but because it was one of the few degrees she could earn while remaining on active duty at Offutt. Also, with a nursing degree she was almost guaranteed a job, whether she stayed in the military or got out.

One of the differences between this war and previous conflicts has been the increased number of women wounded and killed in combat. Salinas didn't treat any female American patients, but Lieutenant Commander Necia Williams, an anesthesiologist, did. Williams and Salinas were both part of Bravo Surgical Company, but it was on Williams' second tour in Iraq, while stationed at a hospital at Al Asad Air Base in the Al Anbar province from February to September 2005, that she treated several female patients.

One of those patients was Gunnery Sergeant Rosie Noel, who had been wounded while riding her bike to the armory to draw her pistol. As she neared the armory, the thirty-seven-year-old Marine heard an explosion. A rocket-propelled grenade had punctured the desert ground in an open area just a hundred meters behind her. The impact wasn't enough to toss Noel off her bike or knock her unconscious, but she did see small pieces of metal flying toward her. The objects reminded her of a scene in the movie *The Matrix* when gray bullets are floating through the air toward their target. But it wasn't bullets soaring her way. It was shrapnel. One shard, an inch and a half long, soared her way, pierced her cheek, and stuck there.

She didn't know it had lodged in her face or that she was bleeding because it had cut the nerves in her cheek. It wasn't until she felt the dampness of blood on her neck that she realized she was bleeding. Noel continued to the armory because she knew someone would be there to help her. All the other buildings between her and the armory were warehouses. Usually during indirect fire, everyone took cover.

She banged on the hatch, leaving a bloody handprint. A corporal answered. Noel identified her unit and sent the young Marine to get her a pressure bandage from his first aid kit. He was taking too long. A pool of blood was forming on the floor below Noel. Having been in the Marine Corps for seventeen and a half years, Noel was used to getting what she wanted, when she wanted it. She was getting impatient.

The corporal grabbed a green T-shirt and radioed for transportation to take Noel to medical. Since everyone had taken cover during the explosion, it took a minute for the corporal to get a response on the phone. Noel got tired of waiting and started walking to the hospital. It was a long walk but what else was there to do? She was bleeding and needed help. Finally, someone picked her up. Now the ride to the hospital was taking too long for Noel. Shuttle buses got in the way, and the driver kept stopping at stop signs. By this time, Noel's right side was drenched in blood. She held the T-shirt in her left hand against her right cheek while she waved her right hand out the window at oncoming traffic. They could see the blood and let her through.

They arrived at the hospital only to find the front hatch locked. The entrances were on the sides and around back. When Noel got inside, she couldn't find anyone.

Great, I'm going to pass out right here in the hospital and no one is going to know.

"Hello, I'm bleeding here," she said as she walked down the hallway.

The medical staff, having sought shelter in the basement, emerged and took Noel to triage. A medic gave Noel a wad of gauze to apply to her wound. The medical staff needed to X-ray Noel's cheek, but as soon as she removed the gauze, blood gushed out. It felt like someone had taken a cup of warm water and poured it down her neck. She immediately put the gauze back over her cheek. The gunny told medical they were going to have to find another way to take the X-ray. A medic was able to take the X-ray with Noel lifting the gauze off her face just enough to distinguish between the bones in her hand and the bones in her cheek.

The X-ray showed Noel had a broken jaw. Initially, because of all the blood, the medical staff thought the shrapnel had gone all the way through Noel's cheek. Instead, it stopped at her jawbone. She had a lot of swelling so they had to put a tube down her throat.

The doc told Noel she was going to be airlifted to Balad to have her jaw fixed and the nerve damage repaired. He also mentioned that, depending on the severity of her wounds, she might have to go to Germany. Each move meant a higher level of care.

"Just stitch me up and send me back to my Marines," she told the doc.

The doc said they couldn't do that.

Noel thought, *What's the big deal? There's a cut in my cheek. Just sew me up. I can walk. I can talk. There's no reason to send me to Balad or Germany.*

She was getting argumentative. It was drilled into her head— Marines take care of their Marines. The mission was what was important. She had to get back to her troops.

She couldn't believe they were going to *make* her leave her Marines.

Rosie would have loved to have gone home, back to the States, but Rosie wasn't in Iraq. Gunny Noel was.

When Noel went to surgery, Williams anesthetized her. But in that brief meeting Noel made an impact on Williams. The anesthesiologist was impressed with Noel's determination to still lead her troops while lying on the operating table.

Noel woke up in a holding ward in Balad, like the medical area Salinas ran. Before the doc briefed her, someone handed Noel a phone to call her mother. Her mouth was so swollen she could barely open it. She reassured her mom that she was okay, but it was a hard concept for her mom to grasp. One of the waiters in a restaurant she frequented had been killed in Iraq.

After they got off the phone, and before the surgeon could brief her, Noel said, "When can I go back to Al Asad?"

Noel didn't know she had a piece of shrapnel taken out of her cheek until the surgeon in Balad told her he had repaired the nerves in her cheek. He told her that he was sending her to Germany so she could have a steel plate put in her jaw and have her mouth wired shut.

Wire my mouth shut? Ha! I don't think that's going to happen.

The doc said he would check back with her later in the day.

As was the case in Salinas's holding ward, not everyone in Noel's area had combat wounds. One had fallen out of the back of a seven-ton truck. Another wanted morphine and was whining. A master sergeant with a dislocated shoulder couldn't get out of bed by himself. Noel watched him ask a nurse half his size for assistance. Noel wanted to tell them to shut the hell up. To her, pain was a good thing. It meant she was alive.

She lay in bed, wondering how she could get back to Al Asad.

It was important for Noel to return to her Marines as soon as possible. She considered every Marine junior to her in the unit as "her Marines." There were hundreds. She had to set the example.

A nurse pushed the gunny in a wheelchair through a series of tents to a comfort trailer where she was able to get cleaned up. Back in Al Asad, before she left for Balad, her sergeant major had pulled together some of Noel's green T-shirts and shorts, tennis shoes, laptop, and other items. He thought she'd be going back to the States. After her shower, Noel put on clean clothes.

By eleven o'clock in the morning, Noel had already pinned her hair back. By noon, she had showered and was in fresh clothes. It was important to Noel that she get cleaned up not only for herself but for the junior Marines around her. She needed to conduct herself as a professional in front of them.

Her belongings arrived in a drab olive bag labeled "Personal Effects Bag." Just receiving the bag and seeing the label was an eye opener. That's when it hit her, when she realized how close she had come to death and how her situation was worse than she had originally thought.

She sat on her bed and went through the items—her military ID card, dog tag, watch, a 21-karat gold bracelet she had just purchased in Qatar, a small angel she carried in her pocket, and the shrapnel the medical staff in Al Asad had removed from her cheek. Until she actually saw it, she had thought little pieces of shrapnel had hit her face and not one big piece. The shrapnel left a three-inch scar.

Looking through the bag made Noel realize just how close her mom had come to receiving those personal items. It also made her think about her own children. Later, she learned some people thought that because she's a mother, she should have gone home. But to her, there's no difference between being a mother or father in war. If they were going to send her home then they should send home every male Marine wounded by shrapnel.

When the doc returned that afternoon, he explained that her jaw was broken but the bones never separated. She wouldn't need surgery. As they conversed, he assessed Noel to see if she was physically and emotionally prepared to return to Al Asad. Was she physically capable of going back to that environment? How would she react during the next indirect fire?

The funny, or not so funny thing, is that there was an indirect fire incident during her twenty-four hour stay in Balad. So the doctor didn't have to wait long to see how Noel would react.

Noel had been told that days, even a week, could pass before another helicopter came in. That wasn't acceptable to her. When a helicopter arrived, Noel was notified. Like a fireman going to a fire, Noel slid her feet into her boots but left them untied and her camouflage blouse unbuttoned. She grabbed her belongings and ran outside to get into line for the flight. There, she finished tying her boots and buttoning her blouse.

When she got back to Al Asad, she could tell the Marines were excited to see her. It boosted their morale to see a wounded Marine return to their unit. You're back? So soon? She felt it was important that they see she was okay. The fear of the unknown in combat is almost worse than the expected.

In Iraq, Salinas's duties expanded daily. Many job descriptions have a long list of tasks an individual is expected to perform, followed by the line, ". . . and other duties deemed necessary." In Salinas's profession, especially in wartime, other duties can take over. The medical staff did what it had to do to make the wounded Marines as comfortable as possible. Oftentimes a wounded Marine arrived at the medical unit in clothes that had been torn up in a battle or accident, or that had to be cut off so medics could get to the wound. The medical staff wasn't thinking about how they were going to preserve the Marine's clothing. They were getting to the patient's wound as quickly as possible. They just took a pair of trauma scissors and cut everything off, including boots. After the patients received medical care, the next step was for the staff to make the patient as comfortable as possible.

If the patient didn't have other clothes with him, the recovering Marine would leave in a thin sheet unless someone gave him something to wear. Salinas willingly gave the shirt off her back, and gym shorts from her already-limited wardrobe, to her patients. When she returned home, her duffle bag was much lighter, but it was all for a good cause.

Once, after handing over a pair of shorts to a Marine with an abdominal wound, someone joked that now the wounded Marine could say he had been in Salinas's pants.

She did the same for a female Marine who was wounded in combat. The patient was in a paper gown because her clothing had been cut off. Salinas, seeing that the patient was about her size, gave her a T-shirt, pair of shorts, underwear, and shower shoes because she had no boots.

Male and female patients received the same treatment and medical attention. Before she left for Iraq, Salinas had a list of supplies to care for her patients. She didn't pack any supplies specifically for treating female patients. The holding ward's primary goal was to stabilize patients and you stabilize male and female patients the same way through blood pressure and vital signs.

A wound is a wound is a wound, whether it's to a man or a woman. The only difference is when it has affected a male or female part of the anatomy. Once you attend to them medically, women and men have essentially the same needs. They want to be reassured that they're going to make it and not be disabled.

If a woman needed a tampon, pad, or ibuprofen for her menstrual cycle, it came from Salinas's personal supply.

In Al Kut, Salinas fulfilled another of those "and other duties." The medics were with a large support battalion. Although the source is still unknown, something the Marines and the medics ate caused an outbreak of diarrhea. The surgical battalion admitted a few dozen with a gastrointestinal bug. At least fifty percent of Salinas's unit had it at one time or another and they were taking in Marines from outlying areas that were affected. The medical staff's first course of action was to get everyone hydrated. One more "other duty" Salinas performed was washing out a Marine's pants and shorts.

On April 25, 2003, Bravo Surgical Company returned to no-lights condition because of fighting in the area. Since there were no lights on anywhere, not even in the city, the stars seemed more vibrant than usual. So did the flashes of nearby sniper fire. Salinas knew she was in danger but there wasn't anything she could do except to maintain a low profile and to not draw attention to herself and the unit.

If, while standing outside her tent and looking up at the sky Salinas saw a shooting star, she may have made a few wishes—for the safety of her children and her ailing mother and brother, as well as for the protection of the Marines, one in particular. Whomever she was thinking about, it most certainly wasn't herself.

When Salinas was preparing to deploy to the Persian Gulf, she knew in the back of her mind there was a chance she could return wounded or not at all. There was a distinct possibility her children would never see her again. Yet if she had to do it all over again she would go back to the desert. "No matter how much it sucked over there—and it did suck over there—I'd go through all that crap again to be able to hold one person's hand and provide a little bit of comfort," she said.

"Millions of Americans do the right thing," she said. "I'm just one person in that million."

Sergeant Angela Jarboe, United States Army.

Roll with It

"Even if I knew what was going to happen, I would go back again."

—Army Sergeant Angela Jarboe

THE DAY AFTER A VAN EXPLODED ON THE SIDE OF THE ROAD IN IRAQ and wounded Army Sergeant Angela Jarboe, someone (an Iraqi insurgent?) uploaded a video of the carefully executed attack for all to see on the Internet. This is modern-day warfare at its best. An American soldier then downloaded it for Jarboe and gave it to her when she returned from Iraq. I sit at her kitchen table, and she plays the video for me. We watch it on my laptop while she stands beside me. Her three boys, all under the age of five, are in another room. They haven't seen it, but her husband, Tony, has.

The video starts with a close-up of two insurgents rigging a stack of 155mm shells—the kind fired by large cannons—into a blue van. Each shell is about a foot to a foot and a half long. They must have used almost a dozen to cause an explosion that could rip the welded armor off a long-haul truck.

Then the camera lens moves to the driver's seat, where an individual is being interviewed and speaking in Arabic. Jarboe and I don't understand what they are saying. Suddenly, the camera is looking behind the van. Jarboe's convoy comes into view. She is a long-haul truck driver. On this day, she is riding shotgun. Her truck is third in the convoy as it approaches the van. The first security truck passes, and then the next. When Jarboe's truck gets next to the van, the van explodes in a bright sudden flash like an overexposed frame of film.

On the morning of January 3, 2005, the twenty-eight-year-old Jarboe was returning in a convoy from Camp Anaconda, an hour and a half north of Baghdad, to Camp Taji, her base camp, a half-hour north of Baghdad. As a member of 3rd Platoon, 594th Transportation Company, out of Fort Campbell, Kentucky, Jarboe had been driving these and other roads in Iraq for the past six and a half months. The 594th's motto is "Roll with It."

She sat in the passenger seat, wearing cammies and with her long brown hair tucked beneath her helmet. All that showed were her green eyes, high cheek bones, and fair skin. She looked a bit like actress Drew Barrymore without make-up. On her right shoulder was a tattoo bearing the name of one of the most important people in her life—her first-born son, Kenneth. Someday, Jarboe planned to have the names of her other two sons, Anthony and Jaylen, etched on her skin.

Jarboe's truck resembled a tractor-trailer with its long open bed used to haul ammo, water, food, equipment, and other supplies. She favored the vehicle because it was one of the fastest trucks in the desert. She could pass other convoys with a load on her trailers going an average speed of 65 miles per hour.

She'd been driving long-haul trucks for eight years, ever since she enlisted in the Army to tear herself away from the wrong crowd. She wanted to get a fresh start. She chose the Army because that was the military branch in which her grandfather and great uncles served. She also wanted to expand her employment possibilities, which were limited in Greeneville, a small town of about 15,000 in northeast Tennessee. The area has a rich, historical background as the home to such famous people as Davy Crockett and President Andrew Johnson. But like Crockett and Johnson, Jarboe wanted to see more of the world and do things she had never done before. Her career choice, driving long-haul trucks, a traditionally male occupation, was consistent with her youthful tomboy nature. She always liked doing "guy stuff," such as four-wheeling, riding on a motorcycle, and bungee jumping. Little did she know she would be driving long-haul trucks in Iraq in an environment more terrifying and dangerous than she had ever imagined. Each time a convoy of trucks left the gates of a secure camp, it was a moving target till it safely passed through the gates at its destination. During each convoy, Jarboe's greatest concern was the fear of the unknown. She had to be alert and aware of her surroundings at all times because she never knew what the insurgents were going to try next.

At night, snipers shot at the drivers with AK-47 assault rifles. Vehicle bombs and improvised explosive devices (IEDs) blew up trucks, crippling the soldiers and their convoys, and making them susceptible to more ambushes. Rocket-propelled grenades exploded beneath and inside trailers, taking out vehicles and drivers. If the trucks were not armored, rocket-propelled grenades could tear holes in their sheet metal sides and spray everybody in the cab with lethal shrapnel. The highway was a shooting gallery . . . worse if you were hauling gasoline or ammo.

In the early days of the occupation, bombs were hidden in trash bins, buried along the side of roads and tucked in drink cans and even road kill carcasses. Soldiers picked up on these techniques and began cleaning roadsides, chopping down trees and clearing brush. The insurgents responded by burying bombs under gravel or asphalt. Each time the soldiers adjusted to an attack, the insurgents readjusted their tactics.

The insurgents were afraid to attack the infantry, with its arsenal of weapons, so they went after the next best thing—their supplies, which were being transported across the wide open Iraqi desert by Jarboe and other truck drivers. This military profession had become so vulnerable in Iraq that the Army began offering huge bonuses to new recruits.

A lot of the new soldiers were scared, but so were veterans such as Jarboe and her platoon sergeant, Laura Mitchell, who had two sons of her own. Mitchell, a fast-talking, no-nonsense soldier, had nineteen years in the Army when she deployed to Iraq for the fourth and final time of her career. Sometimes, as in Mitchell's case, knowing what to expect could be scarier than not knowing. A sense of imminent danger followed the soldiers as they convoyed away from their camp each day. There were no guarantees of what lay ahead. Every mile of every road was a potential trap, an ambush. Every trip was a potential one-way ride.

This was the second deployment for twenty-three-year-old Specialist Joseph Remmers, who drove with Jarboe on January 3 and during most of the convoys leading up to that day. Remmers was tall, with a medium build and blonde hair. If Jarboe had a younger brother in Iraq, she imagined that he would resemble Remmers.

Like Jarboe, Remmers was from a town so small that when you asked him where he was from, he wouldn't say specifically. Instead, he'd say that he grew up forty-five miles from Lincoln, Nebraska. On his first deployment, the convoys drove mostly in the daytime. This made sense to Remmers because driving while it was light gave him a chance to spot the enemy. But between that tour and the next someone decided it would be safer to convoy in the evenings. Remmers didn't agree. The Iraqi insurgents were better organized and more hostile. And in the evening, they could see him but he couldn't see them—a lethal combination.

Despite the heightened level of danger in the desert, Jarboe didn't become overly anxious. She got used to living in fear, so much so that she eagerly volunteered to participate in convoys knowing full well that there was a good chance she wouldn't return alive. She admitted to being scared. She knew she could be maimed or killed, but she didn't let herself dwell on it. That would just make every mission a nightmare. The soldiers were reminded daily not to become complacent.

They convoyed almost every day, hauling supplies to different camps or helping companies relocate from one camp to another. The missions ranged in length from twenty minutes to twenty-one days. Most involved convoying forty-five minutes to Camp Anaconda, six hours to Mosul, one hour to Fallujah, or a half hour to Baghdad International Airport.

Regardless of the imminent danger, Jarboe and her fellow soldiers, male and female, looked forward to the convoys because they wanted to be part of the action. They were prepared to put their lives at risk because that's what they had been trained to do. To travel to Iraq and stay in the same camp day in and day out wasn't what the soldiers had in mind. Staying behind usually meant doing maintenance on the trucks, filling up sand bags to fortify the compound, and picking up trash. The soldiers had the most fun on the convoys because it meant they were away from their company and could breathe. No officers looking over their shoulders. They were busy and focused, their senses heightened and alert. Plus, the soldiers in Jarboe's battalion were like a second family to her. She felt protective of them. When they were traveling into harm's way she wanted to be with them—to take care of and look after them.

And there was another perk: getting outside their Spartan compound and visiting other camps. Mosul, for example, had a full size, indoor basketball court. It also had the best food, including a fabulous stir fry. The soldiers even volunteered to go to Mosul after Iraqi insurgents bombed its dining facility and killed thirteen people. They were willing to put their lives on the line for good food. Jarboe liked going to Fallujah, where she placed second in a weightlifting competition. Nobody could remember how much iron she pumped, but that wasn't the point. The point was doing something, not being bored, getting some creature comforts.

At Camp Taji, Jarboe slept on a bed in an old Iraqi barracks. On the road, the soldiers stayed inside the various compounds. Some bedded down on cots they brought along. Others slept sitting up in the cab of the truck, or lying on the hood or in the trailer. Still others seeking a cooler place to sleep or shelter from the rain slept on a tent cot under the truck. Jarboe preferred to put her cot beside or behind the trailer.

Jarboe's attitude made her one of her platoon sergeant's star soldiers. Mitchell, a woman who had as many as forty soldiers working for her at one time, described Jarboe as the best female non-commissioned officer out there not only because of her enthusiasm but also because she did her job well. "I never had to check behind her."

On this particular morning in early January, Mitchell had assigned Jarboe to another mission but then reassigned her to go to Camp Anaconda so Jarboe could be the convoy commander. But as more security was added to the convoy, Jarboe lost her role as supervisor. She would still be in charge of the soldiers from her transportation company. Security took over the small convoy of five or six trucks. Each of the three security vehicles had turrets with .50-caliber machine guns, and Mark 19 automatic grenade launchers.

Their mission that morning was to take trucks to Camp Ana-conda, thirty miles north of Camp Taji, so the vehicles could be fit-ted with new armor that would give them more protection against ambushes and improvised explosives. The truck Jarboe and Rem-mers drove hadn't been "up armored" yet. At the time, it and many other trucks were "ghetto rigged" with armor—half-inch-thick sheets of metal that hung from the windows on the outside of the passenger and driver's sides of the truck. The truck had air conditioning but the armor prevented the windows from closing. Now the trucks are equipped with ballistic windows that close all the way. They also had a sheet of metal outside on the back of the cab and one that ran across the bottom inside of the windshield to deflect oncoming fire.

Jarboe showered the night before her mission and woke around 2:30 A.M. She grabbed her bags and carried them to her truck. She always brought an overnight bag with a change of clothes in case the convoy had to spend one or more nights at its destination.

Prior to each convoy, the troops were briefed by intelligence about the activities from the past twenty-four hours and what to look out for. The night before, some of the soldiers in Jarboe's company had hauled supplies for the post exchange to Baghdad. It was a routine mission, with the convoy encountering the usual sniper fire. They returned about four in the morning, just as Jarboe was preparing to leave. She ran into Mitchell, her platoon sergeant, in the armor room, where the ammo was stockpiled. Mitchell was turning in her ammo, and Jarboe was drawing hers.

As Jarboe collected her ammo, others in the room, including Mitchell, talked about how dangerous the missions had become. The number of bombings and ambushes had increased. Mitchell and Staff Sergeant Chris Lawson were sitting in a Humvee listen-ing to the radio while soldiers unloaded the trucks from the previous night's mission. The area around Camp Anaconda, where Jarboe was headed, was hot. Mitchell sensed danger and asked Jarboe if she wanted her to go with them. Jarboe said she would be okay. Mitchell was tired but would have gone. Her night was rough, but it would be nothing compared with Jarboe's morning.

On this mission, Remmers drove the truck. Jarboe rode shotgun and manned the radio. There wasn't a lot of room in the cabs but there was enough space for a cooler of ice and water. Some soldiers had a charger that reached from the cooler to the truck's cigarette lighter, keeping the water cold inside.

The seats were vinyl, and could be adjusted by pushing a button that let air in and out, raising and lowering Jarboe. The cabs were equipped with air conditioning that the drivers used even with the windows down, and a heater for use at night when the desert air cooled down. The inside of the trucks smelled like the desert and dirt.

Camp Anaconda was about a forty-five minute drive on a paved road with potholes and no shoulders. Jarboe's convoy completed its mission and was on its way back to Camp Taji. They were twelve miles north of the camp when they ran into trouble. It was 9:30 A.M.

There were always vehicles on the side of the road, so a van parked on a dirt shoulder didn't necessarily raise the suspicions of soldiers in the convoy. Soldiers patrolled the roadside every day, checking those vehicles. The blue van must have arrived after a roadside patrol passed by.

While Jarboe favored the fast speed of the long-haul trucks, they didn't always have the opportunity to drive at high speeds. In convoys, they could go only as fast as the slowest vehicle ahead of them. They couldn't drive off and leave their protection behind.

Speed played a critical role in preventing casualties. Sometimes a small roadside bomb or IED would cripple a slow-moving convoy while the same explosion would merely bruise a fast-moving truck. Driving at a high speed made it difficult for the insurgents to time the explosions.

Remmers kept a distance of about fifty to seventy-five meters between his truck and the truck ahead of him so he would have plenty of time to stop in an emergency. The lead Humvee acted as the eyes of the convoy and guided the trucks behind it. If there were a pothole in the road caused by an earlier explosion, the lead would swerve around it, and the rest of the vehicles would follow. Seldom did anyone fill in the holes left by a roadside bomb, unless it was smack in the middle of a highway. The edges of the roadway were pocked from multiple explosions caused by improvised bombs.

The convoy was traveling about 45 miles per hour, much slower than the 75 to 80 miles per hour Remmers preferred to keep from being ambushed. Neither Remmers nor Jarboe knows why they weren't traveling faster.

The convoy approached a blue van parked on the side of the road. The first gun truck drove by, and then the next. Just as Jarboe's truck came parallel with the van, the van exploded.

Flames shot thirty feet into the air.

Black smoke poured into the truck's open windows, engulfing it and blinding the driver.

The windshield blew out and shattered. Jarboe's instinctive reaction was to look down, even though the truck drivers wore goggles to protect their eyes. She didn't want to risk finding out whether the glass could pierce her goggles and eyes. But the heat was so great that her goggles melted. She tore them off her head.

Jarboe was sitting on the side of the truck closest to the van, and the flames were right in her face. There was no way she could escape from her side of the truck. If she had tried to flee through her door, she would have stepped into an inferno.

Her thoughts immediately turned to her family back home. *I can't die today. I have to get back to my kids, to Tony.* She wasn't scared because she'd always thought that if it were her time to die, she would die, and there was nothing she could do to change it. If it wasn't her time to die, she'd see her family again. It was out of her hands.

Remmers saw a flash of white light and then everything went silent for a second or two. He felt disoriented, like he had just woken from a dream. When he got his bearings, he shouted to Jarboe, "You okay?"

"Yeah—pull over!" Remmers could feel from the bumpy ride that some of the tires had been blown out, and he could see that Jarboe's side of the cab was now on fire. He jerked the truck to a stop across the median that separated the north and southbound lanes.

"Get out!" Jarboe yelled. Remmers' weapon, an M-16, was stuck, and he was trying to free it. He wasn't leaving without it. He knew he would be the first one out of the truck, and he had no idea who or what they would encounter once they left the vehicle. Were there insurgents ready to ambush them? They might be sitting ducks, but at least with the M-16 they'd be armed sitting ducks. Jarboe couldn't find her weapon.

They had been driving in the southbound lane. The northbound lane was on Remmers' side of the truck. Remmers got out and ran across the northbound lane to escape the "kill zone." He didn't know Jarboe was hurt. When he got to the other side of the road, he looked back and saw Jarboe crawling over the driver's seat and trying to get out of the truck. "Hurry up!" he yelled to her. She herself didn't know how badly she was wounded. Her leg hurt but she figured she had just banged her shin hard. It wasn't until she climbed out of the truck and felt her bones rubbing together that she realized her leg was probably broken in several places.

With the truck on fire behind her, Jarboe yelled to Remmers, "My leg's broken!" Remmers didn't hear her, but he and a soldier from one of the Humvees ran back anyway and retrieved Jarboe and laid her down on the side of the road. Remmers checked his back. They needed to get out of there fast. The two male soldiers each took a side of Jarboe and carried her to the other side of the northbound lane.

Both Remmers and Jarboe had minor cuts and blood on their faces from where shards of the windshield had hit them. Remmers still hadn't noticed how badly Jarboe's leg was torn up—he could see she was in pain, but it wasn't like in the movies, no blood spurting out.

Each convoy had at least one combat life saver who was trained in first response and could provide care until a medic arrived on the scene. If the wounded soldier was close to her camp, they'd take her there first for medical care. A female combat life saver from another platoon was on the scene and wanted to splint Jarboe's leg but couldn't. The pain was too great. So Jarboe asked her to hold the wounded leg in a certain position. By now, Jarboe had calmed down a bit. Her sense of urgency had been replaced by relief. She was still alive. Maybe she'd see her family after all.

As she lay on the ground, she could smell the burning ammo from both the truck and the van. But that's about all she'd ever remember. Her awareness of her surroundings faded as she lost more and more blood.

By now, the entire cab of the truck was on fire, and Remmers could hear popping from the ammo cans that held their magazines. It was a good time to get away. They carried Jarboe to a Humvee. It was like carrying dead weight. She held her own but Remmers could tell by her face that she was in shock.

They rushed Jarboe back to Camp Taji, about ten miles away, where she and her company had been stationed for the past six months. Once there, Jarboe was taken directly to a clinic for X-rays and for a shot of morphine to ease the pain.

Back at Camp Taji, soldiers from Jarboe's platoon were still sleeping after their long mission the night before when the van exploded. Staff Sergeant Virgil Taylor was one of the first soldiers at the camp to learn Jarboe had been wounded. He was an assistant truck master, in charge of the numerous missions that the soldiers were assigned. When he learned of the ambush and casualty, he ran to Mitchell's room in the barracks and pounded on her door.

"You have to get up! You have to get up!" he shouted. "She's been hit."

"Whose been hit?" she yelled back.

"Sergeant Jarboe."

Mitchell got dressed and rode in a Humvee to the clinic. All the way there, she chastised herself for sending Jarboe on the mission. She blamed herself for whatever wounds Jarboe had received. In her mind's eye, all she could see were Jarboe's three little boys.

There were three clinics at the camp. Jarboe wasn't at the first one they tried. They found her at the second one. Remmers was standing guard outside. He had nicks and cuts on his face from the glass and he kept repeating, "Fuck, my Oakleys are in the truck."

Remmers was all right, just shaken up, maybe a little in shock. He recounted to Mitchell what had happened.

Jarboe was inside, having her shattered leg X-rayed.

Mitchell wanted to see her but the room was already crowded with docs, nurses, field medics, battalion commander and sergeant major, company commander and first sergeant. The doctor in charge said there were too many people in there. Some left and were replaced by squad leaders and by Mitchell. Outside the clinic, a helicopter waited to medevac Jarboe to a hospital in Baghdad.

Before Jarboe left, Mitchell retrieved a frame holding three pictures, one of each of Jarboe's boys. "This will keep you motivated," the chaplain said to Jarboe, meaning the photos. As Jarboe lay on a stretcher in the helicopter, she could see that Mitchell was upset.

"I'm going to be okay," Jarboe whispered. "I'm going to be okay."

After the helicopter took off, the chaplain hugged and consoled Mitchell. He said, "You gave her the most precious gift. You gave her the photos of her boys." He told her that Jarboe was going to be all right and said a prayer.

Before leaving the clinic, a soldier handed Mitchell a dark green trash bag with some of Jarboe's personal belongings. Without looking at the contents, she put the bag in the Humvee and took it back to her command post.

When she arrived at the post, she was met by other members of her platoon, First Sergeant William Tilton and Sergeant First Class Timothy Krider. They talked for a while, going over the day's events, how the ambush had unfolded, and how Jarboe was doing. Eventually, Mitchell remembered the bag.

"Look, they gave me her stuff," she said.

She opened the bag and, not knowing what was in it, pulled out Jarboe's shirt. It was covered in blood. The blood stained Mitchell's hands red, and she started to cry again. She didn't have a chance to look any further. Tilton snatched the bag from her. "They had no right to give this bag to you," he said as he hugged her. "It'll be all right. It's not your fault."

If Mitchell had looked further into the bag, she would have found Jarboe's bloody Kevlar helmet, load-bearing vest, part of her left pants leg, and her left boot. Krider and Tilton inventoried the items so the Army could replace them. Then they found a trash can and burned the clothing. Some of the items that Jarboe was wearing at the time of the explosion weren't ruined but needed to be washed. Sergeant Daniel Akins cleaned the vest and ammo pouches.

At the hospital in Baghdad, the medical staff asked Jarboe for her wedding ring and wallet because they were taking her to surgery. They cut off her cammies and dressed her in a gown. During the initial surgery, doctors removed shrapnel and put a small external circular fixator on her leg to keep her shattered bones in place before medevacing her to an airbase at Camp Anaconda and then to Landstuhl Regional Medical Center in Germany, the largest American military hospital outside the United States.

On the thirty-minute flight from Baghdad to Camp Anaconda, Jarboe lay on a stretcher in a helicopter. All the occupants had to wear ear plugs because the drumming of the engines inside the metal fuselage was so overpoweringly loud. A line of stretchers stacked three high went from the front to the back of the aircraft. Jarboe was in the middle of one stack. At one point, a wounded soldier below her attempted to stand up and put his hand on Jarboe's wounded left foot for support. She screamed, but he couldn't hear her over the roar of the turbines. Anyway, like all of them he was wearing earplugs.

Jarboe tried to sleep on the next flight, from Camp Anaconda to Germany, but it was hard. A medic gave her morphine to make her more comfortable, but it didn't help much. She had to lie on a stretcher for six hours without moving. She couldn't roll onto her side because her leg was elevated. She arrived in Germany with a severe headache.

Wounded soldiers such as Jarboe go through several echelons of medical care before arriving home. In Jarboe's case, she received treatment at Camp Taji, Baghdad, Camp Anaconda, Landstuhl, and finally Fort Campbell. At each location, the care she received was sufficient for the time but rushed. One of the goals was to get her back to the States as soon as possible, where doctors sometimes had to repair the procedures of previous surgeries.

Jarboe was hospitalized in Germany for a week, where she had more surgery, and then was flown to Blanchfield Army Community Hospital at Fort Campbell, Kentucky, where she spent ten days as an inpatient before starting outpatient physical therapy.

When she arrived at Blanchfield, Jarboe saw her husband Tony and her boys for the first time in more than six months. Kenneth, the oldest at five, looked happy to see her. Anthony and Jaylen were quiet. Tony, who had been taking care of the three boys while his wife was away, now would have one more person to watch over.

I first met Jarboe at Blanchfield Army Community Hospital. It was July 8, 2005, six months after the van exploded and came close to taking her life. She had been going to the hospital twice a week for physical therapy. When I arrived, she was sitting on a plinth, or a patient's table. Jarboe was easy to spot because she was the only female patient in the clinic at the time. All the other patients were male soldiers wearing gray T-shirts with *Army* written in black across the front. The clinic had female patients, some worse off than Jarboe, but they weren't there that morning.

She had her hair parted on the side and pulled back, showing off a pair of gold hoop earrings. Engraved on an eighteen-karat gold necklace were the names of her three sons—Kenneth, Anthony, and Jaylen. The necklace was a gift from the soldiers in her platoon.

But fighting for and getting my attention was not her hair, her earrings, or her necklace, but her lower left leg, where her pants were rolled up past her knee, exposing a contraption of rods, screws, and pins.

Three pins penetrated Jarboe's leg just below the knee to hold her crushed tibia and fibula in place. The pins looked like skewers as they pierced one side of her leg and emerged from the other side. They attached to a metal circular plate known as a halo, which in turn connected to bolts. Three rods helped to hold the apparatus in place.

I stood with trepidation in the doorway of the clinic, not knowing exactly what to expect and not liking how that felt. This was my first meeting with a female soldier who had been wounded while fighting for our country—a sacrifice on which I placed immeasurable value. How was I supposed to approach this casualty of war—this sister, mother, daughter, wife, friend, and soldier? I was fourteen years her senior and not eligible for a military career. Yet, leading up to a series of interviews with Jarboe, I couldn't help but reflect that I had never put my life on the line for my country. It had never occurred to me to seek a military career, and the draft was only for young men. I thought about what choices I would make today if I were just graduating from high school or college. Would a military career have entered my mind before or after 9/11?

I waited for a personal invitation from Jarboe. And I got it. Our eyes met and before I had a chance, she smiled at me. Already she had my attention and my admiration. I left pity and self regard at the door and entered the clinic.

She was wearing a navy blue tank top and light blue sweat pants. A sock and sneaker covered her right foot. Her left foot was bare. She's five feet five inches tall, a characteristic hard to discern when she's sitting down, legs stretched out in front of her. She has a medium build. She had filled out a bit since returning from the war because she hadn't been as active as she used to be. Her wounded leg prevented her from playing around with her children. Her independent and industrious streak had been slowed as she lumbered through the day on crutches.

The day I met Jarboe, I also was introduced to David Boltz, the physical therapy assistant who worked with her. I watched him rub the bottom of Jarboe's left foot with lotion. She squirmed, grimaced, and laughed. The bottom of her foot was extremely sensitive. She could move her toes but couldn't curl them. The muscles that allowed her to move her toes were in her foot; the muscles that enabled her to curl her toes were in her leg, which had no movement.

Boltz had been a physical therapy assistant (PTA) for thirteen years, and had spent two and a half of those years at Blanchfield. Before becoming a PTA, he was in the Army's Special Forces for twenty years and in combat engineering for four years. He had seen about a dozen wounded female soldiers pass through the clinic since the start of the war. Most, if not all, of the wounds had been broken bones caused by motor vehicle wrecks and blasts.

In addition to working with Jarboe, Boltz was treating another wounded female who had worn a halo on her leg for eighteen months, a year longer than Jarboe. The other woman was wounded when an Iraqi insurgent crossed a lane and crashed his vehicle into her tanker truck in Iraq. The wreck shattered her leg.

Jarboe's foot and leg were still swollen six months after she sustained her wounds because they weren't getting the muscle activity necessary to move the fluid along in those areas. Arteries transport blood away from the heart, but the heart isn't a suction pump. The blood and fluids traveling back to the heart needed a push. That's done with muscle movement, what Jarboe didn't have. That's where Boltz came in. The only way to get rid of some of the swelling was by elevating her leg and massaging it to stimulate the fluid. Eventually, Jarboe would have motion in her leg. How much was yet to be determined.

Sometimes Jarboe's knee bothered her but she thought she had a high tolerance for pain. "While it happened, I didn't cry," she said, referring to the explosion. "Maybe I was in shock."

When Boltz finished rubbing Jarboe's foot, the patient stretched her leg and foot for a while on the table. Then she reached for her crutches and walked to the parallel bars on the other side of the room. There, she performed exercises that she couldn't do lying down, such as lifting her leg to the side and behind her. Recently, her physical therapist added an exercise to strengthen Jarboe's arms. She was grateful for this. Her physical therapy could get monotonous. Jarboe struggled to stay motivated, especially when another major surgery was looming.

The external fixator hurt a lot at first and was heavy. The pins were painful. Jarboe took morphine or Demerol every four hours. It took awhile before she could lift her leg off the ground, but that had more to do with her surgeries than with the weight of the halo. At night, she occasionally bumped the pins and rods against her right leg, bruising it. She slept on her back because the halo was round but it didn't go all the way around. It opened in the back like a horseshoe. She could wear only shorts or loose pants. No jeans. The pants she was wearing when we met had a pocket above the knee that she used to hold a child's drink when she and the boys ordered take-out.

Less obvious than the fixator yet also visible were the three scars on Jarboe's left leg. The scar on the top was where it all began, where shrapnel cut and pierced her leg, possibly crippling her for life. A six-inch scar on the left side of her leg and a four-inch scar on the right were made by doctors to clean the wound, to keep out infection, and to align the bones. The scars looked fresh, bright red on her pale skin.

She ended her physical therapy session by filling a plastic bag from the ice machine, sitting back down on the table, and placing the bag on her ankle for fifteen minutes. Her ankle turned red from the ice but she barely noticed the coldness. She recalled spraining her ankle years ago and having to put ice on it. How cold it felt. She wasn't having the same sensation. There were still some spots on Jarboe's leg and foot where she couldn't feel anything. When she was through, she pulled a sock over her left foot.

Before we left the clinic, I asked Boltz how Jarboe was handling her rehabilitation. He hadn't seen her have a bad day. "She has her up days and her down days, but no real bad days. She's mostly positive."

Boltz said women in combat support roles tend to handle their wounds better than the men. They were more aggressive in rehab than men in similar jobs. However, women have more personal-appearance issues. Men don't mind the scars so much. In fact, scars are something to brag about. Jarboe didn't think her self-image had been affected by her wounds and scars. "I know my leg is going to be scarred, but I'm going to walk again," she said. "I'm still going to wear shorts. The scars aren't going to bother me. It doesn't even bother me when people ask about it."

Boltz's wife, Davida, worked in the deployment health clinic and was the primary care provider for some who were wounded in Afghanistan and Iraq. She was Jarboe's care provider, acting as the "gatekeeper" for all of the wounded soldier's medical care. She was also a former Army nurse, and collected World War II and Vietnam books on the women's Army corps.

Davida kept a close eye on all her patients for signs of depression, especially soldiers like Jarboe who had a substantial wound that could alter her self image.

There are psychological surveys about how much crueler women warriors are in battle than men, especially if they have children, because they are ferocious about protecting their young. It goes back to the cave days. The first thought that came to Jarboe's mind after the explosion was that she had to get back to her children. What's the first thought that comes to a man's mind? Davida said men are more self-oriented. They love their kids, but it's not like a mother.

In her practice, Davida has also found that women tolerate pain better than men. She said that sometimes men are like little boys and need to be coddled. The women have a lot of fortitude. In general, female soldiers are tougher than your average woman. This is especially true of career soldiers.

At this point, the war had been going on for two and a half years. More than 1,800 Americans had been killed and many, many more had been wounded. Jarboe was considered one of the lucky ones.

She knew it could have been worse. "I'm just glad I made it home alive to my children and husband."

Yet when I met her, she had already been through seven surgeries and there were more to come. In her next surgery, she would have a bone graft and a rod would be put inside her leg. She would also have surgery on her calf muscle because her foot wouldn't bend properly. Jarobe had yet to turn thirty and already she had to accept physical restrictions, possibly a permanent limp.

In addition to the physical challenges, there would be emotional consequences. It was bad enough that her youngest son, Jaylen, didn't recognize her when she returned. He was only six months old when she deployed. Now she had to cope with not being able to hold him and carry him the way she was able to embrace and cuddle his two older brothers. Kenneth was happy to see her. Her husband told her that when she was gone, he and their sons would be sitting at the kitchen table and out of the blue Kenneth would say, "I miss Mommy." And although she wasn't traumatized by the attack that wounded her, it was not an experience easily forgotten.

The boys and their father weren't the only ones sitting around the kitchen table. On my last morning in the Fort Campbell area, Jarboe and I visited her platoon sergeant, Mitchell, in her home. I was eager to hear the women give voice to their combat experiences. But I have to be honest. Even though I went to Mitchell's home to hear stories about Iraq, never, in my wildest dreams, did I expect to find myself listening to two women, both younger than me, sharing their war stories. These were not the stories of their grandfathers, fathers, brothers, sons, or husbands. They were telling me what they had lived through, and in many cases their stories were just as harrowing as what their male counterparts had faced.

As a female civilian, it seemed the only quality I had in common with the women sitting beside me was our gender. There was just no relating to these soldiers and no putting myself in their boots. To do so would be to minimize their courage and heroism, and to say that I knew what they had lived through. What they experienced in the desert was beyond my comprehension and exceeded what I wanted to imagine for anyone in war.

Between the two of them, Jarboe and Mitchell have five children. I realized that the same could be said if I had been sitting at a table with two soldiers who were fathers. Yet there is still a newness and vulgarity to women in war, to women attacking and even more so, to being attacked. There was a time lag in what we civilians knew, saw, and understood about women in uniform because most of their stories hadn't reached us. Women were in combat, but a part of me couldn't believe it. Their stories still seemed surreal. I never felt comfortable hearing them; only astonished and then a delicate desire for distance.

Mitchell recalled a mission where members of her platoon were traveling from Taji to Kuwait. There were three convoys. Mitchell's platoon was in the third convoy. Early on, they were instructed to take a detour, which meant driving by Fallujah, a hot spot at the time. As they got close to the city, at about two o'clock in the morning, Mitchell noticed an unusual number of Marines on the side of the road, sweeping the area for IEDs. Whenever troops were on foot patrol, the convoy slowed to five miles per hour.

Shortly after the convoy passed the Marines, one of the trucks in Mitchell's' convoy broke down. They were between Fallujah and the front gate of the Baghdad International airport—not a good place to stop. They were out in the open. There were houses but no street lights so it was dark. They couldn't see anything. Typically, they stopped outside safe areas only for emergencies. This was an emergency. They had to drop a trailer and hook it up to a functioning truck. As soon as this was done, they rolled on.

"After that it was like the Fourth of July," Mitchell said. The radios were hot in Baghdad. Everyone was talking, asking for medevac and support.

Next thing she knew, the first convoy was ambushed and soldiers were being medevaced out. Then the second convoy got hit. More soldiers were medevaced out and a truck was on fire. The police, or sheriff as they called them, ordered Mitchell's convoy to stop, which it did for about an hour until receiving permission to continue.

Mitchell's trucks passed the second convoy. They reached the first convoy and were going to pass it when they got hit. An IED exploded in front of and behind her convoy. Her convoy was told to stand fast. The soldiers stayed in their trucks.

Finally, they received the okay to continue. Mitchell was in the seventh truck of her convoy. They had started moving when she saw a light coming from the right. Before she could tell the driver to stop, a rocket-propelled grenade hit her truck. Mitchell felt it explode under her vehicle. The radiator and oil lights went on because the grenade had hit the radiator and oil pan.

Shrapnel hit the ballistic windows, cracking but not penetrating the glass. If they hadn't had ballistic windows, the RPG would have hit Sergeant Chris Beckel in the throat and head. Ballistic windows have the thickness of five panes.

Fortunately for Mitchell, metal plates inside the cab protected her from the RPG. They kept driving after the RPG hit their truck. Later, Mitchell's truck would break down but not before they made it to a Marine checkpoint.

That night, Mitchell got a sense of how Jarboe felt when the van exploded. Although Mitchell wasn't wounded, both her legs had gone numb. She felt the terror of thinking she was wounded.

As Jarboe and I watch the video of the van exploding beside her truck, Jarboe flinches, even though she has watched this video a dozen times already. Flames shoot thirty feet into the air and the van and truck disappear into a boil of black smoke. For a couple of seconds, we can't see anything but smoke.

If I didn't know Jarboe was alive, if I didn't feel her presence beside me, if I hadn't felt her jump when the van exploded, I would have sworn she had been killed in the attack. It seemed incomprehensible that someone could survive such an explosion. "Can I borrow the video?" I ask Jarboe. "I know someone who can translate it." I wanted to know what the Iraqis were saying to one another as they loaded the van with bombs, and what the driver was saying when someone put a microphone in front of him.

"No." She doesn't want to violate operational security. I can't fault her loyalty, but I don't understand. When I returned home, I searched the Internet for the video. I found others, but never the one of Jarboe. Later, Jarboe received authorization to release the video to me.

A year after Jarboe was wounded she still walked with a slight limp but no longer needed crutches or a cane. She was finished with surgery, at least for now. She continued physical therapy to increase the range of motion in her ankle. The Army extended her military contract until she no longer needed medical atten-tion. During that period, she worked in her company's office, managing their paperwork.

Wounded or not, Jarboe had planned to get out of the Army after she returned from Iraq and fulfilled her commitment. She didn't want to go back to Iraq, but not because she was afraid of another ambush. She was thinking more of her children. "I know they need me more than the Army does, especially with them being so young," she said. Her plans included enrolling in college but she hadn't chosen an area of study.

Jarboe admits that when she enlisted in the Army she never envisioned herself in a war, but when you're in the military, you can't think that way, she said. "I went because I had to. I was a soldier before I was a mom."

Epilogue

THE EXPERIMENT INVOLVING THE LARGEST BAND OF SISTERS TO SERVE in combat in U.S. history has been a success. The heroics of America's mothers, daughter, sisters, and wives on the battlefield can no longer be understated. In this war they have proven beyond a doubt that they can run convoys on the most dangerous roads in Iraq, man vehicles and personnel checkpoints, perform route clearance operations, and conduct quick reaction force operations when others got hit on the road with IEDs. They have boldly faced the threat of IEDs. They have been shot at and returned fire.

One member of the band of sisters, Army Sergeant Leigh Ann Hester, became the first woman since World War II to be awarded the Silver Star medal for valor in combat. She skillfully led her team of MP soldiers in a counterattack after about fifty insurgents ambushed a supply convoy they were guarding. A female driver with Hester's unit, Specialist Ashley J. Pullen, received the Bronze Star for her bravery. Pullen laid down fire to suppress insurgents and then exposed herself to heavy fire in order to provide medical assistance to her critically wounded comrades, saving several lives.

More than seventy American women have been killed on the battlefield. That's about twice the number of U.S. military women killed in action in Korea, Vietnam, and Desert Storm combined. More than 430 female warriors have been wounded in combat. Many are familiar with Army Captain Tammy Duckworth, who was co-piloting her Black Hawk helicopter when it was shot down by a rocket-propelled grenade. The explosion damaged Duckworth's right arm and cost her both legs.

Less familiar are the stories of women such as Air Force Staff Sergeant Aime Gaona, who was wounded twice. The first time she was riding in a Humvee that was destroyed by an IED, wounding all four occupants. Gaona suffered a concussion and was hit with a bomb fragment. Two months later a sniper's bullet ripped into her right leg, fracturing the femur.

Army Specialist Crystal Davis lost part of her leg when her vehicle hit an IED. While trapped inside the destroyed vehicle, with her right foot nearly severed, Davis told her cohorts that she would get herself out. She didn't want them to risk coming to her.

Like their male counterparts, these female warriors were eager to put their combat training to use. They stepped up to the challenge, and when they were forced to make split-second decisions, they relied on their training. Lance Corporals Carrie Blais and Pricilla Kispetik volunteered to go with the grunts into a highly volatile town to search women and children on the streets and in their homes. They brought to the battlefield a willingness to do what was needed to accomplish the mission. Lance Corporal Chrissy DeCaprio defended her convoys from the turret of a scout vehicle, and when she returned to the States, she was eager to go back and do it again. She brought confidence to the battlefield and an intense desire to protect her troops. Sergeant Angela Jarboe accepted the fear that went along with driving a long-haul truck on convoys that were ambushed and hit by IEDs on a daily basis.

Captains Amy McGrath and Vernice Armour helped ensure the safety of Marines and soldiers on the ground by seeking out and attacking the enemy from the cockpits of their F-18 fighter jet and Cobra attack helicopter. While taking fire from the enemy, Lieutenant Colonel Polly Montgomery transported troops on and off the battlefield in an aging C-130 and Brown provided lookout for the ground troops.

Lieutenant Estella Salinas and Specialist Rachelle Spors treated the wounded and the dying near and on the battleground. Army Master Sergeant Margaret Furman toted $150,000 to $200,000 in a backpack through the streets of Baghdad for roughly five months to make purchases for the Army. One time, acting as an agent for the Coalition Provisional Authority (CPA), Furman transported $1.5 million from the U.S. government to the Central Bank of Baghdad through the busy streets of Baghdad. Gunnery Sergeant Yolanda Mayo reported the news from Baghdad and throughout Iraq and the Middle East.

This band of sisters is bound by courage, pride, a focus on the mission, a desire to do as well if not better than the men because they know they are being watched closely, a love for their country, and a need to not necessarily stand out as women warriors but to be acknowledged for their contributions.

They bring many attributes to the battlefield, including intelligence, a different perspective to problem solving, quick reflexes, intuition, and a sensitivity that only a mother can offer a wounded or dying Marine or soldier who is crying out in pain. They are empathetic, which may not sound like a big deal, but as Montgomery explained, if she could ease the concern of a pilot in Iraq who had a sick child back in the States, she would be freeing the pilot's mind to focus on his mission. Women are also able to search Iraqi women and children and guard female enemy prisoners of war.

Preparing for and going into combat continues to be different for women, especially those in fighter squadrons who have to go out of their way to fit in. They have to find a balance in doing more to excel and to prove themselves, but not so much that they stand out. This is also true of women serving with infantry, recon, artillery, and other units that are not accustomed to having women around. DeCaprio earned the respect of artillery reservists by bringing them home alive, and Blais and Kispetik earned the respect of an infantry unit by being professional.

What more evidence do the American people need to prove that the experiment of women in combat has been a success? The military no longer differentiates between male and female convoy commanders. When will the American people stop making a distinction?

Marine Gunnery Sergeant Yolanda Mayo said serving her country is a job she accepted freely and without prejudice. "Most of our brothers don't look at us any differently," she said. "It's just the gunny, first sergeant, CO. It's time everyone looked at us this same way."

Since the war in Iraq began in March 2003, some women in the military feel there is a segment of America that wants to hide the fact that women die in combat operations, almost as if they are ashamed they have put women in such a position. But the women want us to know that they put themselves in those positions.

First Lieutenant Lindsay Mathwick of 9th Communications Battalion Motor Transport wrote in an e-mail from Camp Fallujah, "I'm proud to run convoys through some of the most dangerous roads in Iraq and so are the rest of my female counterparts, of which there are many. Women in the military today are in combat operations. We get blown up and shot at just like the guys—the terrorists and insurgents don't differentiate. Stop pretending we're not out there risking and sacrificing our lives just like our male counterparts."

Mathwick's comments are bittersweet. She lost a friend in Iraq. Major Megan McClung was serving with I MEF as head of public affairs for the Marine Corps for Al Anbar province when her Humvee was destroyed by a massive IED. McClung and the other two occupants were killed instantly. McClung was the first female graduate of the Naval Academy to be killed in action since the school's founding in 1845.

DeCaprio volunteered to deploy to Iraq. When she got there, she asked to extend. She fought for the position of .50-cal gunner and proved that she was more than capable of handling the weapon. She told me this not to brag. She said there are definitely some women who can't be put into combat positions, but there are many who can. The same goes for men. Not every man who graduates boot camp will succeed on the battlefield. Not every man will be able to keep a cool head when his team comes under fire. But ask the Marines who served with DeCaprio, and they will tell you they would want her as their team leader over a male any day. She took care of her Marines when they were wounded, and she has seen and heard numerous stories of many other females who have done the same.

"Women can't fight on the front line?" DeCaprio asks disbelievingly. "Is being the .50-cal gunner of the first scout vehicle of a security element of a convoy or security patrol considered front line? Or searching a house of an Iraqi who we needed to detain? That was my job during deployment. We were very successful, and I brought back every Marine that was sent over there with me."

Jarboe was not part of a combat unit, but as a truck driver she provided support on the front lines every day and often took enemy fire. She was in charge of convoys on more than one occasion. She contends that she had the same concerns, worries, and stress as any of her male counterparts when they were in charge. NCOs, male or female, have a duty to take care of soldiers and accomplish their mission. That's their job.

In *Band of Sisters*, you read the stories of about a dozen women who served in combat in Iraq, a mere microcosm of the total but enough to give you a sense of how the experiment is playing out. You may not like what you see. No one enjoys hearing about women being wounded or killed in combat. But these women have served with courage, pride, and physical, mental, and emotional strength.

Few, if any, question the contribution women have made to the war. But not many have given women the praise they deserve, either. Some worry that women in combat will have a negative effect on society. Gunnery Sergeant Mayo doesn't. She said one of the long-term affects of her being in combat is that her daughter, Sydney, has seen how strong her mother is and as a result can stand up to anyone and do whatever she wants to do. If she wants to fly a fighter jet, she can.

Women as fighters have existed for centuries, but Americans have struggled to acknowledge them in that role. Women aren't struggling for sameness. They are struggling for equality. There will never be sameness, nor should there be. My hope is that this band of sisters, especially as they gain the respect they deserve, will bring the qualities and strengths that women possess—on and off the battlefield—to bear on any future military action. In doing so, they won't just be making the military better, they'll be making America better, too.

Afterword:
Where Are They Now?

MARINE CAPTAIN VERNICE ARMOUR RECEIVED THE AIR MEDAL WITH
Bronze Star for individual action and combat "V", Navy and
Marine Corps Commendation Medal with combat "V", Navy and
Marine Corps Achievement Medal, Iraq Campaign Medal, Global
War on Terrorism Expeditionary Medal, Global War on Terrorism
Service Medal, Presidential Unit Citation, Sea Service Deploy-
ment Ribbon, National Defense Medal, certificate of commenda-
tion, and numerous letters of appreciation. Since her last tour in
Iraq, Armour has been working as a program liaison officer at
Headquarters Marine Corps, Manpower and Reserve Affairs,
Manpower and Equal Opportunity. This position deals with equal
opportunity and diversity at HQMC and the DoD level.

Marine Corporal Carrie Blais received a certificate of commendation for the work she did while attached to CLB-2, a Combat
Action Ribbon for the firefight in Haditha, and two meritorious
masts for her work as a mechanic in the desert. She stayed with 2nd
Maintenance Battalion at Marine Corps Base Camp Lejeune for
her entire enlistment. She separated from the Marine Corps Nov.
18, 2006. She joined the Air National Guard to continue to serve
but with a little more stability. She planned to finish a bachelor's

degree in psychology and eventually work in federal law enforcement in New England.

Army Captain Robin Brown left the Army in February 2005 and moved to Corvallis, Oregon. Her husband, Jason, teaches ROTC at Oregon State University. Brown worked as a whitewater river guide for the summer and fall of 2005. Then she decided to run in District 16 for the Oregon House of Representatives. She had a son, Henry "Hank" Paul Brown, on August 30, 2006. Brown and her husband were renovating a 1921 home in downtown Corvallis.

Marine Corporal Karen Cunningham received a meritorious promotion while in Iraq, and was awarded the Navy and Marine Corps Achievement Medal for her work in Al Qaim and Haditha. In addition, she received the Global War on Terrorism Expeditionary Medal, Global War on Terrorism Service Medal, Sea Service Deployment Ribbon, and Armed Forces Reserve Medal. When her commitment to the Marine Corps ended, Cunningham chose to stay with her unit as non-obligation while waiting to hear about a position with the FBI.

Marine Corporal Chrissy DeCaprio earned a combat meritorious promotion for her actions in combat in Iraq, the Navy and Marine Corps Achievement Medal, and a Combat Action Ribbon. She was looking forward to returning to Iraq as a squad leader or patrol leader—in charge of all four vehicles instead of just her vehicle. She loves being a gunner and will take a gun position in a heartbeat but having been promoted she knows she can lead her Marines into combat.

Army Sergeant Angela Jarboe received the Army Commendation Medal and the Purple Heart. After returning from Iraq and completing the majority of her physical therapy, Jarboe was put in charge of the administrative office for the 594th Transportation Company. She was working on a medical discharge and planned to be out of the Army in January 2007. The wife and mother of three boys said her plans for the future are unknown at this time.

Marine Corporal Priscilla Kispetik received a certificate of commendation for the work she did while attached to CLB-2 and a Combat Action Ribbon for being in the firefight in Haditha. She worked with Engineer Maintenance Company, 2nd Maintenance Battalion supporting II MEF. In October 2006, she was promoted to sergeant. Following her promotion, she was detached with Maintenance FWD and trained to return to the desert in February of 2007. When she returns from Iraq, she plans to become a drill instructor.

Navy Aviation Boatswain's Mate Handler Marcia Lillie transferred from the USS *Harry S. Truman* to the USS *Dwight D. Eisenhower*, where she worked in tractors for a while. Then she switched to damage control to maintain the ship's safety equipment. When she leaves the *Eisenhower*, she plans to either go to a shore-duty station or enter the Army.

Marine Gunnery Sergeant Yolanda Mayo returned from Iraq and was promoted to the rank of first sergeant. She is one of only twenty-two Hispanic female E-8s in the entire Marine Corps. That includes master sergeants and first sergeants. Among her other service awards, Mayo received the Joint Meritorious Service Medal for her performance in Iraq. She demobilized in February of 2006. Her current reserve assignment is as the company first sergeant for Charlie Company, 4th Landing Support Battalion, 4th Marine Logistics Group. In her civilian life, Mayo works full time for the Marine Corps as the protocol coordinator for II Marine Expeditionary Force, Camp Lejeune, North Carolina.

Marine Captain Amy McGrath (F-18 back seater) had laser surgery through the Marine Corps, which allowed her to apply for WSO-to-pilot transition. She was accepted and started pilot training in south Texas in the summer of 2004. She flew T-34s and T-45s in south Texas and was winged again, this time as a naval aviator, in March 2006. She flew the F/A-18 and completed the fleet replacement squadron syllabus in Strike Fighter Squadron 106 at Oceana Naval Air Station in Virginia Beach as a front seater. In the summer of 2007, she was operational and back with Marine Aircraft Group 11 in San Diego, where she became a pilot in an operational gun squadron. She was also promoted to the rank of major. During the war in Iraq, she earned eight Air Medals, the Navy Achievement Medal, the Iraqi Campaign Medal, the Afghanistan Campaign Medal, and the Global War on Terrorism Medal.

Air Force Lieutenant Colonel Polly Montgomery completed her tour of command as the 41st Squadron Commander on May 2, 2006. During her eighteen months in command, Montgomery spent twelve months deployed in support of Operation Iraqi Freedom and Enduring Freedom. She logged more than 350 combat flying hours and commanded more than one hundred sorties. Montgomery earned two Air Medals and a Meritorious Service Medal during her tours. The 41st Airlift Squadron was named the outstanding squadron of the 43rd Airlift Wing at Pope Air Force Base, North Carolina, and the 2005 outstanding airlift squadron for all of Air Mobility Command. Montgomery is currently the director of mobility forces with the Joint Special Operations Command at Fort Bragg, North Carolina.

Navy Lieutenant Estella Salinas said she never served a tour for ribbons, medals, or awards. (Author's note: I don't believe any of the women in this book served for the ribbons, medals, or awards.) She doesn't even know what, if anything, she was awarded and has no desire to find out. "What is the reward of such tours? I can recall the hands I held, the brows I wiped, and hair that was gently stroked. Is that not the reward? The plaques I have now just collect dust. The awards I received in the past are in a cabinet and will stay in that cabinet. I do recall a Marine that was sick. He was very tired and had been vomiting and had diarrhea for days in that heat. His clothes and boots were filthy with vomit and diarrhea and of course he had no other clothes. As part of my care for him, I washed out all his clothes and boots. He did not expect that would be part of my care for him. He was shocked and grateful. That is the reward. I received it right there." Following her tour in Iraq, Salinas retired from the Navy and moved to Houston, Texas. She is working at the Michael E. DeBakey VA Medical Center in Houston. Throughout the workday she tries to learn something about each veteran, young or old. In an e-mail Salinas wrote, "This weekend a veteran I had taken care of passed away. It was not unexpected, but it is harder now. After Iraq it is harder for me to see a veteran pass away. Another, well, if he's there tomorrow I will be surprised. I was surprised to catch myself crying. I dreamed of him all night last night. I never did that before. Death is hard no matter where you are. I still want to serve my country in the care of our veterans. I want to be there still."

Army Corporal Rachelle Spors received the Purple Heart for the wounds she received in Iraq, a Good Conduct Medal, and the Meritorious Service Medal. Following her medical treatment at the various hospitals in Iraq and in the States, Spors spent a month at home resting and recovering. Then she returned to Fort Riley, Kansas, where she was given permission to stay on active duty and work at home in Nebraska until she was taken off medical hold. After she was released from medical hold, she went back to the retail job she had before she left for Iraq and waited patiently for the new semester to start so she could finish student teaching and become a full-time Spanish teacher. In August 2006, she began student teaching in the Omaha Public School district and was offered a Spanish teaching position in the same district beginning in January 2007.

Navy Commander Necia Williams was awarded an anesthesiology pain fellowship. She specifically chose to do the fellowship at Walter Reed Army Medical Center because she wanted to work with troops who had been wounded in combat—perhaps because she had a need to know how they fared once they returned to the states. She hoped to focus her research on those who had survived high explosive blasts. A month before she left for Walter Reed, Williams and her husband were living in a motor home at Onslow Beach at Marine Corps Base Camp Lejeune. They had sold their house and were making final preparations for their move north. In an e-mail, Williams wrote, "There were military exercises on base one week. I hear artillery rounds being fired off. I become alert but know that the Marines are training and I'm OK. But the other night after I had fallen asleep a training exercise started and a low-flying helicopter came in near the campground. I awoke suddenly and was on my feet ready to go before I woke enough to realize where I was—in my motor home at the beach with ocean sand outside—instead of desert sand with casualties coming in. It happened again that night after I had finally fallen back asleep. This time I sat bolt upright in bed. My husband, bless his heart, got up and turned on the air conditioning to help drown out the sounds. He hugged me and said 'It's okay.'"

Acknowledgments

I WOULD LIKE TO START BY THANKING PHILIP GERARD, MY MENTOR in the Creative Writing Department at the University of North Carolina Wilmington. The impact of Philip's belief in me and in *Band of Sisters* was monumental from the beginning. There is a direct link between his confidence in me, and my perseverance and ability to make this book a reality. *Band of Sisters* started off as the thesis for my master's of fine arts degree in creative non-fiction. Along with Philip, Phil Furia and John Sullivan provided input as members of my thesis committee. My deep appreciation to everyone in and associated with the creative writing department, especially Tim Bass, Wendy Brenner, Stanley Colbert, Clyde Edgerton, David Gessner, Bekki Lee, Sarah Messer, Bob Reiss, and my classmates, all of whom provided invaluable comments and observations along the way.

Thank you to my editor, Chris Evans, and assistant editor Dave Reisch of Stackpole Books, who believed in the importance of this book and who worked closely with me to take it to the next level, and to my agent, Robert Guinsler of Sterling Lord Literistic, for taking on this project.

Jeri Fountain, my dear friend and pre-editor editor, served in public affairs in the Marine Corps from 1984 to 1990. I'd like to paraphrase what Wilbur said to Charlotte at the end of *Charlotte's Web*: It is not often that someone comes along who is a true friend and a good editor. Jeri is both.

Thank you to my parents, Anne and Herb Holmstedt, my siblings (Herb, Mary, Eric, and Heidi and their wonderful spouses and children), and my special friend, David Weber, for their constant support and encouragement. A sincere thanks to Beth Barton, Dick Bierly, Leanne Lyon Burns, Betsy and Jim Chaffin, Emily and Kevin Delp, Thora Morris, Rodney Priester of Latter Rain Productions, Albert and Shirley Rachide, Mat and Elizabeth Raymond, Jr., Verna Respass, Donald and Sterling Williams, and those who frequent their porch. Writing a book is a journey, a huge undertaking. Thanks for having faith in me.

I work full-time in the Public Information Office at Coastal Carolina Community College. Thank you to the college president, Ronald Lingle, my co-workers Colette Teachey, Jim Phillips, and Leah Swaggerty, and to all my friends and colleagues at the college and in the community. I'm also grateful to *The Daily News* and to First Baptist Church in Jacksonville.

To all the women in the book, and those who helped inform me about American women serving in the war in Iraq, including Margaret Furman, Stephanie Rose Griffith, Elizabeth Wilber, and all the family members, friends, and service members who I interviewed. I appreciate your time, knowledge, and friendship.

Finally, I couldn't have written this book without the support and professionalism of the armed services, specifically the Marine Corps, Army, Navy, and Air Force public affairs offices. I was constantly amazed at their eagerness to help and at their willingness to find women and military specialists for me to interview.

Index

Abu Ghraib prison, 249
aircraft
  C-130 Hercules, 185, 187, 189
  C-130E, 194–95
  C-141, 186
aircraft carriers
  berthing areas, 118
  catapults, 132–33
  chaining aircraft on, 128
  chocking aircraft on, 127–29
  elevators, 119–21
  flight control room, 119–20
  flight deck, 115–17
  flight deck crew, 115–16
  "Ouija board," 123–25
  sexual activity on, 123
  Tractor King, 129
Al Asad, hospital at, 72–77
  sign-out procedures, 73–74
Al Kut, 270–71
  cemetery in, 239–40
Al Zarqawi, Abu Musab, 22–23
Ali Al Salem Air Base, Kuwait, 197
American Forces Network (AFN),
    240–41
Armour, Vernice, 155–83, 311
  at Battle of Fallujah, 178–79
  first African-American female com-
    bat pilot, 155

first African-American female pilot
    in Marine Corps, 155
  fitting into squadron, 176–77
  flight school training, 171–72
  joining training squadron,
    HMT-303, 172–74
  at Najaf battle, 179–82
  operational squadron, 175–76
  promotions and awards, 315
  reconnaissance mission, 161–67
  ROTC involvement, 169–71
  second deployment, 178–82
  tactics tests, 168–69

Babylon, suicide bombing in, 246–47
Baghdad
  convention center, 241
  suicide bombing in, 243–46,
    247–49
Beasley, Dan, 199–200, 202, 203
Blais, Carrie, 1–25, 310, 312
  first official kill of, 20, 24–25
  Haditha school firefight and,
    16–23
  Haqlaniya mission and, 3–4
  personality of, 2–3
  promotions and awards, 315–16
Boltz, David, 299, 300, 301, 302
Brown, Henry "Hank" Paul, 316
Brown, Jason, 51, 316

Brown, Robin, 27–51, 89, 311, 316
  following 3rd Infantry Division
    march toward Baghdad, 46–47
  shot down, 27–42
Butler, Glen, 179

call signs, 100–101, 173
Camp Anaconda mission, ambush
  on, 288–94
Camp Anderson, 258–63, 264–66
  holding wards, 262
  Iraqi patients at, 259–61
Camp Chesty, 266–68
Camp Korean Village (Camp KV),
  56–57, 59
Camp Qatar, 60
Camp Ryan, Kuwait, news bureau,
  237–38
Camp Taji, 294
close air support (CAS), 84
Coalition Press Information Center
  (CPIC), 241
Conway, James, 238
Cunningham, Karen, 21–22
  Haditha mission and, 6–25
  Operation Matador and, 7–8

Davis, Crystal, 310
DeCaprio, Chrissy, 139–53, 310, 312,
  313
  body searches, 144–45
  guarding Highly Valued Detainee
    (HVD), 146–47
  gunner training, 143–44
  patrolling streets outside Camp
    TQ, 145–46
  promotions and awards, 316
  Ramadi convoy mission, 140–42
  rescuing Marines, 151–52
  running convoys, 140–46
  spotting IEDs, 148–53

Fallujah, Battle of, 178–79
fear factor, 45–46
Folgate, Michael, 101, 104, 105

Forward Looking Infrared Red
  (FLIR) system, 110
Frame, Mike, 185, 186
Frushour, Kelly, 219–40
Furman, Margaret, 311, 316–17

GMH Military Housing, 317
Green Zone, 241–42
Grogan, James, 178, 182

Haditha, 2
  mission, 2–25
  school in, 1–2, 4–5, 16–23
  theater in, 23–24
Hampton, Kimberly, 47–49
Haqlaniya mission, 3–4
Hardwick, Ken, 207
Hearst, Pat, 269
helicopters
  Cobra, 155, 157–58, 167–68
  Kiowa, 29, 30
Henderson, Rob, 237
Hester, Leigh Ann, 309
Hooker, Aswald, 67–71, 72
  Relationship with Spors, 59–61
hospital wards, 255–56, 262, 271–72
Houston, Tim, 207

improvised explosive devices (IEDs),
  xx, 148
Innocenti, "Cherry," 83

Jameson, Tricia, 59, 61–65
Jarboe, Angela, 283–307, 310, 313–14
  at Camp Anaconda, 296
  Camp Anaconda mission ambush
    and, 288–94
  convoy missions, 287
  driving long haul trucks, 284–88
  facing emotional consequences,
    303–6
  facing physical challenges,
    297–303
  on flight to Germany, 296–97
  at hospital in Baghdad, 296

promotions and awards, 317
transferred to Blanchfield Army
Community Hospital, 297
video of attack on, 283–84, 306
wounding of, 292–97
Jarboe, Tony, 297
Jarrett, Rachel, 245

Kim, Jaden
call sign, 101
joins Green Knights, 100
Kispetik, Priscilla, 1–25, 310, 312
Haditha school firefight and,
16–23
personality of, 3
promotions and awards, 317
Krider, Timothy, 295, 296

Larsen, Andrew, 90–92, 112
Iraq missions, 106–9
plan of action, 92
Lawson, Chris, 289
Leatherneck, 97–98
Lillie, Marcia, 115–37, 318
chocking and chaining aircraft,
127–29
early years, 125–27
elevator malfunction experience,
120–21
as elevator operator, 119–20
nickname, 127–28
as Ouija board operator, 123–25
as Tractor King operator, 129–37
Lynch, Jessica, xx–xxi

McCall, Jim, 205
McCloud, Scott, 98
McClung, Megan, 313
McGrath, Amy, xiv, xxi, xxii, xxiii,
81–113, 311
Afghanistan missions, 102–5
In air combat instructor training,
105
call sign, 101
destroying bridge mission, 88

first female Marine to fly in F/A-18
in combat, 103
in ground and flight training,
98–100
on her role in war, 109–12
Iraq missions, 106–9
joins Green Knights, 100–2
keeping track of missions, 87
on killing aspect, 111–13
preparing for military aviation
career, 93–100
promotions and awards, 318
in U.S. Naval Academy, 97–98
McGrath, Marianne, 96
Martin, Matt, 63–66
Mathwick, Lindsay, 312–13
Mayo, Yolanda, 217–51, 311, 312, 314
in area of An Nasiriyah, 230–37
bathroom incident, 242–43
at Camp Ryan news bureau,
237–38
in charge of embedded reporter,
228–30
civilian career of, 227
coping with missing her children,
225–26
documentary on Iraqi Armed
Forces female soldiers, 250
at inner-city school in Baghdad,
249–50
as news bureau chief in Baghdad,
240–46
promotions and awards, 318
in public affairs, 219–51
suicide bombing in Babylon and,
246–47
suicide bombing in Baghdad and,
243–46, 247–49
traveling with Recon convoy,
223–25
media, civilian, 220
medics, primary functions of, 56
Meeker, Harmon, 266–67
Merli, Peter A., 31
Messinger, Biff, 29
Messinger, Edwin J., Sr., 31

missiles
  flechette, 166
  SA16, 46
  SA-7, 188
  Scud, 82, 218
  TOW, 158
Mitchell, Laura, 286, 289, 290, 294,
  295–96
  Taji to Kuwait mission ambush
    and, 304–6
Molique, Aimee, 94
Montgomery, Polly, 185–215, 311
  aborted mission and, 206–13
  baptism of fire for, 188–92
  based out of Ali Al Salem Air Base,
    197
  coping with missing her family,
    199–203
  distancing herself from airmen,
    203–4
  first female Air Force commander
    of combat squadron, 187
  flying troops into combat zones,
    195
  promotions and awards, 319
  taking care of airmen, 205
  at 317th Veterans Group Memorial
    Dedication Ceremony, 214–15
  transferring bodies, 196–97
Morris, Steve, 207

Najaf, battle at, 179–82
National Guard, 217
Neely, Bryan, 234–35
Noel, Rosie, 274–79
North, Andrew, 228–30

O'Neill, Sean, 19
Operation Matador, 7–8
Operation New Market, 2–25

packs
  ALICE, 222–23
  MOLLE, 223
Padden, Tim, 186
pilots, biggest fears of, 190

Plummer, Michael Shane, 71–72
Powell, Colin, 248–49
POWs, female, 89–90
public affairs, 219–20
Pullen, Ashley J., 309

Recon Marines, 221–23
Remmers, Joseph, 286, 290, 291
  Camp Anaconda mission ambush
    and, 288–94
reservists, 217
Robinson, Lovette, 269–70
Robinson, Sharita, 65
Ruvalcaba, James, 159, 162, 174, 176

Safwan Hill, strike on, 86
Salinas, Estella, 253–81, 311
  in Al Kut, 270–71
  on awards, 319–20
  at Camp Anderson, 258–63,
    264–66
  at Camp Chesty, 266–68
  children, 268–70
  early military career, 273–74
  early years, 263–64
  "other duties," 279–81
  staff, 265–66
Santere, Dennis, 106, 107–9
Schram, James, 205, 206, 207
Scud alerts, 82–84
Sefzik, Jessica, 77
servicewomen
  casualties in Iraq, xix
  characteristics traditionally associ-
    ated with, 93
  in combat, xii, xviii–xix
  first African-American combat
    pilot, 155
  first African-American pilot in
    Marine Corps, 155
  first Air Force commander of com-
    bat squadron, 187
  history of, xviii
  killed in combat in Iraq, 309–10
  POWs, 89–90
  reasons for joining military, xx

in support roles, xx
winning right to fly fighter jets, 89
wounded in combat in Iraq, 310
sexual harassment incident, 197–98
Sharp, George, 135
Slovitch, Gregory, 245
Spors, Rachelle, 53–79, 148, 311
 ambulance explosion and, 62–72
 on convalescent leave, 78
 convoy to Camp KV, 56–72
 Hooker relationship, 59–61
 injuries sustained by, 72
 physical and emotional reminders
  of experience, 79
 promotions and awards, 320
 transported to Walter Reed Army
  Medical Center, 77–78
Sumner, Jeff, shot down, 27–42
survival vests, 35–36
Szepesy, James, 161

Task Force Tarawa, 217
Taylor, Virgil, 294
Teeden, Mark, 32, 36–42
Thorkelson, Keith, 179
317th Veterans Group Memorial
  Wreath Dedication Ceremony,
  214–15
Tilton, William, 295, 296
torture, systematic, 90
Touchon, Brandon, 189, 192
T-tailer, 187
Twelve O'Clock High (movie), 204

United States Army
 Bravo Company, 1st Battalion,
  82nd Aviation Regiment, primary mission of, 30
 3rd Infantry Division, march
  toward Baghdad, 46–47
 3rd Platoon of the 594th Transportation Company, 284
 313 Medical Company, 55

United States Marine Corps
 call signs, 100–101
 female aviators, 85
 4th Recon, 221
 Green Knights, 82, 103
 ground and flight training, 98–100
 HMT-303 training squadron,
  172–74
 Light Attack Helicopter (HMLA)
  Squadron, 156, 173
 Recon marines, 221–23
 2nd Marine Expeditionary Brigade
  (MEB), 217
 2nd Military Police Battalion, 140
United States Navy
 Bravo Surgical Company, 254–56
 aircraft carriers, 115–33
USS *Harry S. Truman*, 116, 117
USS *John C. Stennis*, 122
USS *Theodore Roosevelt*, 117

Vogel, Dave, 113

Wallace, Chris, 32, 36–42
weapons, chemical, 218
Weapons Missile System (WMS),
  189–90
weapons systems operator, 82
Wertz, Travis, 133
Whittle, Reba, 89–90
Williams, Necia, 73–77, 274, 276,
  320–21
Worthington, Malcolm, 133–34